E
768
.B44

Bell, Sidney.

Righteous conquest;
Woodrow Wilson and
the evolution of
the new diplomacy

154106

DATE			
DEC 0 1 1986			

RIGHTEOUS CONQUEST

KENNIKAT PRESS

NATIONAL UNIVERSITY PUBLICATIONS

SERIES IN AMERICAN STUDIES

General Editor

JAMES P. SHENTON

Professor of History, Columbia University

Sidney Bell

RIGHTEOUS CONQUEST

Woodrow Wilson and the Evolution of the New Diplomacy

National University Publications
KENNIKAT PRESS
Port Washington, N.Y./London/1972

Library of Congress Catalog Card No: 70-189552
ISBN: 0-8046-9023-5

Manufactured in the United States of America

Published by
Kennikat Press, Inc.
Port Washington, N.Y./London

To Alice and Daniel

CONTENTS

Introduction   3

1   Wilsonian Liberalism: Democracy, Reform and
    Expansion   10

2   The Political Economy of Empire   29

3   Latin America: The Opportunity and the First
    Challenge   45

4   Mexico: Guided Revolution to Make the World
    Safe for Democracy in One Country   67

5   Stability *versus* Revolution: The Need for a System
    in Latin America   87

6   Stability *versus* Change Controlled by Others:
    The Need for a World System   108

7   Neutrality *versus* Collective Security   127

8   Security Through Numbers: Cooperation to
    Safeguard a Trade Empire   146

9   From Frontier to Collective Security   172

10 Pax Americana   190

    Bibliography   194

    Index   204

RIGHTEOUS CONQUEST

INTRODUCTION

President Woodrow Wilson crossed the Atlantic Ocean on the *George Washington* early in December 1918 to attend the opening of the Versailles peace conference that promised to inaugurate a new era of international justice and stability. The world had endured the long and terrible years of World War I, a war which had strained the economic and social fabric of its participants, in some cases to the point of rupture. For many Americans of that time and afterward, the voyage stood as a symbol of a noble effort to introduce a new sort of diplomacy, a liberal diplomacy based on morality, fair dealing, and an unselfish disinterest. Wilson's charge to his entourage, "Tell me what's right, and I'll fight for it; give me a guaranteed position," was characteristic of this view. Wilson proclaimed that Americans were the only disinterested people to attend the conference, and complained that they had to negotiate with men "who did not represent their own people."[1]

Wilson's view of himself and the United States as an island of "disinterest" in a sea of special interests has traditionally served as the principle interpretive guide. It has become habitual to view Wilson as an advocate of a "new order" in diplomacy, a David who would do battle with the Goliaths of imperialism, nationalism, power politics and special interest. This view was affirmed by many of his associates and fellow-American peacemakers, even though they disagreed about what went wrong with the dream.

Herbert Hoover explained, for example, that he shared the American dream of a "rebirth of mankind, a new golden age to be brought about by the purification of men, and the triumph of democracy."[2] He was rudely awakened from this dream, he said, by the realization that the ideals were honored only in America. "Ours was the only nation since the time of the Crusades that had fought other peoples' wars for ideals." Hoover went on to deplore that while the Americans had come, "pure in heart," to fight for this dream, the Allies, dominated by "class government," fought merely for their own nationalistic interests.[3] Ac-

3

cording to this definition, the cynical leaders of victorious Europe were so concerned with vengeance, the division of spoils, internal politics, and economic or strategic advantage, that Wilson's goals of a new world of prosperity and peace were lost.[4] Josephus Daniels disagreed. He felt that the fruit of the peace-making, the Versailles Treaty, was an "embodiment of the spirit of the Fourteen Points," and that in the main it was true to Wilsonian goals. It was the later administration of the Treaty, he thought, that veered from the paths of virtue and set the world once more on the road to war.[5]

Charles Seymour, whose personal knowledge was amplified by his career as editor of the *Papers of Edward M. House*, emphasized the necessity of the compromises that produced the Versailles Treaty, and considered them justified by the League of Nations Covenant which, he felt, was the repository of hopes for the "New Order."[6] Henry White agreed that the Treaty was weakened by the self-seeking of the Allies, but that the saving feature was the League Covenant. Through this mechanism, he argued, the worst faults of the peace agreements could be corrected.[7]

The man designated by Wilson to create a favorable press, Ray Stannard Baker, presented Wilson as the protagonist of the "New Order" in deadly combat with the old.[8] The battle produced the Versailles Treaty which represented the "soul of civilization," at once embodying the "fears, greeds, vanities, cruelties [and] pettiness of mankind," and the "highest aspirations and hopes of the world—the League of Nations."[9]

Of the other members of the Peace Commission, Robert Lansing, Secretary of State, was the sole doubter. He did not question the dream, only the possibility of realizing it through the League Covenant. He believed that the League was flawed by being designed to "preserve the artificial structure which has been erected by the compromise of conflicting interests." Lansing argued that Wilson predisposed the conference to failure by his willingness to compromise his principles.[10] He saw the League as a capstone to a new entente rather than as an objective manifestation of disinterested, liberal international morality.

If Woodrow Wilson had been willing to consult advisers, if his plea to be told "what's right" was more than rhetoric, what could these men have told him? Generally they were men who saw Wilson in his own terms, as the champion of what Herbert Hoover called the American dream, and what Charles Seymour called the "New Order." Within that view it is accepted that Wilson came to Paris as the champion of mankind, peace and democracy, that he came unencumbered by any conscious concept of national or special interest that might be at odds with these ideals, or with the actual interests of the great mass of the people of the world who were not truly represented by their own leaders and hence were given hope and voice by Wilson. Clothed with the armor of liberal idealism, Wilson did battle with the disbelievers. Depending on the judgment, he either failed at Paris or met failure at the hands of the United States Senate for perverse or political reasons.

The consequence of that approach has been to direct attention toward the way that the goals of the Allies modified Wilsonian objectives rather than to an examination of the objectives themselves. Since it was assumed that the Wilsonians were "disinterested" and sought only peace, security, and democracy for the world, little analysis has been made of the nature of the ideal itself as policy, and of its relationship to Wilson's definition of the needs and interests of the United States. Part of the conceptual difficulty arises from the vagueness of Wilson's formulation and rhetoric, and is intensified by the tendency to separate Wilson as a disinterested molder of new worlds from Wilson the political leader and Wilson the intellectual concerned with defining the problems of his society and seeking solutions.

Until recently, at any rate, historians tended to concentrate on the question of whether or not particular actions or agreements were "Wilsonian"—that is, in accord with Wilsonian ideals. A number of historians have endeavored to examine ideals as policy, or as particular definitions stemming from specific concepts of the needs of the United States. The orientation of this essay owes much to such pathfinders as Charles A. Beard and Vernon Parrington. Benjamin H. Williams provided a valuable introduction to economic foreign policy in his *Economic Foreign Policy of The United States*, and Howard Kennedy Beale first made this author aware of the significance and implications of noncolonial expansionism, and the interrelation of philosophical ideals and definitions of economic self-interest.

Beard's *The Idea of National Interest*, first published in 1934, must also be mentioned in this context. The subsequent research of historians such as Harley Notter and William Diamond contributed much to a clarification of the nature, meaning, and implications of Wilson's moral and economic thought. Martin J. Sklar's

important unpublished research on "The Political Economy of
Woodrow Wilson" in many ways parallels and contributes to this
essay though from a somewhat different focus. Of most significance is the work of William Appleman Williams, particularly *The
Tragedy of American Diplomacy.*

Information, ideas and insights have been drawn from all of
these historians. This essay is an attempt to extend their work: in
certain areas to add and deepen, and in others to explore new
meaning. The goals of the new diplomacy—democracy, peace and
stability—must be examined for words which convey little meaning in and of themselves. It is vital to know what democracy
meant to Wilson in a world characterized by economic and social
upheaval; what peace meant in a system of competing nations
with disproportionate access to capital, resources, and markets;
and what stability meant in a world of empires, formal and
informal, and of many revolutions.

America's special interests, as Wilson understood them, were
real and urgent, though clothed in terms of international morality and principle. Wilson had evolved an integrated view of an
American society on the verge of social and economic crisis, and
defined national interest in those terms. As was typical of many
Americans of that day, Wilson sought the solution to the problems by looking abroad. When the problems existing within and
among other countries interfered with his concept of American
needs and national interest, Wilson undertook to define a new
system of relationships in order to "make the world safe for
democracy." Wilson fought for this definition of national interest
in Latin America and other regions and then on a global scale in
Paris. It shaped the positions he took and the lines he drew. The
reality of conflicting national interests, the distribution of power,
and the menace of revolution made compromise inevitable at the
peace conference. The more essential had to be preserved at the
expense of the lesser.

Wilson often used the rhetoric of laissez faire liberalism (and
its application to the self-determination of peoples) and the
terminology of "democracy." He accepted those concepts, however, in a special and limited sense. Wilson knew, as did Theodore
Roosevelt and other Progressives, that pre-Civil War laissez faire
had been made possible by opportunities arising from continental
expansion, and realized they were no longer meaningful in the
twentieth century. He accepted the implications of Frederick
Jackson Turner's thesis: the acknowledgment in retrospect of the

role of a frontier of opportunity (or underdevelopment) in domesticating democracy to create a balanced society in which tensions that might have led to internal conflict were dissipated westward along with surplus capital and manpower.[11] And, as with Turner, he recognized that era was gone. He believed that a new consensus had to be forged around a charismatic leader who could create a sense of national purpose and an economic empire abroad to replace continental manifest destiny. Wilson believed in the need for a new moral crusade that would restore a sense of identification and unity through the creation of a "New Order" abroad. The new order would help avoid internal factionalism and conflict through the re-creation of opportunity provided by the growth of the United States in the world economy. An expanding society seeking opportunity abroad would revitalize the concept of laissez faire. This type of expansion was possible, however, only under the direction and guidance of a strong executive who would be capable of transcending factionalism and imposing his own definitions of national direction.

On a domestic level, Wilson opposed social legislation in the name of laissez faire because he felt that it benefitted special groups at the expense of others. But he was not simply a states rights Democrat or an old-fashioned advocate of laissez faire.[12] His political orientation was much closer to the New Nationalism of the theorist, Herbert Croly,[13] and the practitioner, Theodore Roosevelt. Wilson evolved his own version of a neocorporate ideology which held that the leader's function was to harmonize and balance the interests of all conflicting groups. That was not to be done through internal changes, however, but through moral leadership coupled with the establishment of an American frontier of opportunity abroad. The new expansion of opportunity would generate the internal cohesion necessary for a modern variant of classical laissez faire.

Wilson understood something of the problems of a society in which opportunity was no longer adequately generated internally. It was his task, he believed, to restore harmony at home, a sense of general interest, by going abroad economically. He would safeguard the American empire in the area claimed under the Monroe Doctrine and open the door for America's access to the rest of the world. That concept merged with his view of the United States as the nation of the elect capable of regenerating itself by making the world a fit place in which the United States might grow. The result was Wilson's New Order.

This study is concerned with the structure and content of Wilson's thought about the needs of American society and seeks to show how that thought was related to his policy. Arthur Link has pondered the dilemma of Wilsonian principle and practice and concluded that the principle was the reality. The practice was merely forced upon Wilson. Link also presents a survey of the critics ranging from Theodore Roosevelt and William Howard Taft through journalists such as Charles Willis Thompson on to friends such as House who charged Wilson with half-truths or outright lies.[14] Roosevelt called Wilson a "doctrinaire" devoid of the "slightest touch of ethical convictions."[15] Perhaps Felix Frankfurter's comments were more accurate. He believed Wilson was dogmatic. Though Wilson talked of "laying mind against mind," in practice he did the opposite, refraining from discursive argument.[16] Herbert Hoover was perhaps closer to the truth when he commented that Wilson's mind ran to "moral principles," "justice," and "right." In these he held deep convictions. Whatever he concluded was right was "thereafter right as against all comers."[17]

The problem of understanding Wilson resides in the seeming disparity between thought and action. Wilson, as Hoover said, believed in moral principles, but principles are not policies. Wilson defined himself as right, and America as right whenever it was going his way. He gradually reached a definition of America's needs and interests, and this he defined as right. Whoever was opposed was wrong. The coercion of Mexico by the United States was not in conflict with the principle of self-determination, because "real" self-determination came from doing what Wilson thought should be done. Wilson was not concerned with what ordinary men might call principles. He disdained consistency and despised legalisms. Whatever served his conception of justice became right. Thus changing his word, modifying his position in midstream, or engaging in economic coercion were all at one time or another justified as serving the higher morality.

This essay deals with the interaction between Wilsonian thought and practice until the entrance of the United States into World War I. There is a continuity in his growth and development as new ideas and new situations impinge on his thought. From a position of standing aloof and calling on the world to do his bidding through its recognition of his moral principles, Wilson came to realize the extent of American involvement and interdependence. He learned that right was not enough, that to achieve his objectives he had to enter into alliances with other nations, even as the United States competed with them. American entrance into the war marked not a basic change in Wilson's pattern of thinking, but its elevation to a new level. The world was more perilous, and hence the changes had to be more extensive. Come what may, however, the world had to be made safe for American expansion and the American system. But that would reward the world by making it more moral.

Notes and References

1. Memorandum of Dr. Isaiah Bowman, cited in Charles Seymour, ed., *The Intimate Papers of Colonel House* (Houghton Mifflin Co., 1926-1928), vol. IV, 280.
2. Herbert Hoover, *The Memoirs of Herbert Hoover: Years of Adventure, 1874-1920* (Macmillan, 1951), 286.
3. Ibid., 288.
4. Herbert Hoover, *The Ordeal of Woodrow Wilson* (McGraw-Hill, 1958); Herbert Hoover, *America's First Crusade* (Scribners, 1942).
5. Josephus Daniels, *The Wilson Era* (University of North Carolina Press, 1944-1946), vol. II.
6. Charles Seymour, *House Papers: American Diplomacy During the War* (The Johns Hopkins Press, 1952); *Woodrow Wilson and the World War* (Yale University Press, 1921).
7. Allan Nevins, *Henry White, Thirty Years of American Diplomacy* (Harper & Bros., 1930), 441.
8. Ray Stannard Baker, *Woodrow Wilson and World Settlement* (Doubleday, Page and Co., 1922), vol. II, 1.
9. Ibid., 521.
10. Robert Lansing, *The Peace Negotiations* (Houghton Mifflin Co., 1921), 272-277.
11. See Frederick Jackson Turner, *The Frontier in American History* (Henry Holt & Co., 1920), particularly pp. 21-38, 219-221, 243-246.
12. Arthur S. Link, *Woodrow Wilson and the Progressive Era, 1910-1917* (Harper & Bros., 1954), 20.
13. Herbert Croly, *The Promise of American Life* (Macmillan, 1912).
14. Link, *Wilson, The New Freedom* (Princeton University Press, 1956), 67-70, 80-82.
15. Theodore Roosevelt to Frederick L. Smith, December 28, 1918, *Roosevelt Files*, 1909-1919, courtesy H.K.B.
16. Felix Frankfurter, *Felix Frankfurter Reminisces* (Reynal and Co., 1960), 75-76.
17. Hoover, *Ordeal of Woodrow Wilson*, viii.

1
WILSONIAN LIBERALISM

DEMOCRACY, REFORM AND EXPANSION

Woodrow Wilson was born in Virginia in 1856, the year the Republicans campaigned on the slogan of "Free Soil, Free Speech and Fremont" and the issue of "Bleeding Kansas." He left the South for Princeton University in 1875 as Federal Reconstruction yielded to the spirit of accomodation to the new industrialism. During the intervening years he matured in the southern white middle-class tradition of a South despoiled by carpetbag reconstruction. As a product of the generation of the "great barbecue" and the postwar political and industrial colonization of the southern economy, Wilson saw in the world around him the breakdown of that spirit of common purpose which he thought was characteristic of the prewar era of compromise. He feared that the growing concentration of economic power in the hands of self-serving monopolies, and a declining sphere of general opportunity, would generate a spirit of factionalism that would tear American society apart. During his early years as an academic intellectual he was filled with a sense of crisis and upheaval.

Before Wilson became involved in national politics he displayed little concern with foreign policy as such.[1] He viewed America in the classical way as a continental empire held together by balance and compromise. He believed, however, that the balance was being disrupted and that politics was becoming more opportunistic. Local government was marked by corruption and inefficiency; and Congressional government was not functioning as a vehicle of popular representation, but instead was dominated by conflicting factions, boss control, and "government by committee." The turbulence of the 1880s and 1890s, the struggles of the Greenbackers and Populists, the bitter violence accompanying the efforts of labor to organize and gain a greater share in the output of the mines and mills, the criticisms of reformers and rebels could not fail to penetrate the secluded world of the young intellectual.

As a member of the southern gentry and Presbyterian elect,[2] Wilson matured in the Calvinist tradition of leadership whose function it was to provide guidance for the mass of sinners. For generations Wilson's family had been considered among the elect. It was rich in ministers, elders of the church, and professors of theology, and steeped in a consciousness of selection. They had extolled moral achievement and the responsibility of providing leadership and guidance.[3] Arthur S. Link, the most painstaking biographer of Wilson, characterized him as a "citizen of another, invisible world, the world of the spirit," who shared the "absolute conviction that God had ordered the universe from the beginning, the faith that God used men for his own purposes." From such a belief, Link observes, "came a sense of destiny," and a feeling of "intimate connection with the sources of power."[4]

Wilson's youth spanned an era in which old hierarchies had crumbled and new ones arose. It was an age of transcontinental railroads, of mechanization, of the growth of an urbanized and industrialized America. New groups coming to power derived their strength from finance and industry, from the vigorous, and often crude and brutal exploitation of resources and labor. As a student at Princeton, Wilson read Edmund Burke and Walter Bagehot, William Gladstone and John Bright. From them he absorbed the tradition of English liberal conservatism: a belief in economic individualism, laissez faire economics and the liberalizing force of commerce. It was trade, Wilson wrote in 1880 in an essay on John Bright, that was "the great nurse of liberal ideas." It gave men, he said, a broad world view, and its rational principles transformed politicians into statesmen. He defined such liberalism as consisting of free trade, "an extended and purified suffrage, a just and liberal land system, a perfected finance, a worthy, manly, Christian foreign and colonial policy . . . ." In this, he observed, were the "seeds and fruits of enlightened *conservatism*."[5]

The laissez faire that Wilson honored was not a political economy of unrestrained liberty. Through exposure to the works of Francis A. Walker, which he used at Princeton, and from John Bates Clark's *Philosophy of Wealth*, Wilson developed a sense of moral awakening and social cooperation that he integrated with economic liberalism.[6] Competition had to have limits because individuals did not necessarily follow their best interest, and because the multiplicity of individual decisions did not necessarily produce the general welfare. John Bates Clark pointed out that competition in the 1880s had become "incapable of working justice." Combination and factionalism threatened to disrupt society. A new and higher competition must emerge, according to Clark, guided by law and moral force. Wilson saw in Clark's view a moderation and Christianity that appealed to him,[7] but which he found lacking in his time.

While still a senior at Princeton, in 1879, the young Southerner wrote that "our patriotism" was taking on a "tone of despondent solicitude instead of confident hope." He was bothered by anxiety about the future of American institutions and sensed a "prevalent fear" that "grave, perhaps radical defects" in the form of government were undermining liberty and prosperity. Wilson traced the source of the defects to the exercise of power by "irresponsible legislature," and to the "despotic" principle of "Government by Committee."[8]

Wilson saw Congress as an arena of factionalism, rather than the institution representing the general interest, particularly that portion of interest which was the South's. He observed early in 1881 that the South had undergone an economic and social revolution of "almost unparalleled proportions" as a consequence of the Civil War. The South was rebuilding itself economically, but suffered from Congressional interference with the "natural processes of reforming nature" that burdened the South with an "*ignorant* suffrage." Wilson's objection to Negro suffrage was not that their faces were dark but that their "*minds* were dark, . . . ignorant, uneducated, and incompetent to form an enlightened opinion" on public questions. The "southern question," he observed, might "almost cause one to wish that legislation were stopped and legislators stripped of their functions . . ."[9]

Wilson believed that a unified voice was needed to give the country direction and purpose. Without this, the balanced society and purified representation considered essential by James Madison and John Adams could not be restored. He urged a new leadership to replace the voices he believed to be confused and ignorant, selfish and grasping, a leadership that could stand before the nation and restore unity by inspiring a sense of common purpose. To clear the way for such a restored consensus, Wilson advocated a "responsible executive leadership" much on the model of the British parliamentary system. He wanted an executive who could inspire and unite, formulate goals and direction, and thus transcend the conflicts of a multiplicity of wills and interests. He wrote for a form of cabinet government characterized by strong executive power and "ministerial responsibility." Presiding over this would be a President-Prime Minister who could hold power as long as he could muster public support for his policies. This executive would replace Congress as the focus of attention and would be able to appeal to the people through discussion and persuasion. His function and responsibility would be to form an enlightened opinion from which he could draw his strength.[10]

Such a political system did not undercut Wilson's laissez-faire economics. He believed that there had to be a sense of community underlying such economics, which provided the boundaries for the competition of the market place. Such a common interest, shaped by law and morality, did not exist as a natural product of his era, however, and would have to be formulated and guided by executive leadership. Only in that way could a breakdown of agreement on general purpose be avoided. In his major study on *Constitutional Government in the United States*, published in 1908, Wilson stated such ideas with vigor and conviction. He urged the tempering of the confusion of popular government, caused by "multitudinous elections" that promoted the development of factions working at cross purposes, with a new national unity, a "common political consciousness" which would permit concerted action. This consciousness would emerge when the people had a leader who could represent them as a whole, speak for them, formulate objectives on which there might be national accord, and who had the strength of character to create that accord.[11]

Though Wilson's New Freedom campaign of 1912 was later defined by historians as reflecting a "neo-Jeffersonian belief in laissez-faire," stressing local self-government rather than nationalism, his conception of a national leader who held power by making his will accepted was more akin to corporate theory than to laissez-faire liberalism.[12] Liberty was the more significant word to Wilson than democracy. He defined liberty as "the best practical adjustment between the power of the government and the privilege of the individual, with freedom to alter the adjustment." His favorite analogy was of a boat skimming the water, adjusted to the force of the wind. "Throw her head into the wind," Wilson would say, and the boat will "stagger and shake." She will be "in irons." The boat was "free" when she sailed in

perfect adjustment to the wind. Freedom he likened to the
action of a piston-rod in a "perfectly made engine—in adjustment
with a minimum of friction."

There was nothing free, Wilson repeated in this analogy, in the
sense of "being unrestrained in a world of innumerable forces."
"Each force," rather, "moves best when best adjusted to the
forces about it." The freest government was the one in which
there was the least friction between the power of the government
and the privilege of the individual.[13] This freedom, of "liberty,"
was not the product of minimum government, but of the formulation of a "common political consciousness," expressed by a
leader who was in accord with it. The leader was to "win the
admiration and confidence" of the country, and "take the imagination of the people." To the extent that he "rightly" interpreted national thought and boldly insisted on it, he would then
be irresistible.[14]

The leader was to stand above the "impulses," divisions and
factions which Wilson felt dominated Congress, and would draw
opinion to himself through the force of his character and his
ability to transmit his concept of moral principle to the public.
Out of this the national consciousness might be formed, and it
was from the atunement of this charismatic leader to the collective mind that the absence of friction that Wilson called
freedom might appear.[15]

Though Wilson has been labelled Jeffersonian[16] and placed in
opposition to such nationalists as Theodore Roosevelt and Albert
J. Beveridge, he shared their admiration of Alexander Hamilton
as opposed to Jefferson. In the 1890s, Wilson regarded democracy as a mixed blessing and of limited validity. He considered
the tradition of English constitutional training, rather than democracy, to be the great legacy of the United States. Four
centuries of English conditioning, he pointed out, had provided
the leaders of America's revolution with stability, self-restraint,
soberness, and the "temperateness of united action." That disciplined background had produced unity, "one-ness of purpose,"
and cohesion. The American Revolution did not result, Wilson
wrote in 1893, from "hearkening to Rousseau," or by "consort-
ing with Europe in revolutionary sentiment," but was an effort
by Englishmen to preserve their constitutional liberties developed
since the Magna Charta. Americans could be free, Wilson repeated, because they "once had a king."[17]

When Wilson evaluated the architects of American development, as he did in an essay in 1893, he emphasized Alexander Hamilton rather than Thomas Jefferson. Wilson considered the "genius and steadfast spirit" of Hamilton indispensable to the creation of the new nation. No one less "masterful" and "resolute" could "drill the minority, if necessary, to have their way against the majority." or do the organizational work to establish national credit, and with it the national government. Without Hamilton's "conservative genius" to build the "past into the future," American national life would have miscarried. Wilson considered James Madison another "great American" who brought to this country from England the "old and tested convictions of the uses of liberty." The tradition sustained by those men was further strengthened by John Marshall and Daniel Webster.

As for Jefferson, Wilson considered him to have suffered from the "strain of French philosophy that permeated and weakened all his thought." Jefferson had brought a "foreign product of thought" to a locale where "no natural or wholesome demand for it could exist." Wilson admired Jefferson for his qualities as a natural leader and recognized his "almost passionate love for the simple equality of country life" and devotion to "what [Jefferson] deemed to be the cause of all the people." But Wilson considered his "speculative philosophy . . . abstract, sentimental, rationalistic," and "un-American."[18]

Wilson, in elaborating on his views in 1889, divided democracy into two kinds: that which had developed against an Anglo-Saxon background (such as found in the United States), and the variety found elsewhere. The radical thought of the nineteenth century had caused the spread of democracy in the world, but "these were not the forces that made America democratic, nor were we responsible for them." The American leaders of the eighteenth century had not been "carrying out any theory—inventing nothing," but only establishing a "specialized species of English government." Democracy came to the United States, as it did elsewhere, riding the currents of popular education, freedom of thought, and the diffusion of the enlightenment. In the United States, however, it was not the result of "revolutionary theorists," or the discontent of the "pauperized and oppressed," but rather the product of a gradual elevation of the masses toward the level of understanding and of "orderly intelligent purpose" enjoyed by the older upper class. In other words, democracy came not along the path of Rousseau and Jefferson and the

Mayflower Compact, but through the education of the mass of people till they understood the traditions of English liberty upheld by a Federalist and Whig elite. The base of government was broadened as a growing number of people rose to the point where they could share responsibility with the wise and responsible.

This spread of democracy carried a danger to the structure of orderly government. The diffusion of information and education to the masses, Wilson pointed out, may often be "misdirected and unwholesome," sometimes only "feverish and mischievous." It made men conscious of affairs outside the "dull round of their daily lives." It produced light but not necessarily "clear vision." As people became informed they became divided. They received "piecemeal opinion" and lost their common voice. An "aggregate voice" developed, instead of a true sense of community, a voice that was called public opinion, but was incapable of constructive unity. Thus the spread of information tended largely to "confuse and paralyze the mind" with "myriad stinging lashes of excitement."

Far from sharing the Jeffersonian concept of an enlightened, self-governing electorate, Wilson argued that the electorate could not really be self-governing. The mass of people, even if educated and informed, did not possess the vision to create a new consensus. The democratic currents of the nineteenth century, Wilson warned, could not, by themselves, produce republican government. He saw a necessity for a population trained in the capacity for self-government, possessing "practical aptitude for public affairs." Only through the long centuries of English constitutional experience (or the survival of the old "Teutonic" tradition in Switzerland) could "truly organic" government develop. Only against the background of such "organic" government could democracy become something worthwhile.

Wilson believed that American democracy had nothing in common with the "radical thought and restless spirit" called democracy in Europe, or with the popular upheavals of the French Revolution. Americans had demonstrated "self-command" and "self-possession," but democracy in Europe was an act of rebellion and a "destructive force." Democracy had come to the United States "like manhood, as the fruits of youth," and had to be based on the stable foundation of character: it "may no more be adopted than a particular type of character may be adopted."

Wilson felt that the kind of institutions and character found in the United States had to be developed by conscious effort with the aid of "transmitted attitudes." This required long training in self-direction, self-reliance, self-knowledge, self-control and soberness and deliberate judgment. Democracy was possible only "amongst people of highest and steadiest political habit" who were "purged alike of hasty barbaric passions and of patient servility to rulers." Democracy of the type found in the United States was an institution of political "noonday" rather than the "half light of political dawn." It could not sit easily on first generations but had to be strengthened through a long process of social heredity.

Such virtues were found only in the United States and in a few other governments "begotten of the English race," and in Switzerland of the "old Teutonic habit." England had been slow in acquiring democracy only because it had sacrificed itself by sending forth the pioneers with strong instincts for self-government to the colonies. Democracy developed only after a slow process of elevating the masses left behind. In this manner, Wilson distinguished the "democracy" of the English race, which was elitist, ethnocentric, and based on rule by the chosen few of "character," "from the democracy of other peoples, which was populistic and bred by discontent and founded on revolution." One was the slow process of evolution, its level that of "everyday habit, of common national experiences," the other was the "ecstacy of the revolutionist."[19]

This line of political reasoning was Wilson's variant of Anglo-Saxon cultural supremacy, combined with a strong measure of Federalist social doctrine of rule by wealth, talent and education, or its Calvinist counterpart of election.[20] For Wilson, American democracy meant neither laissez-faire individualism nor the crystallization of a majority in pursuit of its own needs and definitions, but rather the elevation or acculturation of the mass to the point where they were disciplined and stable enough to accept the wisdom of a benevolent elite. For the people who were not so trained and elevated, Wilson reserved the judgment of Hobbes and Hamilton—that they were a great beast.

Even though American democracy was of a special nature, having little to do with the passions of discontented European masses, Wilson was troubled by the defects he saw appearing within the United States. His analysis of these cracks, and his absorption of the ideas of Frederick Jackson Turner concerning the role of the frontier in making democracy viable, led Wilson to his doctrine of expansion. That occurred as his fears of "radical flaws" in American democracy continued to grow during the 1890s. It appeared to him that the undisciplined democracy of "majority factions" might overshadow the heritage of Anglo-Saxon constitutionalism. The warnings of James Madison in the Federalist X about majority factionalism in a representative society, unless tempered by checks and balances and "extension of the sphere," were now being verified. [21] In his 1889 address commemorating the centennial of George Washington's inauguration, Wilson warned that though the United States had proven democracy possible in a large nation by its success in integrating 60 million people into one representative system, its national character was now being "diluted." The United States now had to bear the burden of the undesirable influences of European democracy being carried by the "heterogeneous horde of immigrants" whom their home politics had "familiarized with revolution." We were receiving into our own "equable blood . . . the most feverish blood of the restless old world." [22]

Wilson found an explanation for the breakdown of community or common purpose in the pernicious influence of European immigration that did not have the benefit of Anglo-Saxon conditioning. Wilson felt Anglo-Saxon institutions had to be preserved by honoring the traditions from which "our first strength was derived," but they were threatened by "restless forces" and "anarchic turbulence" of European democracy brought to American shores in alarming volume by immigration." The United States no longer seemed able to assimilate and acculturate the incoming flood. Yearly, he wrote, "our own temperate blood, schooled in self-possession, and to the measured conduct of self-government," was receiving a "partial corruption of foreign blood." Europe was exporting its population, its "habits," and its political philosophy, "a readiness to experiment in forms of government," and these alien forces of democracy were to "tell disastrously upon our Saxon habits of government." [23] Wilson was thus arguing, at least in part, that the maintenance of consensus was based on racial culture and conditioning rather than upon a relationship between economic and social conditions.

As competition bred concentration in the age of the trust and the pool, and as periodically the declining rate of growth and change in the organization of the economy produced discontent, many Americans began to re-examine their belief in the assumption that unlimited opportunity was an inherent component of a laissez faire system. The growing gap between agricultural and industrial prices moved farmers to discontent and protest. Many of the new immigrant workers who had come to the United States confident of finding the promised land of opportunity, instead experienced slums, malnutrition, brutal factory conditions, and long periods of unemployment and hunger. And the great strikes and demonstrations of the 1870s and 1880s led to fears of sustained class warfare.

Another long experience with intense depression and bitter discontent came during the 1890s. The conflict between capital and labor became intense at Homestead and Pullman and in the coal fields of West Virginia. Farmers organized to win a larger share of American opportunity. The concerns about the increasing concentration of economic power, political corruption and betrayal, overproduction and unemployment, developing in the context of the rise of the corporation as a new system of power, produced a growing radical challenge to the status quo and an outburst of middle class reformism searching for new ways to make the system function better. For many Americans the quest for regeneration and revitalization led to foreign expansion.

The Progressive Movement was the major bipartisan response to the problems of domesticating the great corporations and integrating them into a system of national economy, and of instituting political and social reforms to ease the pressures that seemed to be fragmenting American society.

Most progressive leaders, as illustrated by Theodore Roosevelt's New Nationalism, turned toward a philosophy of corporatism. This involved a strengthened executive leadership capable of harmonizing conflicting interests and subsuming factional or class conflict in a balanced or integrated society through creating a sense of common interest. The movement accepted the industrial corporation as a necessary economic institution and understood that it was creating a different kind of market place. Freedom, liberty, or democracy, had therefore to be redefined in terms of the new conditions. The old Jeffersonian-Jacksonian formulation was based on a simpler, more individualistic agrarian society. Progressives generally concluded that conflicting interests might be reconciled through new economic growth generated by greater efficiency at home and economic expansion abroad.[24]

Wilson's platform of 1912, which he summarized with the

phrase New Freedom, has traditionally been represented as
"neo-Jeffersonian" laissez faire, states-rightism, and involving a
more limited concept of the role of the federal government than
did the New Nationalism of the 1900s. Actually, however, Wilson's thinking was in many respects quite close to the New
Nationalists. He, too, dealt with the problem of social disintegration, economic stagnation, and the rise of the power of the
corporation, by accepting the inevitability of the corporation as
an economic institution, and by seeking a new and strong national leadership capable of transcending group interests and unifying
contending factions. Wilson believed that American society could
be restored under the aegis of a strong national executive and by
the provision of growth and the restoration of opportunity
through economic expansionism.

The difficulty as Wilson saw it was to reunite the people and
create harmony of thought and action between effective executive leadership and the people as a whole, to induce the people to
support the natural leadership of the best people, those of talent,
wisdom, and "character." Wilson wrote as early as 1908 that
constitutional government became vital only through a "cordial
understanding" between the governed and the governors.[25] He
sought this vitalization of government through the abandonment
of the "Whig theory" of checks and balances which had been
adopted at the Constitutional Convention in 1789 in an "over-
zealous reaction to monarchy." He turned to "Mr. Hamilton's
theory" that government was an affair of "cooperation and
harmonious forces." The Whig theory of maintaining government
at the point of a mechanical balance had resulted in the fragmen-
tation of authority. The multiplication of elective offices meant a
fractionalization of government that emphasized local interests
and special interest at the expense of the unity of the whole.
Wilson concluded that party government made its appearance as
an effort to tie the fragments together, but he argued that no
party manager could piece local majorities together and construct
a national majority. The parties, according to Wilson, had themselves become the body politic, appointing elective officers
through the nomination process. They were trying to bind the
country together by usurping leadership and replacing it with
"organized selfishness." Wilson urged the abandonment of Whig
theory and its replacement with "political responsibility."

Since Anglo-Saxon self-control and self-discipline had broken
down, Wilson believed in the necessity of emphasizing the leader-

ship principle to recreate liberty by submerging factionalism under executive leadership. Once such support was attained, intervention in internal affairs would return to a minimum because the factions and the leader would be in tune. Democracy was not a majority opinion welling up from below but rather the coordination of popular opinion with that of a strong leader who could mold a popular will in accord with his own. He advocated a simplification of politics through a decrease in the number and complexity of decisions the voter had to make on the grounds that the mass of voters could not handle such choices. They should concentrate their efforts on the selection of a few men of "responsibility," a few objects upon which they could "easily centre [their] purpose." That would create a strong executive leadership that would then appeal to the imagination of the mass, submerging the interest of the components and uniting them once more into a political concensus.[26]   But an overriding enthusiasm was needed to transcend faction and create common purpose. Such sense of purpose would replace the self-seeking of groups with a new harmony and "weld our people together" in a "patriotism as pure, a wisdom as elevated, a virtue as sound as those of the greater generation" of a hundred years before. [27] The Spanish-American War turned Wilson's thought toward expansion as the great unifying principle.

Expansion became more and more essential to Wilson's thought after 1900. At first he saw expansion simply as the vehicle for developing the kind of new leadership he thought necessary—a useful kind of tool. He came, however, to consider expansion necessary to the survival of the United States, socially, politically and economically.

Wilson thrilled to the march of the flag across the Pacific in a speech before the New England Society of New York City, on December 22, 1900, and contrasted the contribution of the Puritans to American character, the principles of order, polity, discipline, with the sense of adventure, the restless seeking of the Scotch-Irish of his own ancestry. His forebears, he claimed, provided the aspiration, the daring, the unrest that pushed the United States across the continent. Placing himself in the tradition of aggressive expansionism, he prayed that the Puritan instinct of self-examination "may but precede the expansion of power," and the sense of daring and elevation of the Scotch-Irish may "go with us to the ends of the earth." The United States now faced the challenge of doing new things, and he made the point by offering the following interpretation of George Washington's Farewell Address:

> I want you to discipline yourselves and stay still and be good boys, until you are big enough to stand the competition of foreign countries, until you are big enough to go abroad in the world.

The time had arrived and Americans were ready to venture forth. Wilson called the New England Society to follow the Scotch-Irish across the continent and into the "farther seas of the Pacific;" to follow the "Star of Empire" with those who would "follow anything they think will drop profit or amusement." Wilson urged Americans to cast aside restraint, unify, and face glory.[28]

Wilson had studied with Frederick Jackson Turner at the Johns Hopkins University in the late 1880s, and learned from him the significance of the closing of the frontier. Wilson explained, in an essay published in 1901, that the United States had reached the end of its formulative stage, matured by a century of expansion across the continent, and was now ready to go abroad. Until 1890 the United States had always had a frontier; "looked always to a region beyond, unoccupied, unappropriated," an outlet for its energy, and a new place of settlement and achievement. England had "set her energy free" and given outlet to her enterprise by planting colonies around the world. The United States was doing the same through its own expansion. Thus, to the force of Anglo-Saxon conditioning, Wilson added empire as an engine of liberty.

The Americans, like the English "in every impulse of mastery and achievement," had taken their own continental empire and made democracy workable for the United States. Room for expansion perpetuated the "spirit of initiative and practical expedience," and created a national feeling. It bred "energy, resourcefulness and self-confidence." True, Americans had initially been "fit to be free" by their Anglo-Saxon heritage of self-discipline, organization, obedience to authority and sense of mutual obligation. This heritage was derived from centuries of English leadership by men who were "in a very excellent and substantial sense representative" by being landlords and neighbors of those whose affairs they administered.

Democracy became a viable development in the English political heritage because of the availability of great stretches of open land on the American continent. Opportunity made democracy

work. It provided freedom for every sort of enterprise, and
enabled Americans to determine their own destiny, "unguided
and unbidden . . .using institutions, not dominated by them."
Possessing such freedom, Americans had come to sympathize
with freedom everywhere. Out of their own sense of accomplish-
ment, Wilson maintained, they sought to bring freedom to
others, to export their principles and by so doing to make the
"whole world . . . as happy and well to do as ourselves."[29]

There was a danger now that this Anglo-Saxon heritage of
freedom was being disrupted by mass democracy. The English
liberal tradition had evolved through expansion. It was transplanted to American soil and nourished by the continental frontier. Wilson contended, however, that the capacity for self-
government stemmed from centuries of training and discipline,
the product of a uniquely English heritage. The continental
empire made it possible for democracy to be compatible with
liberty. So long as the frontier could absorb the growing capital,
energies and population, democracy functioned well. The frontier was now closed, however, and democracy in a mass industrial society threatened to swamp the English tradition of
liberty.

Even in the United States, Wilson warned, this "vast and
miscellaneous democracy of ours must be led." Its giant facilities
must be schooled and directed. Liberty requires self-direction
and self-discipline. These qualities were not characteristic of mass
democracy in an industrial society. America needed leadership
and leadership cannot belong to the multitude. Masses of men
cannot be self-directed. The people were now a "thousand audi-
ences who must be unified by organization and persuasion."
They needed leaders who were "impersonated policies." Modern
democracy needed dominant minds with the persuasive power to
shape popular judgment.[30] The United States, though beset by
difficulties within, still possessed the qualities of leadership in
greater measure than other areas. Thus, it was the obligation of
the United States to provide moral leadership and guidance to
the less fortunate peoples of the world.

Wilson urged America to pursue the Star of Empire because of
America's "obligation" to others and also because of its failures at
home. The United States entered a new era with the closing of
the frontier, an era that "had come upon us like a sudden vision
of things unprophesied. . . ." The United States took an insular
empire in the Spanish-American War and this released forces

which must make the politics of the twentieth century radically
different. This change came "at the natural point in our national
development," according to Wilson. [31] The United States needed
a new kind of leadership and unity. Expansion would enhance
the authority and function of the President. The task of adminis-
tering an informal empire abroad would revise the process of
decision-making at home and call forth a new service elite to
replace the chaos and lack of direction of popular democracy. In
the process of expanding American influence the United States
might be able to revitalize its own political structure and get
responsible and centralized leadership instead of "government by
mass meeting." [32]

Wilson rejected the argument that America had to perfect its
own institutions before it embarked on the reformation of the
world. "May it not be," he wrote in 1901, "that the way to
perfection lies along these new paths of struggle, of discipline,
and of achievement." The rewards of the "new duty" might well
be "unified will, simplified method and clarified purpose." Wilson spurned the warning that it would be fatal to be "called off
from a task but half done to the tasks of the world." America
had been neutral too long. "We could not have held off."
Americans could no longer think themselves a "divided portion
of mankind, masters and makers of our own laws of trade." [33]

The first task, Wilson said in 1901, was to extend self-
government to Puerto Rico and the Philippines "if they be fit to
receive it—so soon as they can be made fit." [34] Self-government
was not a product of the destructive forces of mass democracy
unleashed by European revolutions, according to Wilson. It was
not transferrable but rather was based on character traits developed from the "long discipline which gives people self-possession,
self-mastery, the habit of order and peace and a reverence for
law,"—the Anglo-Saxon heritage. This required long training. [35]
The United States could furnish the world with "this long,
tedious education in discipline" that was so necessary to
self-government. [36]

Wilson defined the American obligation to its empire in his
textbook on *Constitutional Government*. America could admin-
ister a just and constitutional government for the well-being of
the Filipinos, but could not permit direct self-government. The
United States should provide authority, teach the Filipinos obe-

dience, self-discipline and self-mastery. "Only a long apprentice-
ship of obedience can secure them the precious possession, a
thing no more to be bought than given." [37] This was Wilson's
version of the "white man's burden" in British liberal
imperialism.

The mission and interests of the United States extended beyond the new insular possessions. The "new frontage toward the
Orient" brought the United States into the mainstream of world
affairs. The East had to be opened and transformed "whether we
will or no," and the West had to impose its standards. The great
civilizing force, "the universal world of commerce and ideas,"
would transform Asia. The United States had the peculiar duty
to moderate this process in the direction of "liberty;" to impart
to the Asian people American principles of self-help, and to teach
the Asians order and self-control in the midst of change. The
Anglo-Saxons would bring to Asia the "drill and habit of law and
obedience," Wilson said, and in the process the United States
would gain a renewal of the "opportunity" on which its "freedom" was based. [38]

The United States could not export its own institutions of
self-government for these would be a "curse" to undeveloped
peoples "still in the child-hood of their political growth." America could export a "spirit of service" and help to provide a
government and rule which would "moralize and elevate." Asia
needed the aid of American character, not its institutions. [39]

This nation, Wilson said, was forced "by history and the
implications of the census of 1890 onto the world scene." It
gained "new frontiers . . . beyond the seas," and a new revolution. The battle of Manila was as important as the battle of
Trenton for American development. It was destined to produce
major changes within the United States. [40] Americans were developing a new sense of nationalism, learning to "stand closer to
other nations and take our measure against them." Empire was
shifting the balance of the federal government. Sectional and
state interests were being subsumed in a national outlook. "We
are sensitive to airs that come to us from off the seas," Wilson
wrote in 1901, and the President and his advisers were becoming
the new focal point and source of guidance in this new relationship with the world. The job was to put leaders of character at
the front and make America "great in the world." [41]

Notes and References

1. Seymour, *House Papers*, I, 176; Arthur S. Link, "Portrait of the President," in Earl Latham, ed., *The Philosophy and Policies of Woodrow Wilson* (University of Chicago Press, 1958), 4; Ida Tarbell, "A Talk with the President of the United States," *Colliers*, LCIII (October 28, 1916), 37; George Frost Kennan, "Russia and the Versailles Conference," *The American Scholar*, XXX (Winter 1960), 14; Arthur S. Link, *Wilson the Diplomatist* (The Johns Hopkins Press, 1957), 4-11.
2. William Allen White, in his biography of Wilson, describes Wilson's background in these terms: "For the Wilsons were not just called and elected of God; they lived in the big brick manse. They associated only with the gentry. Their dictum was received by a congregation of the prominent citizens of Augusta, of Georgia, of the old South, before the Civil War, during the war, and in the decades that followed. The Wilsons were leaders, people anointed, apart, the Really Best People—eminently respectable!" William Allen White, *Woodrow Wilson* (Riverside Press, 1924), 39-40; see also Alexander L. and Juliette L. George, *Woodrow Wilson and Colonel House* (The John Day Co., 1956), 3-21; Ray Stannard Baker, *Woodrow Wilson: Life and Letters* (Doubleday, Page and Co., 1927), vol. I, 6-17.
3. George and George, *Wilson and House*, 3-13.
4. Arthur S. Link, *Woodrow Wilson: The New Freedom* (Princeton University Press, 1956), 62-63.
5. Arthur S. Link, *The Papers of Woodrow Wilson* (Princeton University Press, 1966), vol. I, 610-616. For an excellent analysis of the development of Wilson's economic thought see William Diamond, *The Economic Thought of Woodrow Wilson* (The Johns Hopkins Press, 1943).
6. Francis A. Walker, *Political Economy* (Henry Holt & Co., 1883-1888); John Bates Clark, *Philosophy of Wealth*, (Ginn & Co., 1887). For a discussion of this material see Diamond, *Economic Thought*, 21-34.
7. Diamond, *Economic Thought*, 21-34.
8. Woodrow Wilson, "Cabinet Government in the United States," *International Review*, VI (August 1879), 46-163.
9. Woodrow Wilson, "Stray Thoughts from the South," February, 1881, in Link, *Papers of Woodrow Wilson*, vol. II, 19-25, 26-31.
10. Woodrow Wilson, "Responsible Government under the Constitution," *An Old Master and Other Political Essays* (Harper and Bros., 1893), 141-81.

11. Woodrow Wilson, *Constitutional Government in the United States* (Columbia University Press, 1908), 25-27.
12. Matthew H. Elbow, *French Corporative Theory, 1789-1948* (Columbia University Press, 1953), 11-12.
13. Wilson, *Constitutional Government*, 5-6. This analogy is used in various forms throughout Wilson's public career, whenever he was trying to gain popular support for a policy or a measure—particularly for the Versailles Treaty.
14. Ibid., passim.
15. Ibid., 5-6.
16. Charles Forcey, *The Crossroads of Liberalism: Croly, Weyl, Lippmann and the Progressive Era, 1900-1925* (Oxford University Press, 1961), xxvii.
17. Woodrow Wilson, *An Old Master and Other Political Essays* (Harper & Bros., 1893), 88-89.
18. Woodrow Wilson, *Mere Literature* (Harper & Bros., 1896), 187-199.
19. Wilson, *An Old Master*, 85-103; Woodrow Wilson, "Speech on the One Hundredth Anniversary of the Inauguration of George Washington," April 30, 1889, reprinted in *Selected Literary and Political Papers and Addresses of Woodrow Wilson* (Grosset and Dunlap, 1926), vol. I, 30-39.
20. For a discussion of these concepts in the thought of Theodore Roosevelt see Howard K. Beale, *Theodore Roosevelt and the Rise of America to World Power* (The Johns Hopkins Press, 1956), 27-34.
21. Alexander Hamilton, James Madison, John Jay, *The Federalist* (Tudor Publishing Co., 1937), 62-70.
22. Wilson, "Inauguration of George Washington," ibid.
23. Wilson, *An Old Master*, 108; "Inauguration of George Washington," passim.
24. The literature covering these developments and the political and intellectual responses is prolific. See such works as Harold Underwood Faulkner, *The Decline of Laissez Faire, 1897-1917* (Rinehart & Co., 1951; Thomas C. Cochran and William Miller, *The Age of Enterprise* (Macmillan, 1942); William Appleman Williams, *Contours of American History* (World Publishing Co., 1961); Charles Forcey, *The Crossroads of Liberalism* (Oxford University Press, 1961); George E. Mowry, *Theodore Roosevelt and the Progressive Movement* (University of Wisconsin Press, 1947); Howard K. Beale, *Theodore Roosevelt and the Rise of America to World Power* (The Johns Hopkins Press, 1956).
25. Wilson, *Constitutional Government*, 222.
26. Ibid., 199-222.

27. Wilson, "Inauguration of George Washington," 28-39.
28. Woodrow Wilson, "The Puritan," speech before the New England
    Society of New York City, December 22, 1900, reprinted in *Selected
    Papers*, I, 102-11.
29. Woodrow Wilson, "Democracy and Efficiency," *Atlantic Monthly*,
    LXXXVIII (March, 1901), 289-299.
30. Wilson, *An Old Master*, 109-111.
31. Wilson, "Democracy and Efficiency," 297.
32. Ibid., 299.
33. Ibid., 292-293.
34. Ibid., 297.
35. Wilson, *Constitutional Government*, 52.
36. Wilson, "Democracy and Efficiency," 298-299.
37. Wilson, *Constitutional Government*, 52-53.
38. Wilson, "Democracy and Efficiency," 298-299.
39. Ibid., 299.
40. Woodrow Wilson, "Ideals of America," *Atlantic Monthly*, XC
    (December 1902), 727.
41. Ibid., 733-34.

2
THE POLITICAL ECONOMY OF EMPIRE

Wilson viewed the Spanish-American war as a watershed in American development. It had come in answer to the growing sickness in the body politic. Factionalism and populism were tearing apart the Wilsonian dream of a stable consensus under the leadership of a disinterested gentry. He believed that the new frontier of overseas expansion might provide the means of correcting faults at home.

The new frontier meant to Wilson not only that American principles and character, but also its manufactures, would be exported for the benefit of the world at large as well as the United States. He shared the growing concern with the need for foreign markets and investments, and defined economic expansion as a necessity to make the political economy viable. In his *History of the American People*, published in 1902, Wilson explained that the closing of the frontier meant that the United States had to turn from concentrating on the development of its resources at home "to the conquest of the markets of the world." [1] No longer masters of "our own laws of trade," Americans confronted foreign economic conflict. America's "private business," Wilson had explained the year before, had now to take its chances in competition with the "greater business of the world at large." The national interests, he warned, "must march forward, altruists though we are: other nations must see to it that they stand off, and do not seek to stay us." [2]

Though Wilson spoke much of service to humanity and about the correction of political defects at home, he did not separate those objectives from the pursuit and protection of American markets. He was pleased by the application of the pressure of "our opinion and our material interest in the Cuban struggle." [3] In his view, the American habit of mixing selfish and altruistic motives was a product of the continental frontier of expansion. While sympathizing with freedom everywhere, Americans pursued self-interest in pushing Spain out of the Floridas, and Mexico from the coasts of the Pacific. The aggressive attitude of the United States against French control of the Mississippi, and

the "unpitying force" with which the United States "thrust the
Indians to the wall wherever they stood in our way" were also
part of the American character, and of America's increasing
power.[4]

Wilson was not indifferent to economic pressures for expansion, which had been increased by the depression of the 1890s.
Many saw little chance that the domestic economy could absorb
the manufactured surpluses. Falling prices and the struggle for
profits were forcing improved techniques and cost cutting. As a
consequence, unemployment swelled to 18 percent of the labor
force in 1897.[5] But the exports of manufactured goods doubled
between 1893 and 1899, and that gain helped bring recovery, as
did the great wheat harvest of 1897. The United States was also
beginning to export capital. The Boer War stimulated that development and by 1902 the United States had loaned the British
government $208 million and the German government $20
million.[6]

More important than the loans, American investments in raw
materials extraction, railroads and canals, industrial plants, and
bonds mounted rapidly in the early 1900s. In the period between
1897 and 1914, American direct investments abroad more than
quadrupled from $634.5 million to $4,652.5 billion, and port-
folio investments jumped from $50 million to $861.5 million.[7]
In the years when the European market took less capital and
fewer goods, surplus funds were used for recapitalization and
concentration at home under the leadership of such financiers as
John Pierpont Morgan. Those uses tended to increase efficiency
and thereby compounded the problem.

As the American economy struggled with the difficulty of
creating domestic demand to absorb the production of industry,
and thereby control the business cycle, Wilson and other observers emphasized the need for expansion into world markets. That
meant challenging Europe for the trade of the Far East and Latin
America. Wilson defined economic expansion as inevitable, oblig-
atory, and the means of creating new viability in the American
system. He warned the American Bankers' Association in 1908
about the danger of the "atomizing of our social structure,"
which was stemming from "sharp class contrasts and divisions,"
the "sharp distinctions of power and opportunity." The whole
structure of society, he warned, was being criticized and
"changes of the most radical character were being discussed."

The contest, he explained, was between the great concentrations of capital and the "less concentrated, more dispersed, smaller and more individual economic forces." The "organic connections" of society were threatened by the domination of concentrated capital being used to deprive the masses of economic opportunity. The efforts of the great corporations to accumulate a greater share of the national wealth at the expense of the whole people were permitting "socialist remedies to be taken seriously." To prevent recourse to radical measures Americans had to "open our minds wide" to the "new circumstances of our time."

Wilson asserted that stagnation was the cause of the troubles in the American economy. "You know," he told the bankers, "that even the colossal enterprises of our time do not supply you with safe investments enough for the money that comes in to you." As a consequence, banks were investing in speculative and questionable ventures "at a fearful and wholly unjustifiable risk in order to get the usury they wish from their resources." Wilson warned that the reserves of capital had to be used to provide growth and expanding opportunities for all. Statesmanship, he said, was being forced upon bankers and all those in control of the vast accumulated wealth of the country.[8]

The United States was entering a new and confusing age in the field of economic enterprise, Wilson observed in January 1909, and there were no standards of comparison. Economic institutions and policies had to be adjusted to the new world. In order to avoid destruction, corporations had to reform themselves and pursue their self-interest by cooperating with a broader social interest. Wilson warned that the era of corporate giants struggling with each other for the spoils was past. A new and enlightened conception of class interest was necessary.[9] Through that analysis, Wilson arrived at the central formulation of his new liberalism: the idea of enlightened corporate leadership allied with his new political leadership in the common purpose of promoting economic growth as the dynamic force to reunite American society through prosperity and opportunity. Wilson was slow to formulate his conclusion as starkly as Albert Beveridge had done in 1898:[10]

American factories are making more than the American people can use; American soil is producing more than they can consume. Fate

has written our policy for us; the trade of the world must and shall
be ours.

But he was approaching the question from a somewhat different
direction, and hence did not arrive at the same position until
1909.

As a man being considered for political office, Wilson stressed
two themes in his public speeches and articles during that year.
One was the need for a new elite leadership capable of reuniting
the country. The second was the need for tariff reduction to
permit the United States to shake off industrial inefficiency
nurtured by artificial production and create new opportunities
through market expansion. He identified the Republicans as
protectionists, the bulwark of partisanship and local interest
which promoted disunity and dissolution. Protectionism meant
the dispensing of government favors, bossism, and corruption. It
helped foster economic inefficiency and prevented the American
economy from becoming competitive in the world market.

Wilson was not arguing merely as a Democrat, nor as an
advocate of states' rights. He believed that protection had been
functional when the United States was underdeveloped. He had
approved, he said, of Hamilton's original program of protecting
infant industries to promote growth, for it had been "idle to ask
an undeveloped continent to put its faith in the natural laws of
trade and production," to try to build its wealth "on the demand
for what it has and buy what it has not."

As the United States reached economic maturity, however,
protectionism ceased to be a virtue and became instead a prop
for inefficiency and special privilege. As long as the United States
had a growing domestic economy the system worked. Isolation
from the world market was not burdensome. But protectionism
now served as á barrier to further growth. It promoted monopoly
and permitted the accumulation of enormous fortunes without
contributing to efficient growth: monopoly was "crushing competition." Wilson did not blame the corporate leaders, whom he
called the men of "extraordinary genius," for the emergence of
the large corporation was a natural and inevitable economic
evolution. But the great industrial corporations had attained the
size and organization that permitted them to "invade foreign
markets and sell to all the world."

The maintenance of protectionism served to perpetuate a
prosperity that was uneven and selective. Wages were ;being
maintained by the aggressiveness and determination of organized

labor rather than by the prosperity of the corporate system. The efforts of the great corporations to maintain control of the market narrowed the area of opportunity for others. The result was the development of serious stratification: a small privileged class possessing great influence in the "committee government" of Congress, and a vast underprivileged body which "forces its way to a share of the benefits" only by threats and strikes and is steadily "deprived of a large percentage of what it thus gains by rapidly rising prices." Wilson had progressed beyond the belief that dissent and factionalism were caused by the passionate blood of European immigration which could not be assimilated, and now explained those phenomena by the narrowing of the base of economic opportunity.

Wilson did not propose "sweeping the whole system away." "The system," he warned, "cannot be suddenly destroyed." That would pose a grave danger to national life. He preferred a slow process of reform through tariff reduction that would realize Hamilton's "old purpose." The time had come to promote the collective interest of a truly national economy rather than those of diverse special groups. The test of the wholesomeness of American economics would be the ability of industry to compete in world markets."

Wilson continually stressed the need for industrial efficiency to improve America's competitive power in the world market. That would enable the United States to resume its economic growth and regenerate economic opportunity, thereby creating a sense of identification with the system which would eliminate discontent, factionalism and disunity.'² Once factionalism was subsumed in a new sense of community and national purpose,'³ economic individualism would again become meaningful. But if that did not occur, then the United States would "stagger like France through fields of blood" before "she again finds peace and prosperity under the leadership of men who know her needs.'''⁴

As Wilson made the transition from resident of Princeton to Governor of New Jersey, his thoughts began to reach men more influential in the national economy. He continued to advocate a program of reform based on the driving force of economic expansion. He argued the need to destroy the connection between special interest groups and government in order to permit wider freedom of economic opportunity. Economic growth would revitalize "democracy" through cooperation, strong executive leadership, the reduction of the role of Congress, and the simplification and narrowing of the choices the voter was called on to make. Wilson continued to advocate his version of cabinet government, or, as he called it in 1910, government by council, which would have the power to appoint key officials instead of having them elected. That would permit the desired concentration of responsibility at the top. The voters could then narrow their attention to the more important question of choosing a leader with whom they had empathy. The people could then allow that leader to distribute authority instead of having to go through the laborious and confusing process of decision making by headcount, by voting for a whole hierarchy of officialdom. This new process would permit the emergence of a "leadership of the whole" rather than that of conglomerations of factions.[15] This was the essence of the version of corporatism labeled the "new democracy."[16]

When Wilson addressed the convention of the American Bankers Association in 1908, he elaborated his corporatist view. He pointed to the dangers of social atomization that were becoming increasingly evident and explained them as the result of distinctions of power and opportunity.[17] This dissolution of social unity was a very dangerous development because Wilson felt that American society could only exist as an organic whole. The parts, by themselves, were not capable of life.[18]

As a consequence of the disintegration, many were turning to the principles of socialism. Wilson believed that, in principle, socialism was hardly distinguishable from democracy. The object of both was to "effect such an organization of society as will give the individual his best protection and his best opportunity, and yet serve the interest of all rather than the interest of any one in particular." The programs of socialism, however, were either "utterly vague" or "entirely impracticable." Even so, because there was no "organic harmony," socialism looked "hopeful and attractive." It could not be pushed aside or defeated by "mere opposition or denial." It had to be replaced by "wiser and better programs."[19]

The center of power in the United States lay not in government, Wilson pointed out, but in capital, and it was the task of the men representing capital to take the lead in recreating an organic community of interest. Capital must reorient itself toward serving the interests of the people as a whole. "Voluntary cooperation" must forestall coercion by the state.[20] Bankers and

businessmen must meet their obligation to "be public men serving their depositors and the enterprises whose securities and
notes they hold." It was necessary for "men of every class" to
concern themselves with the public welfare as they had never
before. Statesmanship was being forced upon bankers, and upon
"all those who have to do with the application and use of the
vast accumulated wealth of this country." [21]

As candidate for Governor of New Jersey in 1910, Wilson
expanded on his program of reform based on the subsuming of
class interest into national interest. The driving force was to be
economic expansion. He told the New Jersey Bankers' Association in September that a "new standard of honesty" and new
opportunity for enterprise depended on the ability of government and business to work together to stimulate the rate of
growth of the economy. The resources of the country, Wilson
warned, were approaching exhaustion, and the future was with
those who could "husband them, renew them, economise," and
"combine resources" to promote efficiency. The future belonged
to the man who could compete, without patronage and protection, with the German manufacturer and miner. As the United
States had once conquered the world by its visions, by "feeding
. . . [the world's] hope of a political millennium," now it would
have to "conquer once more by endeavor," by competing in a
world drawn into one community and in which "it will be a day
of shame for any race that cannot stand on its feet and take the
fruits of the game according to its merits." The time had come,
Wilson told the New Jersey bankers, when "if you cannot be
statesmen you cannot be bankers." [22]

Two years later, as a Presidential candidate, Wilson stressed his
old theme that the closing of the frontier had created the
necessity for "the conquest of world markets." [23] In an address
before the National Democratic Club on January 3, 1912, he
described 1898 as the turning point in American development
that marked the end of an inward oriented economy. The United
States needed "to give scope to our energy," and he urged tariff
reduction so that American industry might become more efficient and able to win foreign markets. America also needed a
merchant marine to transport its surpluses. Restricting the merchant fleet had deprived the country of the carrying trade of the
world which it might have controlled "to the exclusion of other
nations." Capturing markets abroad, he proclaimed, would allevi-
ate unemployment and social distress at home. [24]

The economy, he argued a bit later, was confined at home and developing inefficiency, waste, unemployment, corruption and suffering. Though exports had been rising, industrial production continued to create surpluses. America needed markets abroad and ships of its own, for the nation which "carries the world's goods can generally see to it that its merchants get the markets." According to Wilson, productive capacity had far outstripped the power to consume. "In order to relieve the plethora," in order to "use the energy of the capital of America," the country had to "break the chrysalis"—"the conditions of America are going to burst through it and are now bursting through it."

Americans could not fight the Spanish-American War, Wilson cried, and "still keep your gaze directed inward." The nation needed a national spokesman, a "single will," a strong, guiding executive, "because it had no choice—it must have it." The country required efficient industry and leadership to enter "the general field of competition which includes the whole globe." This was the century in which America was to "prove once more whether she has any right to claim leadership of the world of originative economic effort." [25] Again and again Wilson stressed the closing of the old continental frontier and the necessity of a new one in world trade. That was essential to prevent disturbance at home. The closed frontier, said Wilson at Richmond, Virginia, on February 1, 1912, meant the end of the ability of people to flee from "intolerable conditions" in "crowded" America. For as America "turns upon herself her seething millions . . . the cauldron grows hotter and hotter."

Americans were no longer free to "release themselves," and were faced, for the first time, with the necessity of acquiring a "modus vivendi in America for happiness." The United States had "never had to finish anything before; there was always room to move on." Now Americans were faced with the problem of "making things work." Once having made this point, however, Wilson backed away from the implications. The modus vivendi he sought would be found by again moving on. Overseas economic expansion might make the system viable. The "great, irrepressible energy of America is doing more than it can keep within its own shops and limits," Wilson went on, and it had to be released for the "commercial conquest of the world." [26] America had to "fling our own flag out upon the seas again," and take possession of "our rightful share of the trade of the world." [27]

The "rank and file" of Americans were finding it hard to

sustain life because of the growth of privilege. Economic opportunity had narrowed in the face of corporate concentration. The
great questions of "right and justice" were questions, now, of
national development, of the restoration of economic opportunity. A "great readjustment" was necessary to again provide
opportunity and to utilize the forces of the whole society.
Americans must work together to conserve national resources,
organize their productive potential, and expand their economy.
"Our industries have expanded to such a point that they will
burst their jackets" if they cannot "find a free outlet to the
markets of the world." Though Wilson sought new opportunity
at home as the means of reuniting society, he stressed the
argument that "our domestic markets no longer suffice. We need
foreign markets." [28]

Wilson used this conception of a New Freedom to oppose
Theodore Roosevelt's "New Nationalism." Though the two candidates clashed over the extent of the role of the federal government in controlling corporations and adjusting social
imbalance, [29] they agreed on some basic points. Robert H. Wiebe
makes the point that both candidates "accepted the legitimacy of
power residing in voluntary groups, they assumed the responsibility of the national government for guidance, and they conceived
of that guidance in bureaucratic terms." [30] This was one common
denominator of their progressivism. Both believed the old definitions of individualistic liberty stemming from a laissez-faire system were made irrelevant by the new economic organization.

They also accepted the emergence of an economy dominated
by large corporations as a necessary consequence of modern
industrial conditions. Roosevelt argued that the effort to restore
competition "as it was sixty years ago" was foolish and "doomed
to failure." His purpose was not to "strangle business as an
incident of strangling corporations," but to help "legitimate
business" in order to safeguard the interests of the people as a
whole. Great corporations that had attained their position
through efficiency were not only legitimate but necessary. They
were, he said, a "weapon in the great field of industrial competition." It was only the corporation that engaged in corrupt
practices and unfair methods which had to be curbed. [31]

Wilson shared the view, despite the apparent contradiction in
some of his campaign rhetoric, that the rise of the corporate
system was a necessary and natural consequence of American
development, an essential part of industrial efficiency. And effi-

ciency was the key to the "righteous conquest of the markets of the world." "Business is going to be done by corporations," he proclaimed in 1912. "The old time of individual competition is gone by." Only the corporations could conduct business on "a great and successful scale."[32] The United States could never return to the "old order of individual competition." Organization on a "great scale of co-operation" was "normal and inevitable."[33] Wilson also agreed with Roosevelt that the danger was not a result of size *per se* (even if that size tended to restrict individual competition), but in inefficient size that restricted economic growth by diverting capital from productive channels to the enrichment of small groups of monopolists.[34]

Wilson believed that the energies of the corporation had to be redirected toward a social function, the "reintegration" of an "atomizing" society. Capital had to be made to serve the interests of the whole by being oriented toward productive growth. To this end the various classes had to "co-operate and work for the public interest."[35] Where Roosevelt distinguished between the good and the bad trusts, Wilson preferred to talk of efficient and competitive "big business" as opposed to the inefficiency of the trusts. The distinguishing factor was efficiency rather than size or share of the market. Though Wilson made references to wanting the "pigmy to have a chance to come out," he also made it plain that he saw the future in terms of "the development of business upon a great scale, upon a great scale of co-operation."[36] The evidence suggests very clearly that Wilson's definition of the good corporation developing on a great scale was very similar to Roosevelt's "good trust," and that the "trust" denounced by Wilson had the same characteristics reserved by Roosevelt for the "bad trust." Neither really advocated the old concept of laissez faire.

The substantive difference between the two men concerned government participation in reform. The New Nationalists advocated a program of government action to correct some of the social abuses and restore a better balance between conflicting interests.[37] Wilson recognized the existence of discontent, and acknowledged the danger of group antagonism and conflict. But he emphasized the importance of promoting economic growth. An expanding economy, he argued, would effect the necessary social reform as an automatic consequence. His general program stressed reforming the tariff "which cuts us off from our proper part in the commerce of the world," monetary and banking changes to promote the more effective use of financial resources for growth (particularly in foreign trade), measures to encourage greater efficiency in agriculture by applying science and private credit, and the better utilization and conservation of natural resources.[38]

An understanding of this underlying pattern helps resolve the seeming paradox of referring to the Wilson period as an era of "democratic reform" while at the same time describing Wilson as a very reluctant reformer. Wilson believed that if the Federal Government paved the way for economic growth, social reform would generally take care of itself (with some local help). The chief object of the revision of the Articles of Confederation, Wilson had explained in 1909, was "undoubtedly economic regulation." The central power given Congress concerned the regulation of commerce. With the creation of a national economy, the "development of the resources of the country, the command of the markets of the world" became more important than any political theory of "lawyer's discrimination of functions." But the federal government should not delve into "moral and social questions."[39] Though the necessities of party politics caused Wilson to make references to social welfare legislation, he generally opposed specific reforms in the "moral and social area," and tried to honor his belief that internal reform would follow the economic development generated by expansion abroad.[40]

Arthur S. Link has documented Wilson's opposition to measures of domestic social reform and his reluctant acquiescence in their passage into law. While Wilson acknowledged the need for an income tax to replace the tariff as a source of revenue, for example, he fought any effort to use the measure as a means of redistributing income. He opposed Federal control of banking, supporting instead a bill by Carter Glass which was designed to "serve only the business community" and to "reinforce private control over banking and currency." Similarly, he opposed the exemption of labor organizations from antitrust prohibitions and court restrictions, accepting a compromise only when three Democratic Congressmen threatened to bolt to the Republicans on the antitrust program. In the same manner, Wilson protested against a child labor law, the extension of suffrage to women (until the "war for democracy" forced it), government financing for land banks, and government commissions to regulate business. Wilson's special conservatism is perhaps best revealed by his favoring the introduction of a greater degree of segregation for

Negro employees of the Federal government "for their own good."[41]

Wilson fought for the promotion of an expanding economy as the means of rehabilitating American society while rejecting measures of assistance to particular groups such as labor because the latter approach, he said, would isolate the interests of particular groups from that of the "great body of fellow citizens who sustain and conduct the enterprises of the country."[42]   Tariff reform was for him the principle means whereby businessmen would be subjected to the "stimulation of a constant necessity to be efficient, economical, and enterprising." They would be prodded to become masters of "competitive supremacy," and become workers and merchants better than "any in the world."[43]   Tariff reform was not simply party doctrine, but the key to the expansion of foreign trade that would regenerate consensus and community through the reinfusion of opportunity. The Underwood Tariff was designed, according to Wilson, to place domestic industry in a position to compete with European manufactures by reducing or abolishing rates only where it could be shown that "American products occupied a dominant position in the world market."[44]

Currency and banking reforms were considered auxilliary to tariff revision. They were designed to give industry the tools to exploit its new freedom.[45]   Wilson also called for antitrust legislation to clarify the relationship of the corporation to the law, rather than to restrict the corporation further. And he wanted government commissions established on the principle of helping business to pursue foreign markets. Wilson presented his general program as a series of measures to facilitate an American assault on foreign trade, and summarized his efforts in a speech of September 1916 before the Grain Dealers' Association. He opened with his familiar reference to American production having "burst its jacket," and then recounted his efforts to rectify the situation. The Federal Reserve Act, he said, provided a national banking structure to assist American commerce throughout the world, and to clear the way for the United States to "take her place in the world of finance and commerce upon a scale she never dreamed of before." The Bureau of Foreign and Domestic Commerce, now utilized in "studying the foreign commerce of this country as it was never studied before," was to provide information and guidance for the promotion of foreign trade. The Federal Trade Commission was formed to coordinate relations between business and government, to show the way in which government could help rather than hinder enterprise, and to play the role for industry that the Department of Agriculture played for the farmer. In short, Wilson argued that his efforts were creating "instrumentalities of knowledge" which would enable American businessmen to "know what the field of the world's business is and deal with that field upon that knowledge."

To utilize such information most effectively, Wilson urged businessmen to stop acting separately. They should instead join "trade associations and study their problems as partners and brothers and co-operators." Americans must cooperate, Wilson urged, "the Government with the merchant, the merchant with his employee, the whole body of producers with the whole body of consumers," to insure that "the right things are produced in the right volume and find the right purchasers at the right place." With all groups working together, "we realize that nothing can be for the individual benefit which is not for the common benefit." Wilson urged exporters to combine to gain an advantage over foreign rivals, and for that purpose supported the Webb bill to exempt combinations of exporters from the Sherman and Clayton Acts. He also reiterated his long standing support, including governmental action where it was necessary, for the expansion of an American merchant marine to carry American goods in the interest of American trade. In conclusion, he stressed the development of friendly relations with customers in the republics of South America. This program was the "loom all ready upon which to spread the threads which can be worked into a fabric of friendship and wealth such as we have never known before!"[46]

Wilson's New Freedom was a highly nationalistic, coordinated campaign to expand American trade throughout the world on the basis of domestic integration and cooperation, and with the leadership of a strong executive. It was predicated upon the extension of an American liberal empire that would replace territorial expansion as the engine of domestic prosperity and tranquility. The test of this program would be the reception it got abroad, particularly in Latin America. It was there that Wilson learned of rival nationalism, rival expansionism and revolutionary zeal that would challenge his claims to the moral leadership of the world.

Notes and References

1. Woodrow Wilson, *History of the American People* (Harper & Bros., 1902), vol. V, 296.
2. Wilson, "Democracy and Efficiency," 295.
3. Woodrow Wilson, "Cleveland as President," *Atlantic Monthly*, LXXXIX (March 1897), 289-300.
4. Wilson, "Democracy and Efficiency," 294-295.
5. Alexander Dana Noyes, *Forty Years of American Finance* (G. P. Putnam's Sons, 1909), 273-274; Foster Rhea Dulles, *Labor in America* (Thomas Y. Crowell Co., 1955), 166-182; Harold Underwood Faulkner, *The Decline of Laissez Faire, 1897-1917* (Rinehart & Co., 1951), 262.
6. Noyes, *Forty Years*, 281-283.
7. Faulkner, *Decline of Laissez Faire*, 68-86; Thomas C. Cochran and William Miller, *The Age of Enterprise* (Macmillan, 1942), 202-210.
8. Woodrow Wilson, "Address Before the Annual Convention of the American Bankers' Association," Denver, September 30, 1908, published in Ray Stannard Baker and William E. Dodd, *The Public Papers of Woodrow Wilson: College and State* (Harper and Bros., 1925), vol. II, 54-56.
9. Woodrow Wilson, "Robert E. Lee, an Interpretation," Address delivered at the University of North Carolina, January 18, 1909, *College and State*, II, 64-83.
10. Claude Bowers, *Beveridge and the Progressive Era* (Riverside Press, 1932), 69.
11. Woodrow Wilson, "The Tariff Make-Believe," *North American Review*, CXC (October, 1909), 535-556.
12. Woodrow Wilson, "The Ministry and the Individual," Address at the McCormick Theological Seminary, Chicago, November 2, 1909, *College and State*, II, 178-187; Woodrow Wilson, "Political Reform," Address before the City Club of Philadelphia, November 18,1909, *College and State*, II, 188-192.
13. See Wilson's analogy of liberty on page 13.
14. Woodrow Wilson, "Address to the Pittsburgh Alumni Banquet," April 16, 1910, *Public Papers*, II, 202-3.
15. Woodrow Wilson, "Hide and Seek Politics," *North American Review*, CXCI (May 1910), 585-601.
16. See Herbert Croly, *The Promise of American Life* (Macmillan, 1909) for an exposition of the ideology and rhetoric of the "new democracy."

17. Woodrow Wilson, "The Banker and the Nation," Address before the American Bankers Convention, Denver, September 30, 1908, *Select Papers*, II, 187-188.
18. Ibid., 188.
19. Ibid., 188-189.
20. Ibid., 189-192.
21. Ibid., 193-197.
22. Woodrow Wilson, "Address Before the New Jersey Bankers' Association," May 6, 1910, ibid., 225-233.
23. See Chapter I.
24. Woodrow Wilson, "Address Before the National Democratic Club," New York, January 3, 1912, *Select Papers*, II, 334-336.
25. Woodrow Wilson, "Address Before the Real Estate Men of Boston," Boston, January 27, 1912, ibid., 354-366.
26. Woodrow Wilson, "Address Before the General Assembly of Virginia," Richmond, February 1, 1912, ibid., 367-388; "The Tariff and the Trust," February 24, 1912, ibid., 405-408; "Government in Relation to Business," Annual Banquet for the Economic Club of New York, May 23, 1912, ibid., 435-437.
27. Wilson, "Government in Relation to Business," ibid., 436.
28. Woodrow Wilson, "Speech Accepting the Democratic Nomination for the Presidency of the United States," Seagirt, New Jersey, August 7, 1912, *College and State*, II, 452-474.
29. For an excellent brief analysis see John Morton Blum, *Woodrow Wilson and the Politics of Morality* (Little Brown and Company, 1956), 58-63.
30. Robert H. Wiebe, *The Search for Order, 1877-1920* (Hill and Wang, 1967), 217-218.
31. Theodore Roosevelt, *Outlook*, IC (November 18, 1911), 65.
32. Woodrow Wilson, "Address at Nashville, Tennessee," February 24, 1912, *College and State*, II, 410-411.
33. Wilson, "Speech Accepting the Democratic Nomination," ibid., 464.
34. Wilson, "Address at Nashville, Tennessee," ibid., 411-412.
35. Wilson, "Address Before the Annual Convention of American Bankers' Association," ibid., 54-56.
36. Woodrow Wilson, *The New Freedom* (Doubleday, Page and Co., 1913), 164-169.
37. See Forcey, *Crossroads of Liberalism*. For an interesting study of the definitions of the New Nationalism see the above. Also see Mowry, *Theodore Roosevelt and the Progressive Movement*, 120-141.
38. Woodrow Wilson, "Special Address to Congress," April 8, 1913, Ray

Stannard Baker and William E. Dodd, *The Public Papers of Woodrow Wilson: The New Democracy* (Harper and Bros., 1926), vol. I, 34-35. (Hereafter cited as *New Democracy*).

39. Woodrow Wilson, *Constitutional Government in the United States* (Columbia University Press, 1908), 173-196.

40. See Arthur S. Link, *Woodrow Wilson and the Progressive Era* (Harper and Bros., 1954), 20-21, for the conflict in interpretation of the "democratic reformer" and his "reluctant reforms." See Introduction, supra, for the development of Wilson's thought on corporate freedom and efficiency.

41. For Link's description of Wilson's opposition to this type of reform, and his concentration on attempts to provide facilities for corporate growth as the chief vehicle of reform, see Link, ibid., 20-80; Wilson, *The New Freedom*, 199-276.

42. Woodrow Wilson, "Freedmen Need no Guardians," *Fortnightly Review*, IC (February, 1913), 209-218.

43. Woodrow Wilson, "Special Address to Congress," *New Democracy*, I, 34-35.

44. Ibid.; Wilson, "Address Accepting the Democratic Nomination," *College and State*, II, 459; Link, *Woodrow Wilson and the Progressive Era*, 38. See also Frank W. Taussig, *The Tariff History of the United States* (G. P. Putnam's Sons, 1931), 409-446. Taussig draws the proper distinction between competitive tariffs and free trade.

45. Woodrow Wilson, "Address to Joint Session of Congress," June 23, 1913, *New Democracy*, I, 37-40.

46. Woodrow Wilson, "Address Before the Grain Dealers' Association," Baltimore, September 25, 1916, *New Democracy*, II, 312-321.

3
LATIN AMERICA

THE OPPORTUNITY AND THE FIRST CHALLENGE

Latin America provided President Wilson with the opportunity and the necessity of shaping the "fabric of friendship and wealth" in accordance with the imperatives provided by his economic, moral, and political principles. There is general agreement among historians that the "record of American interference in Mexico, Central America and the Caribbean region from 1913 to 1917 was unparalleled before or since in the history of the western hemisphere."[1] At the same time, Wilson's New Diplomacy is often regarded as an effort to break with the "dollar diplomacy" of the Taft Administration and as the harbinger of a new era of international morality and mutuality. Professor Link explains the "apparent contradiction between New Freedom profession and practice"[2] as the result of Wilson's inability to put his principles and intentions into practice. This was caused by prior commitments, by present necessities, and by an "ignorance of foreign conditions." According to this analysis, Wilson and Bryan failed to "meet their own criteria" because of the "naiveté" of their underlying assumptions that "moral force controlled the relations of powers, that reason would prevail over ignorance and passion in the formation of public opinion," and that men were "automatically progressing toward an orderly and righteous international society." This view distinguishes between "realists" such as Theodore Roosevelt, who felt that men were motivated by greed and ambition more often than "Christian Love," and "Idealists," such as Wilson, who felt that "altruism was enough."[3]

The difficulty with an interpretation based upon the existence of a dichotomy between profession and practice is that the historian often creates a conflict that was not apparent to the protagonist. Such was the case with Wilson.[4] Wilson conceived of himself as a most moderate reformer, rather than a radical innovator, who relied on economic efficiency and an aggressive pursuit of trade expansion as the major engines of reform. "Shall we adopt Thorough as our motto and sweep the whole system away?" Wilson asked in 1909. "By no means," he answered.

45

"The system cannot be suddenly destroyed. That would bring our whole economic life into radical danger.⁵ The United States was, according to Wilson, a "business country," and business was "intolerant of ill-considered and rapid change . . . profoundly distrustful of everything it regards as experimental." Wilson took pains to point out that he was sound with respect to that basic principle.⁶ Addressing an audience at the McCormick Theological Seminary in 1909, Wilson avowed himself an "unabashed disciple" of the "doctrine of expedience." "You cannot carry the world forward as fast as a few select individuals think," he warned. Leaders must content themselves with "a slackened pace and go only so fast as they can be followed." They must not be impractical or impossible. Those who would lead must not "insist upon getting at once what they know they cannot get." Christianity, he said, did not come into the world "merely to save the world . . . to set crooked things straight: the end and object was the individual," who should content himself with telling the world what was wrong and not be "fool enough to insist that it adopt [his] program for putting it right." Speak the truth often enough and "the theme will sound familiar."⁷ That was not the counsel of a man who sought to impose a new morality or a radically different pattern of relationships on an unwilling world.

Latin America provided the primary area in which Wilson could apply his concepts of a new order dedicated to the economic well-being of the United States. When he took office, to be sure, he inherited certain problems and commitments in that region; but his statements and actions indicated that he did not consider himself trapped by the past. He accepted the challenge to solve the difficulties and meet the obligations within the framework dictated by his expansionist thesis, his Anglo-Saxonism, and his conception of American moral superiority.

The economic commitments of the United States in Latin America were large and growing rapidly. American long-term investments in Mexico and Central America had increased from $195 million in 1900 to $740 million in 1912. During the same period, investments in Cuba and the West Indies had grown from $60 million to $200 million, and in South America from $35 million to $175 million. Indeed, by the time of Wilson's inauguration, half of the foreign investments of the United States were in Latin America.⁸ The region had absorbed $135,363,245 of American manufactures during 1912, and exported to the United

States $247,094,781 worth of raw materials and tropical food products.[9]

As a President critically concerned with the expansion of the American economy abroad, Wilson could not avoid regarding Latin America as an area of great potential. He accepted the situation he inherited and defined the protection of the position of the United States in Latin America as of central concern. He saw the region becoming ever more closely entwined with the economy of the United States, and he accepted the premise that the government of the United States would act as arbiter of the rules of the game.

Wilson repeatedly stressed the conviction that the opening of the Panama Canal would mean a growing market for American production, and would thereby make an important contribution to the prosperity of the United States. Combined with the insular harvest of the Spanish-American War, the construction of the Canal gave the United States a physical stake in the Caribbean and in Central America;[10] and, during the first decade of the century, "dollar diplomacy" had done much to extend the economic and political influence of the United States. Political and economic penetration of Panama, Cuba, Nicaragua, Haiti and Santo Domingo had led to, and been assisted by, the Roosevelt Corollary. That doctrine provided impetus as well as justification for interposing the United States between Central America and European investors. "By arranging timely Latin American revolutions, by interfering in foreign elections and appropriating foreign customs, the American government sought to make the Caribbean exclusively an American sea and the canal exclusively an American enterprise."[11]

One sympathetic analysis of this expansionism is provided by Dana G. Munro in his study of the era, *Intervention and Dollar Diplomacy in the Caribbean 1900-1921*.[12] Munro writes as a participant[13] who shares the basic assumptions of liberal interventionism, but who believes Americans must learn from its mistakes.[14] The basic assumption, which did not change greatly when new individuals assumed responsibility or even when a different political party took control,[15] was that the United States had prior and paramount strategic interests in the Caribbean in terms of commerce and naval deployment, and that those interests were jeopardized by foreign intervention to secure either territory or trade and by domestic political instability and economic backwardness in the area. Having evaluated the politics of Central America and found them wanting, it was the responsibility of the United States to intervene to promote stability, democracy and isolation from Europe.[16] Revolutions were to be discouraged because they were "the chief cause of controversies with European powers since they endangered foreign lives and property and disrupted the government's finances so that it could not meet foreign claims." Economic improvement had to be promoted in order to secure political stability. Munro asserts that, though State Department officials sometimes "held out the hope of increased trade and new fields for American investment," it is doubtful whether "these considerations really had any great influence in the formulation of policy."[17]

If this contention is accurate, it contradicts the concern with the commercial implications of the Caribbean, particularly after the opening of the Panama Canal, that Munro also posits. If commercial concern is discounted, then all that remains are a desire for naval efficiency [18] and a quest for stability in the area. The argument thus dismisses as secondary the broad definitions of American interests made by several Presidents (most particularly Roosevelt, Taft, and Wilson), by Secretaries of State from William H. Seward to Robert Lansing, and by the various commercial conferences held under the auspices of the United States. It appears far more accurate to interpret the quest for political stability in the Caribbean and the exclusion of European competition as an effort to prepare the way for broad economic expansion.[19]

The situation in Nicaragua offers a good example of the relationship of principle to practice in Wilson's New Diplomacy. Nicaragua had been a major arena of dollar diplomacy after President Jose Santos Zelaya antagonized American interests from 1907 to 1909 by policies that directly challenged the Central American aspirations of the United States. He negotiated a loan of £1,250 million with a London syndicate, he countered the efforts of the United States to secure control of the alternate canal route by inviting the Japanese to enter into negotiations, and he followed a policy of granting monopolies to Nicaraguans and Europeans (thus arousing the antagonism of American concessionaires).[20]

A revolt erupted in 1909, and the revolutionaries were financed by large grants of mysterious origin channelled through Adolfo Diaz, a thousand-dollar-a-year bookkeeper for the American owned La Luz y Los Angeles Mining Company.[21] When two Americans who had enlisted in the rebel forces were executed for trying to destroy a government troop ship, Secretary of State Philander C. Knox terminated diplomatic relations with the Zelaya government, even though Zelaya claimed that the Americans were not entitled to diplomatic protection because of their belligerent status. Secretary Knox developed an argument in the course of this affair which is significant in its own right, and also because Wilson's position was very similar. The Secretary based his action on several specific charges: first, Nicaragua had violated conventions with other Central American States (conventions to which the United States was not a direct participant); second, the Zelaya government was oppressive, as was revealed by "any tendency to real patriotism" being rewarded with imprisonment; and third, the execution of the two Americans was a violation of the "enlightened practice of civilized nations" because they were officers connected with the revolutionary forces and were entitled to be treated as prisoners of war.

Knox concluded that the revolution against Zelaya represented the "ideals and will of a majority of the Nicaraguan people more faithfully than [did] the Government of President Zelaya," and that the government was unable to provide protection for American citizens and interests.[22] Knox thus took the key positions that became basic to Wilson's New Diplomacy. He reserved the right to determine the extent to which a foreign government represented the "ideals and will" of its people, and used that authority as the basis for supporting a "good revolution" against a "bad" seizure of power. And he asserted that an American interest in Caribbean stability was sufficient, when threatened by a local government, to justify intervention.

Acting on the advice of President Diaz of Mexico, Zelaya abandoned his struggle to remain in power. He was succeeded by Dr. Jose Madriz, elected President by the Nicaraguan Congress. Regardless of the technical legitimacy of this succession, or the respectability of Madriz, Knox continued to withhold recognition. He instead supported the rebels on the ground that America opposed not only Zelaya, but the "system for which he stood."[23] Knox thus proclaimed the right of the United States to deny the legitimacy, not only of an individual, but of an entire political faction. The United States then prohibited the Madriz government from establishing a blockade of the rebel forces, supplied arms and men in support of the rebels, and landed

American troops to participate in the hostilities.[24] The actions
helped the rebels win the struggle.

Recognition of the new government of Juan Estrada was made
conditional on the acceptance by the revolutionaries of certain
agreements know as the Dawson Pact. They provided that a
constituent assembly would be formed which would elect Estrada and Diaz as president and vice-president, that Zelaya's Liberal
Party would be barred from participation in the election, and
that the new constitution to be written and adopted by the
assembly would revoke the monopolies granted by Zelaya and
guarantee the legitimate rights of foreigners. American investors
were also to receive preferential treatment on damage claims.
Still another agreement provided for a loan from the United
States to refund the foreign debt, thus undercutting British
influence, and secured by control of the customs. It further
provided that the presidential succession would remain with the
Conservative (revolutionary) Party.[25]

With those limits established, the United States granted recognition. The "ideals and will" of the majority were guaranteed by
determining in advance the composition and policies of the new
government. The Knox-Castrillo Draft Treaty of June 6, 1911,
provided for a loan of $15 million and further negotiations were
undertaken to secure an American option on the alternate canal
route and for a naval base at Fonseca Bay. President Taft urged
ratification of the arrangement by arguing that Nicaraguan in-
debtedness to another power might involve the United States to
prevent forceable collection. He added that it was American
policy to aid countries near the Panama Canal to promote the
development of their resources and to reorganize their fiscal
systems in order to promote stability and expand commerce with
the United States. Finally, Taft believed that a suitable loan
policy might forestall further revolution.[26]

As negotiated with American bankers, the loan agreement
provided for the reorganization of the National Bank with a
controlling interest passing to American hands; for the improvement of the National Railway under American direction; and for
a lien on customs with the administration of the customs handled
by Americans.[27]

Led by Democrats, the Senate reacted unfavorably to the
Draft Treaty. Senator Cullom told Knox on June 12 that the
treaty did not have "a ghost of a chance" for ratification.[28] He
was correct. It died in the Senate Foreign Relations Committee

on May 8, 1912, despite efforts by Secretary Knox and various chambers of commerce.[29] The State Department then supported a loan contract that provided for American control of the National Bank; currency reform with reserves deposited in an American bank; and a lien on customs and liquor taxes. A provision was inserted whereby American investors obtained the right to "solicit the State Department" for protection against violation of the agreement, or for aid in imposing its fulfillment. Disputes over the interpretation of the new arrangements would be decided by the Secretary of State.[30]

These negotiations, which continued until the Taft Administration left office, were justified in the name of peace, stability, and prosperity. Munro is no doubt correct in asserting that the United States was not motivated by a specific policy of forcing concessions for American businessmen, though that did occur. The primary objective was stability in Central America under the auspices of an informal protectorate based on the Roosevelt Corollary. Elihu Root, Theodore Roosevelt's Secretary of State, explained the point in January 1905:

> The inevitable effect of our building the Canal must be to require us to police the surrounding premises. In the nature of things, trade and control, and the obligation to keep order which go with them, must come our way.

The United States, he later added, must control the canal route without conquest of territory because it would be inadvisable to "dilute the electorate" with people so different in race and customs.[31]

Wilson made a basic assumption at this time that revolution represented no question of policy but rather merely rival strong men who aroused ignorant mobs for whatever loot and satisfaction power might bring.[32] But there was significant political conflict in Nicaragua. The battle between the Liberals (with artisan and small farmer support) and the Conservatives (backed by the leading families who controlled commerce on Lake Nicaragua and the cattle ranches around Granada) had been long and bitter.[33] American marines and money did not settle the matter. Exposure by the Liberals of the provisions of the Dawson Agreement served to intensify domestic hostility and increased the resentment toward the United States. American Minister Elliott Northcott reported that the "overwhelming majority of Nicaraguans" were antagonistic toward the United States, and that

President Estrada was maintaining his power only through the threat of American intervention.[34] When the new National Assembly mustered enough courage to repudiate the commitments exacted from its preceeding members and proposed a new constitution, Estrada retaliated by dissolving the Assembly in April, 1911. But the threat of a revolt caused Estrada to resign. He was replaced by Adolfo Diaz, who enjoyed the assistance of an American warship for "moral effect."[35] Diaz attempted to handle the recalcitrant Assembly by requesting a treaty with the United States that would permit the United States to intervene in Nicaragua on much the same basis as provided in the Platt Amendment.[36] A new revolt erupted in the summer of 1911 and was suppressed by the deployment of 2,725 United States Marines. American military pressure combined with his control of the election machinery secured the re-election of Diaz.[37]

The quest of the United States for stability in Nicaragua was motivated by more than a political or moral concern for that country. The Liberal-Conservative conflict in Nicaragua was part of a regional struggle to reunify Nicaragua, Guatemala, El Salvador, Honduras and Costa Rica. One of Zelaya's projects had been to attempt to restore the old federal union of Central America, and thereby establish control over the alternate canal route through Costa Rica and El Salvador (as well as Nicaragua). The movement for unification meant working with revolutionary groups wherever Conservatives held power. In an effort to prevent the spread of revolt through Central America, and to calm the hostility to the Roosevelt Corollary and the Dominican intervention of 1907, President Roosevelt and Porfirio Diaz of Mexico applied pressure for the creation of a system of mediation. That led to the Washington Conference of 1907 which, among other things, created a Central American Court of Justice and adopted a convention against exporting or aiding revolutions in neighboring countries. The United States was not a signatory power, but it exercised dominant influence on the Court (which opposed Zelaya). Zelaya rejected such a "pan-American" approach in favor of Central American federation opposed to the dominance of the United States.[38]

The United States justified intervention against Zelaya on moral, political, and economic grounds. Morality was invoked against the "destructive character" of the Zelaya regime and in support of the desires of the United States to support "legally constituted good government for the benefit of the people of

Nicaragua." The economic aspect was defined as the protection of American trade and investments which were defended as essential to the development of the area. And the political issue was held to involve the "moral mandate" of the United States to exert its influence for the preservation of general peace in Central America and the enforcement of the Washington conventions.[39]

American intervention and the efforts of the United States to secure an option on the canal route aroused opposition in the neighboring states (particularly El Salvador). The American Minister to Nicaragua sent a warning, seen by President-elect Wilson, that the Liberals of El Salvador might provoke a war that would upset the Diaz regime in Nicaragua.[40] Wilson was thus faced, on the eve of his inauguration, with the threat of further revolt or war in Central America, European financial influence in the American sphere, potential competition for the Panama Canal, and nationalistic antagonism that threatened the United States' definition of a Central American system.

Some of the same ingredients, though in a different ratio, awaited Wilson in Mexico. Porfirio Diaz had governed as dictator of Mexico for 35 years. He had promoted peace and economic development by destroying political opposition, by buying the support of the large landowners with permission to expropriate much peasant land, and by attempting to bring modern capitalism to Mexico through foreign investment on favorable terms. To facilitate economic development, Diaz had abandoned the older Spanish and Indian concepts of government ownership of subsoil rights in order to free petroleum and other mineral resources for the landowner and concessionaire. During his regime a large part of the land, including almost all mining and manufacturing properties, a substantial part of the commerce, and extremely profitable oil concessions, had passed into foreign hands.[41]

The United States had through the years acquired a stake in Mexico which Wilson was bound to protect by inclination as well as necessity. American investment in railroads, mining, oil and land totalled more than one billion dollars in 1913, and between 40,000 and 75,000 Americans lived in Mexico as supervisors and other employers.[42] Growing American domination of the Mexican economy produced a rising wave of nationalistic sentiment, anti-Yankee literature, and invitations to European investors to counterbalance the position of the United States. Under the impetus of the Petroleum Law of 1901, which permitted concessions, Harry Doheny and other Americans had rapidly developed extremely productive oil fields. Porfirio Diaz granted concessions to British interests headed by Lord Cowdray for the purpose of creating competition for American influence, but the result was a struggle for control of Mexico's oil. Francisco Madero's insurrection of 1910 appeared to have the backing of American oil interests. Then General Victoriano Huerta seized power in February, 1913 and acquiesced in, if he did not order, the assassination of Madero. It soon became apparent that General Huerta enjoyed European (particularly British) support.[43]

Wilson took office confronted by serious challenges to America's sphere of influence. Revolution and war threatened Central America, and the efforts of the United States to limit European penetration and investment were jeopardized in Mexico and along the alternate canal route. Wilson viewed the opening of the Panama Canal as the harbinger of great new opportunities in South America. He thought in terms of a shift in trade patterns comparable to the rise of Atlantic commerce after the opening of the New World. The "opening gate at the Isthmus . . . will open the world to a commerce she has not known before, a commerce of intelligence and sympathy between North and South."[44] Wilson believed that the new era signalled by the closing of the frontier and the coming of the Spanish-American War involved the orientation of South America toward the United States and away from European influence. If Americans were to "emancipate" the Latin American states from European enterprise through the liberating effects of American commerce, Wilson argued, then they would have to prove to be "their friends and champions upon terms of equality and honor.[45] Wilson soon made it apparent that the United States would champion them regardless of their desires and would do so, furthermore, on somewhat less than equal terms.

Wilson first formulated a position in the cabinet meeting of March 11, 1913. He described his objective as the cultivation of the friendship and confidence of the Central and South American republics, and the promotion of common interests and cooperation. Cooperation, however, was considered possible only when "supported by the orderly processes of just government based upon law" as opposed to "arbitrary or irregular force." Just government depended on the "consent of the governed," and freedom required "order based upon law and upon public confidence and approval." Wilson said he would lend "influence of every kind" to the realization of order, legality, and popular government, but that he had no sympathy for those who seized power by force. He ended by disclaiming any dishonorable intentions of American aggrandizement. "The United States has nothing to seek in Central or South America except the lasting interests of the peoples of the two continents," the security of popular government, and the development of trade to mutual advantage.

Thus Wilson defined a broad area of involvement and intervention, wherein the United States would pass judgment on political developments in Central America and use its influence to shape those events. Wilson assumed a special relationship between the two continents that would facilitate trade, and that it was the task of the United States to promote the defined political preconditions that would make cooperation possible. He noted in the Cabinet discussion that "agitators of certain countries wanted revolution and were inclined to try it on the new administration." He made it clear that they would have no such opportunity if he could prevent it.[46] This statement, released to the press the following day, has been interpreted as a "repudiation of dollar diplomacy,"[47] but it substantially repeated the arguments made by Taft and Knox in defense of their Nicaraguan intervention.

Wilson was soon given a chance to reveal the meaning of his words. Adolfo Diaz of Nicaragua, threatened by political instability, appealed to Wilson on April 12, 1913, to bolster his regime by signing a new treaty along the lines of the aborted Knox-Castrillo Treaty.[48] Diaz needed help to stabilize financial conditions to continue in power, but loans were not forthcoming without State Department support.[49] The question was whether an unpopular regime would continue to be kept in power in Nicaragua by American support. But the principles of legitimacy and constitutionalism, which had been defined as prerequisites for cooperation, were vague when applied to the shifting tide of revolution and counter-revolution. Wilson lacked, moreover, detailed knowledge of the social and political issues around which revolutions turned in Central America.[50] But he did have a sense of moral righteousness and a belief that that which preserved the system the United States was building in Latin America was good—and that which jeopardized it was bad. Perhaps he still believed what he had written in 1907, long before he was plagued by such decisions:[51]

> Since trade ignores national boundaries and the manufacturer insists on having the world as a market, the flag of his nation [must] follow him, and the doors of the nations which are closed against him must be battered down. Concessions obtained by financiers must be safeguarded by ministers of state, even if the sovereignty of unwilling nations be outraged in the process. Colonies must be obtained or planted, in order that no useful corner of the world may be . . . left unused.

Wilson's belief that the agitators and revolutionaries were going to "try it on the new administration" was supported by State Department information that revolutions were brewing throughout Central America and that much of the ferment was caused by resentment of American influence "in almost all the Latin American Republics." According to these reports, at least eight states of Mexico were planning to secede and join the revolutionary movement.[52]   Other reports circulated in the press that General Huerta of Mexico was supporting the threatened revolt to distract the attention of the United States from the struggle in Mexico. According to those accounts, Archbishop Eulogio Gillow, an Englishman who had "great influence over the Mexican people," would recruit the Zapotecan Indians of southern Mexico in a general revolt to penetrate the coffee belt of Guatemala and sever the Pan-American Railway. That would be the signal for revolts in Nicaragua, Honduras and El Salvador.[53] Lurid reports circulating in the press gave no indication, however, of any reasons for the popular readiness to revolt. There were only vague references to bandits, the thirst for power of ousted leaders, support from "many prominent men" in the United States who "would see a repetition of events which resulted in the acquisition of . . . Mexico's largest State by the Northern Republic.[54]

The New York Times, in a eulogistic editorial on Wilson's anti-revolutionary statements, commented in Wilsonian style. The trouble, said the editors, "is that these peoples are fundamentally unlike the people of this country, or the people of England, of Germany, or of France." A great part of the population of Latin America was "hopelessly ignorant," had no opinions on public questions and no "conception of conscience as applied to political action." Those of high intelligence, "often of pure Spanish blood, free from that racial admixture which has been so prolific of evil . . ." remain aloof from politics.[55]

Wilson believed that the "moral forces" of his administration would be sufficient to work "great reforms" in the Latin American Republics. But time was needed to create the necessary electoral machinery, modeled after that of the United States, "the best yet tried."[56] For, in addition to the inherent problems of that approach, American policies had generated opposition. Wilson's friend and early supporter, Thomas Nelson Page (later made Ambassador to Italy), commented that "on this continent we are the most universally hated people."[57] Secretary of State William Jennings Bryan was also disturbed by the growing opposition to the cycle of instability, intervention and loans leading to further instability, intervention and loans.

He criticized the practice of allowing particular groups of private investors to gain such control of the Nicaraguan economy that their power and influence undermined the very stability the United States was trying to preserve. He expressed concern about the way that loans, for which the bankers demanded large securities and high interest rates, led to requests for government intervention to eliminate or lower the risks, or to insure payment. On the other hand, Bryan feared that the failure of the United States to pursue the traditional policy might open the door for European investment and influence.[58] Zelaya's efforts to secure a British loan had only been blocked by revolt. American pressure had forced Cuba to reject British railroad investments in 1912.[59] And the British were preparing to recognize Huerta in Mexico.[60] The danger of European penetration was considered by the Wilson Administration as the "hard reality" which it had to block promptly and effectively.[61]

Wilson and Bryan acted within the Roosevelt Corollary to the Monroe Doctrine. They interpreted it as a justification for interposition by the United States to collect debts and keep order in Central America, and as a rationale for replacing European investments with American capital. That outlook guided Wilson's extension of Taft's "dollar diplomacy," though the President contributed his sincere belief in Anglo-Saxonism and the obligation of the superior races to keep order and promote peace, development and trade among the lesser breeds. From a Latin American point of view, however, European influence meant competition for the United States, and that provided Latin America with maneuverability and economic and ideological alternatives.[62]

Wilson saw the issues as those of safeguarding backward people from evil foreign concessionaires, and of substituting good, wholesome, liberating American capital for foreign economic exploitation. He accepted the reward of increased American trade as the deserts of the just as well as a necessity.

After the Senate Committee on Foreign Relations refused to approve the Nicaraguan Draft Treaty, American bankers Brown Brothers and J. and W. Seligman advanced smaller loans in return for American control of customs, the National Railway and the National Bank. By May of 1913, however, the bankers were warning the State Department that they would be forced to withhold further credit unless the Government extended protection and support. Nicaragua would then turn to Europe. The Latin American Division of the State Department warned Bryan of the desirability of obtaining a canal option and a naval base at Fonseca Bay, and of continuing the Mixed Claims Commission to insure cooperation between Nicaragua and American bankers. The Mixed Claims Commission was preferable to an all-Nicaraguan commission because it would insure acquiescence by Europe in the "paramount influence and importance of the United States Government in Central America." All, however, was contingent on an American loan.[63]

Faced with the dilemma posed by Nicaragua's need for a loan and the opposition of the Senate to the Knox-Castrillo Treaty, Bryan and Wilson devised an alternative. They called for an option on a canal route and the naval base in return for a loan carrying less severe conditions.[64] Thus the New Diplomacy followed the path and the assumptions of the old, even though it modified some of the details. The resulting agreement provided for a canal option, a naval base, a lease on the Corn Islands, and a $3 million loan. It also included a prohibition against Nicaragua granting similar concessions to any other power.

To secure the agreement (and shore up the Diaz Administration), the arrangement also authorized American intervention under terms similar to the provision in the Platt Amendment.[65] Wilson gave this agreement his "entire approval" and hoped that it would be approved by the Senate.[66] Bryan warned that the alternative would be the overthrow of the Conservative government by revolution. Nothing was to be gained, he said, by "throwing this government into chaos merely to see which faction can win in the fight that would ensue."[67] Thus, as stated in

Wilson's overview of March 11, popular government was defined in terms of law and order.

The United States thus chose to intervene in behalf of those who would best promote "good government"—regardless of whether they enjoyed popular support. Wilsonian principle resulted in support for a regime that Ray Stannard Baker described as "the creature of the United States Government."[68] Bryan upheld the proviso for intervention by arguing that Nicaragua understood that it had benefitted Cuba, and that Diaz had become convinced of the disinterestedness of the United States.[69] The Latin American republics, Bryan pointed out, were "our political children." They looked to the United States for guidance and for a model. It was the duty of the United States, therefore, to look after them.[70]

Some of the children resented parental authority, however, and Latin America was described as a "hornets' nest of protest." El Salvador attacked the protectorate clause as weakening the autonomy of all Central American states and undermining the "special historical relation" among them.[71] Senator William Borah, the lone Republican to join the Democrats in opposing the Knox-Castrillo Treaty, now condemned the new treaty as exploitive.[72] Senator George Norris protested that it made dollar diplomacy look like "the proverbial 30 cents."[73] Georgia Democrat Augustus O. Bacon, on the other hand, greeted the treaty as the introduction of a new policy that would doubtless be extended to other Central American States when the necessity should arise. *The New York Times* editorialized that the "dawn of a new era" has arrived with the "cheerful acceptance and amplification" of dollar diplomacy.[74]

The opportunity for a change of approach came when Bryan proposed a plan designed to provide economic support for Nicaragua, increase the influence of the United States, and prevent revolution without provoking Central American hostility. Direct loans from the United States Government, secured by Nicaraguan bonds bearing 4½ percent interest, would bring those results. The United States would raise the money by issuing 3 percent bonds, and the difference would be refunded to Nicaragua in return for prompt payment. Bryan thought that approach would avoid situations in which bankers demanded high interest rates for Central American loans, justifying them on the ground of high risks, while at the same time they demanded that the risk be eliminated through government intervention. No wonder, Bryan said, "the people of these little republics are aroused to revolution."[75]

The program, he concluded, if applied generally throughout Central America, would help restore financial stability and at the same time create a more favorable climate for American influence. It would prevent revolutions and stimulate trade with the United States.[76] But Wilson was not prepared to move that close to government financial responsibility, and rejected the Bryan plan with the comment that it would "strike the whole country . . . as a novel and radical proposal." The President continued to rely on private loan agreements accompanied by the usual economic controls.[77]

The Bryan-Chamerro Treaty was signed despite strong opposition on August 5, 1914, after the protectorate clause was dropped. As finally ratified in 1916, the treaty provided for a grant of perpetual proprietary Canal rights to the United States.[78] The United States also received leases for naval bases at each terminus of the Canal route. In return the United States agreed to pay $3 million which went to satisfy creditors.

As a consequence of the economic dislocation caused by World War I, and by the high costs of American supervisory personnel who controlled customs and administered finances, Nicaraguan financial and political instability continued.[79] American bankers extended credit and expanded their control over the Nicaraguan economy, particularly the National Bank and the Railway.[80] Though the United States tried to control the Nicaraguan election of 1916 through the use of diplomatic pressure, American gunboats were required to keep order and to insure that the right candidates were chosen.[81] The New Diplomacy expanded American control in Central America, guaranteed security of the Canal, and placed American economic influence across the path of the British.[82]

Charles M. Pepper, Foreign Trade Commissioner during the Roosevelt Administration and Commercial Adviser to the State Department under President Taft, documented the continuity of the New Diplomacy with the old.[83]

> The national policy of the United States coincides with the economic tendencies of the Caribbean area . . . . This is one of the few instances in which no break is shown, and no national administration overturns the policies of its predecessor. The policy adopted by President Taft's

Administration in relation to Central America as embodied in the
Nicaraguan Treaty was accepted and carried forward by President
Wilson's Administration . . . . The Marines are few in numbers, but their
presence is a distinct moral force. It gives encouragement to the
development of Nicaraguan resources, and it is an invitation for the
investment of foreign capital.

Behind Wilson's concern for constitutionality, stability, and
progress in Central America lay the fear that revolution would
disrupt the desired community of nations learning good government (defined by Wilson's conception of the Anglo-Saxon tradition) while the United States liberated and elevated them with
infusions of American capital and trade. But important as Nicaragua was as an example of Wilsonian aspirations and actions to
create a liberal empire in Latin America, Mexico soon became the
classic illustration of the President's approach.

Notes and References

1. Link, *Wilson: The New Freedom*, 327; Ray Stannard Baker has
   applied the term New Diplomacy, see Baker, *Woodrow Wilson: Life
   and Letters*, IV, 55.
2. Link, *Wilson: The New Freedom*, 319-320.
3. Ibid., 279-280.
4. Throughout Wilson's political career he was given to vague statements
   of principle which he seldom defined specifically. Walter Hines Page,
   Colonel House, Robert Lansing, Joseph Tumulty and many others
   have commented on this as a tactic. Richard P. Longaker commented: "Wilson doubtless sensed that the legislative mills roll more
   easily when greased with moralism. Moralism led to near tragedy in
   Mexico and to confusion in World War I when the President threw a
   sentimental curtain around the reality of America's position. Al-
   though his morality in these instances was self-righteous, oversimpli-
   fied, and contradictory, in others it was used effectively as a technique and basis of leadership." Richard P. Longaker, "Woodrow
   Wilson and the Presidency," in Earl Latham, ed., *The Philosophy of
   Policies of Woodrow Wilson* (University of Chicago Press, 1958), 75.
   In 1895 John Bach McMasters commented that Wilson could "talk
   about potatoes and make it sound like Holy Writ." Cited in Eric
   Goldman, *John Bach McMasters* (University of Pennsylvania Press,
   1943), 68.
5. Woodrow Wilson, "The Tariff Make-Believe," 535-536.
6. Woodrow Wilson, "Iroquois Club Address," February 12, 1912, *College and State*, II, 392-395; "A party at once conservative in respect

of law and radical in respect of the service we mean to render the people. Our policies do not cut to the alternation of institutions, but to the effectuation of measures," *Harpers' Weekly*, LIV (April 9, 1909), 9.

7. Woodrow Wilson, "The Ministry and the Individual," McCormick Theological Seminary, Chicago, November 2, 1909, *College and State*, II, 178-179, 184-185.

8. Department of Commerce, *American Direct Investments in Foreign Countries*, Trade Information Bulletin No. 731, 837-838; H. E. Fisk, *Inter-Ally Debts*, (Bankers' Trust Co., 1924), 306.

9. Charles M. Pepper, *American Foreign Trade* (The Century Co., 1919), 221-222. See pages 214-231 for an analysis of South America as a market for the United States.

10. Dana G. Munro, *Intervention and Dollar Diplomacy in the Caribbean, 1900-1921* (Princeton University Press, 1964), 4-7.

11. Thomas C. Cochran and William Miller, *The Age of Enterprise* (The Macmillan Co., 1951), 208. See Benjamin H. Williams, *Economic Foreign Policy of the United States* (McGraw-Hill, 1929), 52-56; Thomas Parker Moon, *Imperialism and World Politics* (The Macmillan Co., 1926), 423-434; Samuel F. Bemis, *The Latin American Policy of the United States* (Harcourt Brace and Co., 1943); and Wilfred H. Callcott, *The Caribbean Policy of the United States, 1890-1920* (Johns Hopkins Press, 1942).

12. Munro, *Intervention and Dollar Diplomacy*.

13. Munro was a student in Central America between 1914 and 1916 and was later a State Department officer, ibid., viii.

14. "A study of this experience should be of some value at a time when we face a far more dangerous situation in the Caribbean than we did in 1900. We are acutely aware today of the importance of promoting stable, democratic government and improving living conditions in the region in order to check the further advance of communism . . . . We can at least perhaps profit from the lessons of history to avoid some of the mistakes that were made a half century ago." Munro, ibid., vii-viii.

15. Munro, ibid., 7.

16. Ibid., see Chapters One and Twelve.

17. Ibid., 534-535.

18. Alfred Thayer Mahan, *The Interest of America in Sea Power* (Little, Brown and Co., 1897).

19. For illustration of the concern for the economic interests of the United States in the Caribbean, see: *The Proceedings of the First Pan-American Financial Conference*, May 24-29, 1915 (Washington; G.P.O., 1915); Hon. Edward N. Hurley, "Co-operation and Efficiency in Developing our Foreign Trade," *Senate Document 459*, 64th Congress, 1st Session, 1916; William McAdoo, "Prosperity and the Fu-

ture," *Documents of a Public Nature*, vol. III, 1915-1916, 64th Congress, 1st Session; J. F. Normano, *The Struggle for Latin America: Economy and Ideology*, (Houghton Mifflin Co., 1931); Charles M. Pepper, *American Foreign Trade* (The Century Co., 1919). Mr. Pepper was Commercial Adviser to the State Department, 1909-1913; Howard K. Beale, *Theodore Roosevelt and the Rise of America to World Power*, (The Johns Hopkins Press, 1956).

20. See Isaac Joslin Cox, *Nicaragua and the United States* (World Peace Foundation, 1928), 706-707; Scott Nearing, *Dollar Diplomacy* (B. W. Huebsch and the Viking Press, 1928), 151-152.

21. United States Senate Foreign Relations Committee, *Convention Between the United States and Nicaragua*, Part 1, 32, 63rd Congress, 2nd Session, 1914.

22. William Jennings Bryan to Nicaraguan Chargé d'Affaires, December 1, 1909, *Foreign Relations, 1909*, 446-452.

23. Cox, *Nicaragua*, 708.

24. See diplomatic correspondence, May 1910, *Foreign Relations, 1910*, 752, 758-763; Cox, *Nicaragua*, 709; Nearing, *Dollar Diplomacy*, 153-154.

25. See Dawson Agreements, October 27, 1910, *Foreign Relations, 1910*, 763-764; Consul Thomas C. Moffat to Bryan, October 12, 1909, *Foreign Relations, 1909*, 452; Nicaraguan Minister of Foreign Affairs to Special Agent Dawson, November 5, 1910, *Foreign Relations, 1910*, 626.

26. William H. Taft, June 7, 1911, *Senate Document Exec. B.*, 62nd Congress, 1st Session; June 28, 1911, *Senate Document Exec. C.*, 62nd Congress, 1st Session, 1912.

27. *The Convention Between the United States and Nicaragua, Hearings on Nicaraguan Affairs*, Part VI, 174-202, 62nd Congress, 2nd Session, 1913.

28. Munro, *Intervention and Dollar Diplomacy*, 194.

29. Ibid., 203.

30. *Hearings on Nicaraguan Affairs*, Part VI, 205-206, 63rd Congress, 2nd Session, 1914; United States Senate Subcommittee on Foreign Relations, *Hearings on Foreign Loans*, February 25-26, 68th Congress, 2nd Session, 1926.

31. Munro, *Intervention and Dollar Diplomacy*, 113.

32. This attitude, shared by Wilson and extensively applied in Central America, Mexico, and Russia is summed up in Munro, 7-12.

33. Hubert Herring, *A History of Latin America* (Alfred A. Knopf, 1961), 462-464; Cox, *Nicaragua*, 704-706.

34. Minister to Nicaragua Northcott to Knox, February, 1911; March 27, 1911, *Foreign Relations, 1911*, 655-659.

35. Correspondence between Northcott and Knox, February to May, 1911, *Foreign Relations, 1911*, 655-659; text of the new Nicaraguan

Constitution proposed by the Assembly in *Foreign Relations, 1912,* 993-1011. It prohibited "compacts or treaties ... contrary to the independence and integrity of the Nation, or which ... affect its sovereignty." Foreigners had to press claims through the same channels as Nicaraguans, and alienation or leasing of public revenues was prohibited.

36. Chargé d'Affaires Gunther to Knox, December 21 1911, *Foreign Relations, 1911,* 670-671.

37. *Hearings on Nicaraguan Affairs,* Part VI, 210-216; 239-249; Part IX, 400-401; Cox, *Nicaragua,* 719-720; Nearing, *Dollar Diplomacy,* 164-165.

38. Herring, *Latin America,* 449-464; Cox, *Nicaragua,* 705-707; *New Pan Americanism* (World Peace Foundation, 1916), Part III, 116-138, Appendix, xxii; Munro, *Intervention and Dollar Diplomacy,* 141-155.

39. Acting Secretary of State Huntington Wilson to Northcott, September 4, 1912, *Foreign Relations, 1912,* 1043.

40. Northcott to Knox, February 2, 1913, *Foreign Relations, 1913,* 1035; Cox, *Nicaragua,* 718.

41. See Howard F. Cline, *The United States and Mexico* (Harvard University Press, 1953), 51-56, 112-134; Frank Tannenbaum, *Mexico: The Struggle for Peace and Bread* (Alfred A. Knopf, 1950), 46-58; Henry Banford Parkes, *A History of Mexico* (Houghton Mifflin Co., 1938), 277-308; Carleton Beales, *Porfirio Diaz, Dictator of Mexico* (Lippincott, 1932).

42. Burton J. Hendrick, *The Life and Letters of Walter Hines Page* (Doubleday, Page and Co., 1923), I, 178-179 (hereafter cited as Hendrick, *Page*); James Fred Rippy, *The United States and Mexico* (Alfred A. Knopf, 1926), see pages 311-331 for an account of American economic penetration.

43. For a description of anti-American nationalism and the invitation to the British, see Rippy, *United States and Mexico,* 325-331; United States Senate, Fall Committee Report, "Investigation of Mexican Affairs", *Senate Document 285,* I, 218-219; X, 25-32, 66th Congress, 2nd Session, 1920; Edgar Turlington, *Mexico and Foreign Creditors* (Columbia University Press, 1930), 237-240; Link, *Wilson: The New Freedom,* 348.

44. Wilson, "Address Before the Southern Commercial Congress," Mobile, October 27, 1913, *New Democracy,* I, 65; "Speech Accepting Democratic Nomination," August 7, 1912, *College and State* II, 356-360; "Address Before the General Assembly of Virginia," Richmond, February 1, 1912, *College and State,* II, 375-376; "Address at Nashville," February 24, 1912, *College and State,* II, 409. For a discussion of trade prospects, see Pepper, *American Foreign Trade,* 183-247.

45. Wilson, "Mobile Address," *New Democracy,* I, 65-66.

46. The text appears in *The New York Times,* March 12, 1913. For a

discussion see Ray Stannard Baker, *Woodrow Wilson: Life and Letters* (Doubleday, Doran and Co., 1926), IV, 64-66 (hereafter cited as Baker, *Life*); and David F. Houston, *Eight Years with Wilson's Cabinet, 1913-1920* (Doubleday, Page and Co., 1926), I, 44; E. David Cronin, ed., *The Cabinet Diaries of Josephus Daniels, 1913-1921* (University of Nebraska Press, 1963), 67.

47. For this view see Link, *Wilson: The New Freedom*, 319-320; Samuel Flagg Bemis, "Woodrow Wilson and Latin America," in Edward H. Buehrig, ed., *Wilson's Foreign Policy in Perspective* (Indiana University Press, 1957), 120-122.

48. Adolfo Diaz to Wilson, April 12, 1913, Wilson Papers, Library of Congress (hereafter cited as WW Mss.); see also Link, *Wilson: The New Freedom*, 332.

49. Northcott to Knox, February 2, 1913, *Foreign Relations, 1913*, 1035; Memorandum of the Latin American Division of the State Department, May 22, 1913, *Foreign Relations, 1913*, 1042.

50. See the memo of John Bassett Moore, Wilson was "not conversant with foreign conditions. Of international law he knew little and of diplomatic history scarcely none," John Bassett Moore, *Collected Papers*, VI, 435.

51. Wilson, May 4, 1907, WW Mss.; Harley Notter, *Origins of the Foreign Policy of Woodrow Wilson* (The Johns Hopkins Press, 1937), 148.

52. *New York Times*, March 9, 1913.

53. Ibid., March 12, 1913.

54. Ibid., March 9, 1913.

55. Ibid., March 13, 1913.

56. Ibid.

57. Ibid., February 2, 1913.

58. Baker, *Life*, IV, 431-433.

59. Acting Secretary of State Huntington Wilson to American Minister, March 5, 1912, March 14, 1912; President Jose M. Gomez to American Minister, March 23, 1912, *Foreign Relations, 1913*, 383 ff.

60. Baker, *Life*, IV, 431-433.

61. *New York Times*, March 12, 1913.

62. See study by Brazilian scholar J. F. Normano, *The Struggle for South America: Economy and Ideology* (Houghton Mifflin Co., 1931). Of particular interest is his correction of overemphasis given to United States-oriented Pan-Americanism by his discussion of the alternatives of Pan-Hispanism (Spain), Ibero-Americanism (Portugal), and even regional ties to Great Britain, France, Germany and Africa. Charles M. Pepper, in *American Foreign Trade*, discusses the extent to which racial and intellectual ties lead away from "Pan-Americanism" as defined by the United States. Even geography did not make manifest an orientation of South America toward the United States. The length of the steamship routes from New York and London to Brazil

varied by only 400 miles. "Except for its propinquity to the Caribbean coastal ports, the United States relatively has no marked advantage over Europe in transportation routes," Pepper, *American Foreign Trade*, 203.

63. Latin American Division memorandum, May 22, 1913, *Foreign Relations, 1913*, 1040-1042.

64. Bryan to Wilson, May 24, 1913; Wilson to Bryan, June 19, 1913, WW Mss.

65. For details of the early drafts see Link, *Wilson: The New Freedom*, 333-334.

66. Wilson to Bryan, June 19, 1913, WW Mss.

67. *New York Times*, June 19, 1913.

68. Baker, *Life*, IV, 438.

69. Link, *Wilson: The New Freedom*, 338.

70. *New York World*, August 3, 1913.

71. See Bryan to W. J. Stone, July 2, 1913, cited in Link, *Wilson: The New Freedom*, 335; Baker, *Life*, IV, 437; correspondence between minister of Costa Rica, Chargé d'Affaires of El Salvador, and Bryan, July, 1914, *Foreign Relations, 1914*, 959-963.

72. Johnson, *Borah*, 342.

73. *New York Times*, July 22, 1913.

74. *Boston Transcript*, July 21, 1913, cited in Link, *Wilson: The New Freedom*, 336; *New York Times*, July 21, 1912.

75. Memorandum, Bryan to Wilson, July 20, 1913; Bryan to Wilson, August 16, 1913, WW Mss.

76. Baker, *Life*, IV, 433-435; Bryan to Wilson, August 6, 1913, WW Mss.

77. Wilson to Bryan, March 20, 1914, WW Mss; Brown Bros. and Seligman to Bryan, October 2, 1913; October 8, 1913, *Foreign Relations, 1913*, 1055, 1061-1063; Link, *Wilson: The New Freedom*, 337; Baker, *Life*, IV, 437-438.

78. Thomas A. Bailey, "Interest in a Nicaraguan Canal, 1903-1931," *Hispanic American Historical Review*, XVI (February, 1936), 2-28.

79. Cox, *Nicaragua*, 721.

80. Munro, *Intervention and Dollar Diplomacy*, 395-397.

81. Ibid., 406-413; Cox, *Nicaragua*, 721.

82. Cox, *Nicaragua*, 739-777; Link, *Wilson: The New Freedom*, 342-345.

83. Pepper, *American Foreign Trade*, 244-245.

4
MEXICO

GUIDED REVOLUTION TO MAKE THE WORLD SAFE
FOR DEMOCRACY IN ONE COUNTRY

Mexico proved a severe testing ground for Wilson's principles and purposes. General Huerta was unable, after seizing power, to overcome or suppress his opponents. Reports of continuing threats to American lives, property and commerce reached Washington. Troops and gunboats had been readied by President Taft should intervention prove necessary. Taft refrained from the use of force to establish order because of the fear that American military invasion of Mexico would be "practically synchronous with the massacre of many innocent American citizens . . . possibly result[ing] in war."[1] *The New York Times* demanded intervention, however, to protect American interests. Only a strong man could restore order. "It is a Porfirio Diaz or a Roosevelt that Mexico needs."[2] General Leonard Wood, Army Chief of Staff, expressed the conviction that intervention would mean a long and costly war that would unite the warring factions of Mexico.[3]

President Wilson confronted the problem generally ignorant of conditions in Mexico, and was reluctant to accept the advice of his institutional advisors.[4] He did listen, however, to the principle investors in Mexico in making his first attempts to formulate policy. New York banker James Speyer told Wilson that General Huerta was depending on American recognition to raise money for payments on a $10 million loan coming due in June 1913. If Huerta failed to obtain a new loan it might mean the collapse of his government, and that would force American intervention.[5] Utilizing this weakness, a plan was prepared by Julius Kruttschnitt of the Southern Pacific Railroad Company (of Mexico), Harry Doheny of Mexican Petroleum, and representatives of Phelps, Dodge and Company, and the Greene Cananea Copper Company.

They proposed to exchange American recognition for Huerta's promise to hold elections in the part of Mexico he controlled. The rebel Constitutionalists would then hold elections in their area, and both sides would promise to honor the results. That would stabilize the situation and end further revolutionary struggle. Otherwise, the group of businessmen pointed out, war and "banditism" would exhaust the country, endanger lives and property, and extend the American losses that were running to millions of dollars a day. They warned that foreign powers were "seeking to undermine the influence of the United States in Mexico." By this they meant that the British were threatening to recognize Huerta, and that Lord Cowdray (chief competitor for Mexican oil concessions) was using his influence to obtain a large loan for Huerta in Great Britain. If the British helped Mexico, then "American prestige will be destroyed . . . and the commerce of the United States will suffer untold loss and damage."[6] This advice, though it may have come from a special interest group, corresponded very closely to Wilson's definition of national interest and moral principle, and the President was responsive.

The plan gained additional favor by being recommended by Wilson's friend, Cleveland H. Dodge, of Phelps, Dodge and Company, and the National City Bank.[7] Wilson followed the approach in drafting a note to Ambassador Henry Lane Wilson in Mexico. He warned Huerta that a continuation of the existing state of affairs would "disturb most dangerously" Mexico's international relations, and that the United States would not agree to any settlement made with European support in exchange for "special advantages."[8] Simply enough, the United States would not stand for a British loan coupled with further concessions for Lord Cowdray. As had been demonstrated in Nicaragua, investment and loans were considered an American prerogative. Without American recognition there would be no loans, and without loans there would be no financial stability in Mexico. The policy encouraged the Constitutionalists, and intensified political instability.

Bolstered by the promise of British recognition to be followed by the recognition of other European and Latin American states, Huerta refused to deal with the representative of the United States as long as the United States withheld recognition from Mexico. That action led Wilson to doubt Huerta's "trustworthiness."[9]

Huerta's seizure of power and his use of force against opposition offended Wilson's sense of political morality. The President was firm in his belief that he was the intuitive spokesman for American national morality[10] and, just as he was the interpreter of national morality, so the United States should be the interpreter of international political morality. "Our flag," he proclaimed in 1914, stands for the "assertion of the right of one nation to serve the other nations of the world."[11] Wilson believed the United States was born of the Christian principles of "self-sacrifice and devotion," and its "reason for existence" was to direct men toward the "paths of liberty and mutual serviceability;" to point out the "high road" for those not fortunate enough to share the Anglo-Saxon heritage.[12] So long as Wilson defined the "high road" in terms of safeguarding American capital and influence, there was no necessary conflict between Wilson's political morality and his sense of political economy. Both led to the pursuit of economic expansion abroad.

Huerta's "arrogance" in rejecting Wilson's overtures, and his flirtation with the British, provoked Wilson to change his position. A new plan was submitted by Kruttschnitt on May 26, 1913, which eliminated any recognition of Huerta. It offered, instead, the good offices of the United States in paving the way for a general election in which Huerta would not participate. Bryan seized this proposal as "a way out," and Wilson agreed.[13] New instructions were prepared by Wilson in which he proclaimed his conviction that in Mexico there was a "fundamental lack of confidence" in the government, and the United States would arrange an armistice and conference of all leaders if Huerta would assure an early election and declare himself not a candidate.[14]

Huerta rejected Wilson's offer. By the end of March, 1913, Huerta was recognized by Great Britain and other European nations, and by all Latin American nations except Argentina, Brazil, and Chile. The ABC powers waited for the decision of the United States. Wilson's bargaining strength, the Mexican need for recognition to obtain a loan, was ebbing away.

Colonel Edward Mandell House, Wilson's intimate adviser, was increasingly concerned with the growing rivalries between European power blocs. He was thinking about a program of cooperative expansion in underdeveloped areas carried on under the open door policy as an alternative to a European war which would ultimately affect the United States. House believed that Anglo-German tensions might be eased if the United States were to provide a sphere in South America for Germany to "exploit . . . in a legitimate way" through emigration and by developing resources.[15] He considered the possibility of a "sympathetic understanding" developing among the United States, Great Britain, Germany, and Japan on the basis of "insuring peace and the proper development of the waste places" on condition of equal access.[16]

As far as Wilson was concerned, however, the idea of international cooperation in an open door development program for underdeveloped countries could not apply to Central America and Mexico. His objective of protecting American interests and supporting the Monroe Doctrine functioned well with his view that European influence was pernicious. The British interest in Mexican oil, based on the recent conversion of the British fleet to oil, was a challenge to the supremacy of the United States in that area. Regarding British loans as exploitative, while American loans were conducive to self-determination, Wilson undertook to isolate Huerta by making it clear to Britain that Mexico was part of the American sphere.[17]

In the early part of July, 1913 House made that point to Lord Edward Grey, the British Foreign Secretary, with reference to Mexico. He implied that the decision to withhold recognition from Huerta might be waived if early elections were held.[18] Lord Grey indicated that Britain's recognition was "only provisional." They then turned to the question of the Panama Canal Tolls Controversy and Lord Grey received a vague promise of a favorable settlement at the appropriate time.[19] The conversations with Lord Grey produced an understanding that Huerta would be left to the United States, and that Wilson would work out a satisfactory solution to the tolls question.[20]

That was enough to discourage British loans to Huerta. And, as the economic situation in Mexico was becoming precarious, Wilson made another effort to bring Huerta into line. He sent John Lind, former Governor of Minnesota, to deliver a threat of American action if "effective government" was not established. "The United States," he said, "does not stand in the same case with the other great governments of the world in respect to . . . Mexico." It offered its good offices not only because of friendship, but because the nations of the world expected the United States to act as Mexico's nearest friend. Wilson ended the note with the warning that the disorder in Mexico was incompatible with the fulfillment of its international obligations, with civilized development, and with the maintenance of tolerable political and economic conditions in Central America. The terms proposed by Wilson involved an armistice and an election. As in dealing with Zelaya in Nicaragua, Huerta would be barred from running for office.[21]   The proposal was made more palatable by the offer of a large loan to Mexico as the reward for compliance.[22]

The reply from Huerta reached Washington on August 26. Frederico Gamboa, the Mexican Foreign Minister, delivered a blistering rejection. If Mexico were to permit the United States to intervene in Mexican politics, "not only would we forego our sovereignty," Gamboa wrote, "but we would as well compromise for an indefinite future our destinies as a sovereign entity." All future elections would be jeopardized by submitting them to an American veto.[23]   Wilson replied the following day in a special message to Congress that justified his policy of intervention. He argued that American intervention strengthened rather than weakened Mexican sovereignty. He argued that "peace, stability and contentment" in Mexico would result not only in an enlarged field for American commerce and enterprise, but also in an expansion of the area of self-government in Mexico. Returning to his earlier discussion of the effects of the Panama Canal on American trade, he now argued that the two continents were waiting for Mexican development to enable Mexico to share in the new sphere of trade.

Wilson defined American policy as "assisting in the establishment of peace" and the creation of a "universally acknowledged political authority." He repeated his belief in the incompatability of disorder in Mexico with that country's ability to meet its foreign obligations and with the maintenance of political and economic stability in Central America. Wilson then explained that the rejection of his offer of assistance to Mexico was caused by the Mexican failure to "realize the spirit of the American people in this matter." He felt that the pressure of "moral force" would win the day and that the United States would triumph as "Mexico's friend sooner than as her enemy."[24]   Thus, intervention was not really intervention because the intentions of the United States were for the best and the consequences would be beneficial to Mexico.

The illusion that Wilson was concerned primarily with representative government instead of compliant government was shattered after Huerta and the Constitutionalists rejected his demands for a settlement through elections. When the Catholic party, a reactionary minority group, nominated Frederico Gamboa as its candidate in the coming elections, Wilson immediately promised recognition and financial support, even though both the Constitutionalists and the Liberals boycotted the election. [25]

The Mexican elections were scheduled for October 26, 1913, the date on which the provisional government would expire. That event would also end interim British recognition. Walter Hines Page wrote Wilson on August 25 that the time had arrived for joint Anglo-American intervention to establish order. It was the duty of all great nations, he wrote, to intervene "as they did in the case of the Boxer riots in China." Such a venture would make it clear to Central and South American nations that they "must keep orderly government" or the great powers would "forcibly demand quiet on their borders." Such joint intervention would promote a "new era of security" and safeguard investments. An Anglo-American police force would make the world understand that the time had come for "orderliness and peace," and for the "honest development of backward, turbulent lands and peoples." [26]

Despite the objectives, which corresponded rather closely with his own, Wilson was not amenable to accepting a British role in Latin America. That became clear on October 11, 1913, when the new British Ambassador, Sir Lionel Carden, raised the question of extending support for a "strong man" such as Huerta, and indicated his doubts about the "haphazard election." [27] Wilson was angered by the implication of British support for Huerta, and invoked the Roosevelt Corollary. In a draft note that the State Department's legal adviser, John Bassett Moore, finally prevailed upon Wilson not to send, the President asserted the unwillingness of the United States to "have an American republic exploited by the commercial interests of our own or any other country through a government resting on force." Forgetting Adolfo Diaz in Nicaragua, Wilson denounced Huerta for relying on foreign assistance rather than on the "sympathy of his own people." As the United States had shown in Cuba, where it provided assistance in securing independence from a foreign power, so the United States "would assist in maintaining Mexico's independence of foreign financial power." [28]

In an address before the Southern Commercial Congress, meeting in Mobile, Alabama, on October 27, 1913, Wilson again outlined his attitude toward the relationship between Latin America and the United States. The speech has often been described as providing the core statement of the idealism of the New Diplomacy, yet Wilson opened with his repeatedly invoked description of the changes in the patterns of commerce. The

Panama Canal would open to the world a commerce of "intelligence, of thought and sympathy between North and South." That is, there would be more trade with the United States and less with Europe. Wilson drew a distinction between foreign concessionaires who "exploited" and American businessmen who were "invited to make investments." Investors from the United States could provide "emancipation" from the "subordination . . . to foreign enterprise" that made inequitable deals and exacted high interest rates. Emancipation would come through intimate relations with the United States. The people of the United States would show themselves the "friends and champions" of Latin America. A closer association would promote the development of constitutional liberty, "human rights, national integrity and opportunity against material interests." "America was created to realize a program like that."[29]

Wilson's belief in the peculiar virtues of the American branch of the Anglo-Saxon political tradition was now used, under the pressure of competition for concessions, against Great Britain itself. Page exulted on October 25 that "the future of the world belongs to us . . . The great economic tide of the century flows our way. *We* shall have the big world questions to decide presently . . . ."[30]   Page reported that Lord Grey was moving toward a recognition of the need for a cooperative policy in Mexico to retain the friendship of the United States in the face of troubled conditions in Europe. Page had promised Lord Grey that the American solution would restore order in Mexico. If this should fail, "the United States might feel obliged to repeat its dealings with Cuba."[31]   In Washington, meanwhile, Wilson conferred with Sir William Tyrell, Lord Grey's secretary, and defined his purpose as being to "teach the South American Republics to elect good men." When Sir William expressed the view that it was difficult to make such a judgment, Wilson replied with a scale of measurement for Huerta, Pancho Villa and Carranza.[32]

House then instructed Ambassador Page on the Wilson Doctrine. The policy of the Administration, he said, was to withhold recognition from any Central American government that was not formed along constitutional lines. Revolutions, he explained, were instituted solely for the purpose of loot, and if the loot was not forthcoming then revolution would cease. To eliminate the profitability of revolutions, foreign investors would be discouraged from "controlling these unstable governments."[33]   The implication was that the United States would exert influence to prevent revolutionaries from negotiating with foreign financiers and concessionaires.

Page in turn lectured Lord Grey on the "Wilson doctrine." Lord Grey asked what would happen if intervention would prove necessary, and Page replied: "Make 'em vote and live by their decisions." And if they did not do so? "We'll go in again and make 'em vote again." "And keep this up for two hundred years?" asked Grey. "The United States will be here for two hundred years and it can continue to shoot men for that little space till they learn to vote and rule themselves." When Page described this conversation in a dispatch to Wilson, he jeered at the inability of the British to understand idealistic shooting instead of merely shooting to keep order as the British had done in India. "A nigger lynched in Mississippi," Page marveled, "offends them more than a tyrant in Mexico." [34]

The British were offered a choice between "cordial cooperation" with the hint of a "sympathetic alliance . . . , the protection of British investments in Mexico combined with a favorable settlement of the Panama Tolls Controversy and being forced to accept a policy Wilson was determined to follow at all costs." [35] The British chose cooperation. Under pressure from the British Foreign Office, Lord Cowdray withdrew his requests for concessions in Colombia, and Britain withdrew support from Huerta. Wilson had won a clear field in Mexico. [36]

Unfortunately for Wilson, however, the Mexican contenders were not ready to accept an American solution to their problems. Wilson favored the Constitutionalists, supporters of Carranza, as successors to Huerta. He considered military intervention and possible occupation of Northern Mexico to protect foreign interests, [37] but Carranza rejected the idea of American intervention. All he wanted, Carranza wrote, was sufficient arms to permit the revolution to run its course and to allow the rebels to destroy the power of the military and the landed aristocracy. Wilson, not comprehending revolutionary objectives, replied that he would not assist, even indirectly, if "they took so narrow and selfish a view." Wilson proclaimed that the Constitutionalists "do not understand constitutional processes." [38] Wilson's desire for the establishment of order and the Constitutionalist's desire for basic change were beginning to conflict. [39]

As the fighting continued in Mexico, new threats to foreign investments were reported. The railroads were disrupted, interest payments were suspended, and foreign business in Mexico suffered. Foreign investors turned to the United States Government to honor its promises of protection. The Roosevelt Corollary, the American deal with the British, and the Anglo-Saxon mission to bring stability and civilization were being put to the test. Wilson was presented with the alternative of direct intervention or support for the Constitutionalists to help them establish order. He had to pacify the Europeans who were not receiving their interest payments, and at the same time steer American public opinion "on the right path."[40]

Wilson weighed the alternatives and decided the danger of direct military intervention in Mexico was too great. The United States had to choose a "legitimate" champion to secure order. Wilson decided to support Carranza in exchange for promises that Carranza would "respect property," uphold "just and equitable concessions," and oppose "confiscation and anarchy." Thus, safeguarding American interests as best he could, Wilson made his choice.[41]

President Wilson then began to examine the question of revolution in Mexico from a new perspective. Wilson told the British Foreign Office on January 29, 1914, that triumph by the Constitutionalist movement was the only possible solution for the Mexican difficulty. The revolutionaries, Wilson said, had a program which went to the "root of the causes which have made constitutional government . . . impossible." The Constitutionalists had become more than "mere rebels."[42] With this justification, Wilson advised the European powers of his intention to lift the arms embargo and allow a revolutionary settlement of the situation in Mexico to take place—with the support of the United States.[43]

Wilson's strategy was to permit arms to be shipped to Mexico for the Constitutionalists. Huerta was to be denied access to the arms. When Wilson and Bryan had devised their policy for eliminating Huerta through general elections (late in July, 1913), they had replaced Henry Lane Wilson, who was sympathetic to Huerta. They sent a friend of Bryan's, former Governor John Lind of Minnesota. Lind may have known nothing of Mexican affairs but he was a good progressive Democrat. When Huerta indignantly rejected the proposal to hold elections from which he would be barred, Lind warned that the United States might allow the Constitutionalists to purchase arms, and as a last resort, use military force itself.[44] The time had come to act on those threats.

After consultation with Lind on January 2, 1914, about aid to the Constitutionalists, [45] Wilson decided they needed more American help in order to win. The alternative was to send an American force into Mexico. [46] Raising the arms embargo was not enough to end the fighting. Furthermore, open dissent was reported between Carranza and Pancho Villa. [47] In the face of increased involvement by the United States, Huerta gained increased support from landholders and the Church. By March 1914, these elements provided Huerta with a loan large enough to prosecute the war. [48]

Wilson, who had earlier condemned revolutions as banditry, now perceived broader implications. It was not a mere struggle for personal power, but a revolution as "profound as that which occurred in France." [49] Lind advised Wilson that the time had come to deny Huerta access to the Gulf ports, thus depriving him of access to arms. Wilson acted at the "psychological moment" [50] provided by the Tampico Incident. A naval detail, seeking to purchase gasoline, landed behind Federalist lines without permission and were arrested. The Mexican commander apologized and ordered them released. Over the opposition of Bryan and Josephus Daniels, Secretary of the Navy, Wilson ordered the North Atlantic Fleet to Tampico and threatened to seize the port and Vera Cruz and blockade the Mexican coast. Wilson also considered dispatching an expeditionary force to Mexico City. [51] When news arrived of an approaching German arms shipment, Wilson sent in a naval force on April 21, 1914, to seize the customs house at Vera Cruz. "It's too bad, isn't it," the President commented, "but we could not allow that cargo to land. The Mexicans intend using those guns upon our own boys." [52] On the other hand, Wilson avowed that he expected the American force to be given a friendly reception by the Mexican people. [53] His more pessimistic estimate was correct. Vera Cruz was secured only with the aid of four thousand marines and sailors, and a costly battle involving the Mexican garrison and the cadets of the Naval Academy. Casualties were high and there was a great hostile reaction to the use of force by the United States.

Thousands of Mexicans volunteered to fight the invaders, and American flags and consulates were burned. [54] Anti-American riots spread to Costa Rica, Guatemala, Chile, Ecuador and Uruguay. American imperialism was denounced in the Latin American press. [55] Carranza, who was supposed to benefit from this action, demanded the United States leave Vera Cruz. [56] Wilson responded by stopping the flow of arms to the Constitutionalists.[57]

The Administration was stung by criticism at home from financial leaders, church groups, anti-imperialist societies and labor and socialist groups who did not regard war as the best method of protecting American interests in Mexico.[58] Representative Frank W. Mondell of Wyoming denounced the Tampico action as the misuse of patriotism to hide an inept foreign policy. Mondell claimed the landing was a ruse to get rid of Huerta that violated all the arbitration treaties signed by Bryan.[59] Within the Senate, appeals to patriotism were countered by denunciations of demagoguery.[60] Henry Cabot Lodge supported Wilson's action, but the episode seems to have crystallized his intense dislike of Wilson. He confided to Brooks Adams that "this Administration is incompetent to a terrifying degree. . . . To sacrifice American lives and money for the purpose of putting one Mexican rather than another in control of Mexico City seems to me as wrong as anything can be."[61]

The newspaper accounts of American casualties and the call to the flag rallied many behind the President. Wilson had expressed the belief that the country needed a strong executive who could unify the people behind a moral banner, and a measure of that objective was accomplished. The House and Senate overwhelmingly endorsed Wilson's actions.[62] Volunteers rushed to the colors. Theodore Roosevelt expressed a desire to return from Berlin and raise a brigade of cavalry to fight in Mexico if only there was "a real war" instead of talk.[63] Even Lind asserted that Huerta was blocked from supplies, and the Constitutionalists would be able to push forward. "The end would not be far off for Huerta."[64] Edith O'Shaughnessy, the wife of the American chargé d'affaires in Mexico City, commented that the seizure of Vera Cruz would cost the Huerta government close to a million pesos a month through losses of customs house revenues. Not understanding the intricacies of Wilson's moral purpose, she mused bitterly: "Might is Right. We can begin to teach it in the schools."[65]

Despite the support it won, the Vera Cruz incident marked the failure of military intervention as a policy. Wilson acknowledged this later, in 1916:[66]

America cannot reap the harvest of her influence unless the soils of the world are kindly and genial and yield to her influence, and they will yield not to hatred, not to enmity, but to sympathy and co-operation.

At the time, Wilson was surprised by the extent of hostility at
home and abroad. To calm the growing indignation, he attempted to justify the right of intervention on the basis of the
exalted nature of the American political and moral heritage. That
led him into a greater acceptance of the principles of "good"
revolutions, and to a ͵ ͺeal to the concept of Pan Americanism to
support that kind of discrimination between contending forces.

Wilson abandoned all efforts to halt the revolutionary struggle.
He turned instead toward developing an American definition of
legitimate revolution. In an interview given on April 27, 1914,[67]
Wilson said that though he sought the establishment of "orderly
and righteous government," his "passion" was for the "submerged eighty-five percent" of the Mexican people who were
struggling for liberty. Liberty was not something to be handed
down from above but was attained by the forces "working
below, underneath, by the great movement of the people."[68]

The old order of the hidalgos was dead in Mexico, Wilson said,
and it was his duty to aid in composing the differences among
the revolutionary factions so that a new order based on "human
liberty and human rights shall prevail." Wilson then defined the
characteristics of such a new order. Foreign exploitation would
not be permitted, only efforts by legitimate business interests to
develop rather than exploit Mexico. The land question so basic to
the revolution, would be settled by "constitutional means such as
that followed in New Zealand."[69] Wilson said he would insist on
that point. He then went on to explain that the American
presence in Mexico was based on the necessity to oust those in
control before Mexico could "realize her manifest destiny."
Wilson referred to the difficulties of handling a situation in which
so many elements were "without our control and our territory."

The duty of the United States was not to act as a policeman
who established order and then left, but rather to provide a
"strong guiding hand of the great nation on this continent." The
nation must "assist these warring people back to the path of
quiet and prosperity." After that was accomplished, the United
States might leave the Mexicans to work out their own destiny,
"watching them narrowly and insisting that they shall take help
when help is needed."

Wilson thus moved to the concept of revolution from below,
but kept the proviso that limits would be set from the outside.
To those who argued that Mexicans were not fitted for self-
government, Wilson made substantially the same reply he had

given about the Filipinos in 1909. "When properly directed," he said, "there is no people not fitted for self-government." Though the peons of Mexico were not as capable as other people, "ours for example," that did not mean they never would be. Wilson ended his prescription for guided revolution by pointing out, once more, the trade implications of the Panama Canal. The United States desired to convince South America that "their interests are identical with our interests" and that the United States had no plans of "self-exaltation." This country desired only the "peace and prosperity of the hemisphere."

Wilson justified military intervention, on an ex post facto basis, by an appeal to moral sanction. He explained that the Marines had been sent to Mexico in the service of mankind. The United States desired to serve because Americans, wanting themselves to be free, knew how *they* would like to be served. It was a "proud thing" to die in a "war of service." [70] As he told the graduating class at Anapolis on June 5, 1914, this was all part of the civilizing mission of the Navy. Their function was to "keep the world straight," to go to sea "like adventurers enlisted for the elevation of the spirit of the human race." Wilson believed that the Mexicans would come to respect the "strength of character" of the marines who fought at Vera Cruz, men who went "quietly like self-respecting gentlemen about their legitimate work." They "used force like men of conscience." [71]

Wilson's unilateral proclamation of the right of the United States to "fight wars of service," the natural implication of the Wilson Doctrine, was not overwhelmingly applauded by those who anticipated being served. Indeed, the conflict between the United States and Mexico appeared to widen. Border clashes occurred and anti-American riots broke out in Mexico City. American citizens and American property were attacked, and there was increasing talk of a general war. [72] Such developments prompted Argentina, Brazil and Chile to offer to mediate between the United States and Mexico to "prevent further bloodshed." [73]

France and Great Britain indicated that they would also be willing to help, but the Wilson administration was not interested. The Latin American proposals were regarded with greater favor. Wilson admitted that "we have been in a blind alley so long that I am looking for an exit." The overtures of Argentina, Brazil and Chile appeared to offer a way of improving strained relations with Latin America while settling the conflict on terms favorable

to the United States. [74] Wilson's concept of settlement involved
Mexico's acceptance of the Wilsonian formula for a new government. That was the only way of stabilizing the situation on terms
acceptable to the United States. He informed the mediators that
the United States would accept no decision that did not eliminate Huerta and provide for a provisional government committed
to reform. [75]

In his instructions to the American commissioners who attended the mediation conference held at Niagara, Ontario, Wilson
said the objective was to depose Huerta and complete the trans-
fer of power to the Constitutionalists. The new government
would then have to commit itself to constitutional agrarian
reform and to political reform of a nature satisfactory to the
United States. American troops would remain until the United
States was "finally and truly satisfied" that such a program
would be honored. The only questions left open for discussion
involved the method of transferring power. Wilson wanted it
"moderated," and the arrangements to insure a permanent accommodation. Otherwise the settlement would have to come by
force of arms, "either ours or those of the Constitutionalists." [76]

Carranza refused to accept Wilson's efforts to dictate the
composition and politics of the new government, to select the
candidates for a provisional presidency, or to set up a reform
program for the future government. [77] The American Commissioner, Joseph R. Lamar, reported that the ABC mediators agreed
with Carranza, and also revealed strong sympathies for Latin
American sovereignty and a "deep seated fear of the United
States." [78] Torn between Carranza's refusal to permit the United
States to define limits on the revolution, and the insistence of
Wilson that the conference do nothing else, the mediators produced a meaningless protocol. It called for the formation of a
provisional government pledged to amnesty and free elections,
and to pay compensation to foreigners for losses they had suffered. The representatives of the Huerta government, the Constitutionalists, and the United States all expressed dissatisfaction
and refused to sign the document. [79]

General Huerta was unable, however, to secure a foreign loan.
American forces had denied him the customs revenue and foreign
arms, and he was suffering significant military defeats. He resigned on July 14, 1914. Wilson was forced to deal with Carranza
who had become more uncooperative. Facing that challenge,
Wilson maintained his opposition to revolution unless controlled

and directed along lines of American definition. In Central America and Mexico, Wilson adhered to the Roosevelt Corollary and a commitment to the political and economic priorities of the United States. This was coupled with the premise that American influence was liberating compared to the exploitive nature of European influence. Wilson's policy was challenged by nationalism and revolution. He had to resort to a military campaign in Mexico to bring pressure against Carranza. The larger nations of South America, Argentina, Brazil, and Chile, for example, were outside of the Monroe Doctrine sphere and could not be subjected to the Roosevelt Corollary. In this area Wilson appealed to mutuality, cooperation, and Pan Americanism. Wilson sought to further both approaches through Anglo-American understanding based on British recognition of the priority of the United States in the Central American and Mexican Monroe Doctrine sphere and a policy of "sympathetic co-operation" with the British in the area further south.

Notes and References

1. *New York Times*, February 8, 1913; February 10, 1913.
2. Ibid., February 14, 1913.
3. Ibid., February 15, 1913.
4. Charles Willis Thompson, veteran Washington correspondent, described this characteristic: "Nobody who was competent to tell him [Wilson] the truth about Mexico could get his ear, could even get to his presence. It soon became a stock joke . . . that the only way to get to him was to tell Tumulty that you had never been in Mexico . . . . Having made up his mind, he did not want to have it disturbed by upsetting information." Charles W. Thompson, *Presidents I Have Known* (Bobbs-Merrill Co., 1929), 261. Felix Frankfurter made substantially the same comment in *Felix Frankfurter Reminisces* (Reynal and Co., 1960), 75-76. Robert Lansing commented: "Possibly his idea is that an empty mind is more receptive of the truth than one affected by experience and study . . . . Yet when one considers how deep the roots of political controversies are in history, social, and industrial conditions and racial traits this reason hardly satisfies." Lansing Diary, March 20, 1919. Herbert Hoover refers to Wilson's "Presbyterian conviction of being right. What they concluded was

right, was thereafter right as against all comers." Herbert Hoover, *Ordeal of Woodrow Wilson* (McGraw-Hill, 1958), viii.

5. James Speyer, Memorandum, May 5, 1913, WW Mss; John Bassett Moore to Woodrow Wilson, May 3, 1913, WW Mss.

6. Julius Kruttschnitt to Colonel House, May 6, 1913; Colonel House to Wilson, May 6, 1913, WW Mss.

7. Cleveland Dodge was a classmate, political supporter, and financial contributor. He provided funds to support Walter Hines Page's embassy in London. See Alexander L. George and Juliette L. George, *Woodrow Wilson and Colonel House* (John Day Co., 1956), 102, 123, 184; Charles Seymour, *The Intimate Papers of Colonel House* (Houghton Mifflin Co., 1926), I, 127, 165.

8. Baker, *Life*, IV, 248-249.

9. Ibid., 947.

10. For a discussion of this facet of Wilson's character see Link, *The New Freedom*, 61-86. Lansing commented: "His judgements were always right in his own mind, because he knew they were right. How did he know . . .? Why he *knew* it, and that was the best reason in the world. . . . When reason clashed with his intuition, reason had to give way." Lansing Diary, November 20, 1921.

11. See Chapter One, supra.

12. Woodrow Wilson, "The Meaning of the American Flag," June 15, 1914, *New Democracy*, I, 134; "Address before the Federal Council of Churches," Columbus, Ohio, December 10, 1915, ibid., 437-438.

13. See Baker, *Life*, IV, 249; Julius Kruttschnitt to Bryan, May 26, 1913; Bryan to Wilson, May 27, 1913, WW Mss.

14. Baker, *Life*, IV, 254.

15. House Diary, January 22, 1913.

16. Colonel House to Johann von Bernstorff, May 9, 1913, House Diary. Theodore Roosevelt expressed the same idea: "If China became civilized like Japan; if the Turkish Empire were abolished and all of uncivilized Asia and Africa held by England or France or Russia or Germany, then I believe we should be within sight of a time when genuine international agreement could be made by which armies and navies could be reduced so as to meet merely the needs of internal and international police work." Allan Nevins, *Henry White: Thirty Years of American Diplomacy* (Harper & Bros., 1930), Appendix I, 500.

17. For a discussion of the "closed door" policies of the United States, see Benjamin H. Williams, *Economic Foreign Policy of the United States* (McGraw-Hill, 1929), 317-331, 100-216.

18. Wilson's insistence that Huerta had pledged early elections stemmed from the interpretation he gave to the *Pacto de Ciudadela* (Pact of the Embassy), signed in the American Embassy by Huerta and Felix Diaz. The pact provided for the deposing of Madero and making

Huerta provisional president. Diaz was designated Huerta's successor.
Howard F. Cline, in *The United States and Mexico*, page 132, points
out that Wilson misunderstood *proxima* (next) to mean early. Wilson's denunciation of Huerta for failing to hold *early* elections as
"promised" indicates his acceptance of the Pact as binding and this
undermines his criticism of Huerta's illegality.

19. House Diary, July 3, 1913.
20. Hendrick, *Page*, I, 246.
21. Wilson's instructions to Lind were reprinted in *Foreign Relations,
    1913*, 821-822. The threat, the justification for intervention, the
    self-proclaimed special position, even the disclaimer of self-interest,
    were duplications of the arguments used by Taft's administration.
    Wilson's moral rhetoric and denunciations of concession seekers gave
    it additional color. Much has been made of the fact that Wilson
    foreswore conquest. This had not been an issue since the conquest of
    the Philippines. Theodore Roosevelt's comment on the Cuban revolt
    of 1906 had much the same content, though it revealed temper-
    amental differences: ". . . All that we have wanted from them was
    that they should behave themselves and be prosperous and happy so
    that we would not have to interfere. And now, lo and behold, they
    have started an utterly unjustifiable and pointless revolution and may
    get things into such a snarl that we have no alternative save to
    intervene—which will at once convince the suspicious idiots in South
    America that we do wish to intervene after all, and perhaps have
    some land-hunger!" Theodore Roosevelt to Henry White, September
    13, 1906, Nevins, *White*, 255.
22. *New York Times*, August 9, 1913.
23. John Lind to Bryan, August 22, 1913, August 25, 1913; Chargé
    d'Affaires O'Shaughnessy to Bryan, August 27, 1913, WW Mss.
24. Special Message to Congress, August 27, 1913, reprinted in *New
    Democracy*, I, 45-51.
25. Chargé d'Affaires O'Shaughnessy to Bryan, September 24, 1913, WW
    Mss; *New York World*, September 26, 1913.
26. Hendrick, *Page*, I, 194-195.
27. *New York Times*, October 22, 1913.
28. Baker, *Life*, IV, 279-280; Bryan to Ambassador to Mexico, October
    27, 1913, WW Mss.
29. Wilson, "Address Before Southern Commercial Congress," Mobile,
    October 27, 1913, *New Democracy*, I, 64-67.
30. Page to Wilson, October 25, 1913, WW Mss.
31. Page to Bryan, October 29, 1913; November 8, 1913, in Hendrick,
    Page, I, 199-200.
32. Ibid., 204.
33. Colonel House to Page, November 4, 1913, House Papers; see also
    Hendrick, *Page*, I, 205-206.

34. Page to Wilson, November 16, 1913, Hendrick, *Page*, I, 188-189.
35. Colonel House to Page, November 14, 1913, ibid., 206-207, 209-210; Wilson to Lord William Tyrrell, November 22, 1913, WW Mss; House Diary, November 12, 1913, November 13, 1913. In January 1914 Wilson and House agreed to explain to the Senate that it was better to make concessions on the Panama Tolls issue than lose British support for the American policy in Mexico, Central America, and South America, Seymour, *House*, I; 204.
36. Page to Colonel House, November 26, 1913, House Papers; Lord Tyrrell to Wilson, November 22, 1913, WW Mss; Hendrick, *Page*, I, 209.
37. House Diary, October 30, 1913.
38. Special Agent William Bayard Hale to Bryan, November 14, 1913, Bryan to Hale, November 16, 1913, cited in Link, *The New Freedom*, 383.
39. By mid-December an American naval force had to intervene off the east coast of Mexico to prevent the Constitutionalists from attacking Tampico and Tuxpam in the oil region, Link, *The New Freedom*, 387.
40. John Lind to Wilson, January 8, 1914; James W. Gerard to Bryan, December 20, 1913, WW Mss.; House Diary, January 16, 1914; Wilson to Mary A. Hulbert, February 1, 1914, WW Mss.
41. Luis Cabrera to William Phillips, January 27, 1914, January 28, 1914; Phillips to Wilson, January 28, 1914, WW Mss.
42. Bryan to Page, January 29, 1914, *Foreign Relations, 1914*, 445.
43. Bryan to all Diplomatic Missions, January 31, 1914, ibid., 446-447.
44. *New York Times*, August 9, 1913; Frederico Gamboa to John Lind, August 16, 1913, *Foreign Relations, 1913*, 827, John Lind to Bryan, August 18, 1913, WW Mss.
45. Memorandum, January 2, 1914, WW Mss.
46. House Diary, January 16, 1914.
47. John Lind to Bryan, February 24, 1914, State Department Papers.
48. John Lind to Bryan, March 8, 1914, ibid.
49. Woodrow Wilson to Lindley M. Garrison, August 8, 1914, WW Mss.
50. Samuel G. Blythe, "Mexico: The Record of a Conversation with President Wilson," *Saturday Evening Post*, CLXXXVI (May 23, 1914), 4.
51. Link provides a good account of the strategy in *The New Freedom*, 395-599; see also *New York World*, April 16, 1914, April 21, 1914; *New York Times*, April 16, 1914; Baker, *Life*, IV, 117.
52. Joseph Tumulty, *Woodrow Wilson as I Knew Him* (Doubleday, Page & Co., 1921), 192. The implication would seem to be that Wilson was thinking of intervention regardless of the arms shipment.
53. Baker, *Life*, IV, 330; Wilson to Thomas D. Jones, April 22, 1914, WW Mss.; Thompson, *Presidents I Have Known*, 267.
54. Link, *The New Freedom*, 399-400.

55. Ibid., 405.
56. *New York Times*, April 23, 1914.
57. Carranza to Bryan, April 22, 1914, *Foreign Relations, 1914*, 483-484; *New York Times*, April 24, 1914.
58. The documentation of the letters of protest to Wilson is summarized in Link, *The New Freedom*, 404-405; see also April and May, 1914, WW Mss., and *The New York Times* and the *New York World* for these months.
59. *New York Times*, April 16, 1914.
60. Ibid., April 23, 1914.
61. Cited in John A. Garraty, *Henry Cabot Lodge* (Alfred A. Knopf, 1953), 305.
62. *New York Times*, April 23, 1914; April 24, 1914.
63. Ibid., April 23, 1914.
64. *New York Sun*, April 23, 1914.
65. Edith O'Shaughnessy, *A Diplomat's Wife in Mexico* (Harper & Bros., 1916), 290.
66. Woodrow Wilson, "Address at Shadow Lawn," New Jersey, November 4, 1916, *New Democracy*, II, 392.
67. Blythe, "Mexico," 3-4.
68. Compare this with Wilson's definition of liberty as a product of the Anglo-Saxon heritage. This might explain how liberty could be derived from below while at the same time requiring guidance from above.
69. The *Plan de Ayala*, proclaimed by Emiliano Zapata, provided for the seizure by arms of all land "usurped by *hacendados, cientificos*, or *cacicques*, through tyranny and venal justice." Special tribunals would be set up to process such claims. The plan further called for the expropriation of large haciendas for distribution to the peasants. Indemnity for such property confiscated would consist of one third of the value of the land. The text of the plan is printed in Nathan L. Whetten's *Rural Mexico* (University of Chicago Press, 1948), 111-112. The Decree of 1915, later incorporated into the Constitution of 1917, also provided for expropriation.
70. Woodrow Wilson, "Address at the Brooklyn Navy Yard," May 11, 1914, *New Democracy*, I, 404.
71. Woodrow Wilson, "Address to Annapolis Graduating Class," June 5, 1914, ibid., 127-134.
72. *New York Times*, April 25, 1914.
73. *New York World*, April 25, 1914.
74. Woodrow Wilson to Dr. Jacobus, April 29, 1914; WW Mss.; Henry Cabot Lodge, *The Senate and the League of Nations* (Charles Scribner's Sons, 1925), 19.
75. Confidential Memorandum to Special Commissioners, May 25, 1914, WW Mss.
76. Bryan to Special Commissioners, May 24, 1914; May 27, 1914,

Foreign Relations, 1914, 506-510.

77. Special Commissioner Lamar to Bryan, June 12, 1914; June 16, 1914, ibid., 528-538.
78. Special Commissioner Lamar to Bryan, June 16, 1914, ibid., 538.
79. Secretary to the American Commission, H. Percival Dodge, to Bryan, June 5, 1914; July 3, 1914, ibid., 547-549, 554-556.

5
STABILITY *VERSUS* REVOLUTION

THE NEED FOR A SYSTEM IN LATIN AMERICA

While Wilson struggled with the problems of order and stability in the Western Hemisphere, the situation in Europe became precarious. The acquisition of an overseas empire, and the rapid extension of foreign trade in the preceding decades, tied the United States to the problems of the European balance of power. As the British accommodated themselves to dollar diplomacy in Central America, Anglo-American cooperation was strengthened. Great Britain, though the largest exporter to Latin America, was considered less a rival in the Western Hemisphere than Germany.[1]

German-American friction had developed out of the confrontation over American agricultural exports, the struggle for the Spanish islands in the Pacific, a conflict over Caribbean naval bases, and investment rivalry in Latin America. Tariff wars re-enforced the mutual resentment.[2] By the end of the 19th century, the rivalry between the two latecomers on the imperial scene was clear to most observers. The tension was overshadowed, however, by the more grim and implacable Anglo-German rivalry.[3]

British naval supremacy had been the bulwark for the Monroe Doctrine and the shield for American expansion.[4] Despite some friction, Anglo-American cooperation in empire building and spreading Anglo-Saxon civilization became more pronounced after 1900. Theodore Roosevelt wrote of the kinship of the two nations in blood, principle, and political and social ideals, and he warned in 1900 that disaster for the British Empire would mean war for the United States with one of the continental military powers.[5] Roosevelt supported an "English-speaking commonwealth south of Zambesi," while Britain recognized the United States as the guardian of the Western Hemisphere.[6] Captain Alfred Thayer Mahan conceived of an Anglo-American world system based on control of the Suez Canal and the Panama Canal. Together, the two nations could control the entrance to the Indian Ocean and the Pacific, and the access routes to the Far East.[7]

Roosevelt argued for the "civilized nations" to cooperatively expand over the "barbarous nations" in the interests of peace,[8] and for the English domination of South Africa and American domination of the Western Hemisphere in the "interests of civilization."[9] President Wilson and House held an essentially similar conception of an American mission to spread Anglo-Saxon guidance and civilizing influence based on an empire of trade.[10] Wilson came to the Presidency believing in the necessity of expanding American trade and investment abroad. This involved a secure base in the Monroe Doctrine area and an open door for American trade in Europe and Asia. Stability and peace were the prerequisites, but revolution in the Western Hemisphere and the increasingly critical situation in Europe threatened those essentials.

Even as the new President occupied himself with the selection of a cabinet, his friend and adviser, Colonel Edward Mandell House, discussed with Wilson his concern about the dangers of Anglo-German conflict. He believed the imperial rivalry might be lessened by drawing Germany into an Anglo-American program of cooperation, expansion, and investment. The friction might be reduced if Germany were provided with a sphere of "legitimate exploitation" in South America wherein it could participate in the "development of its resources" and settle German surplus population. Such an agreement would involve an understanding about the Monroe Doctrine and would serve to stabilize expansion in South America.[11]

With the approval of the President, House attempted to obtain initial responses to his idea. Utilizing the services of James Speyer, a New York banker with German and American connections, House attended a luncheon with the German Ambassador Count von Bernstorff.[12] House spoke of a "sympathetic understanding" among the three powers so that, by mutual endeavor, they might "ensure peace and the proper development of the waste places." That would help maintain the open door and equal opportunity for "everyone everywhere." Von Bernstorff suggested China as a fruitful field for such concerted action.[13] House also approached Walter Hines Page. He responded enthusiastically, agreeing that it was time for the great world powers to combine to "clean up the tropics." Such cooperation would permit armies to be transformed into "sanitary police, as in Panama," allowing them to "forget the idea of fighting and at last dissolve."[14]

The first step, Page suggested in June, 1913, would be to reach an understanding with the British on the Panama Tolls and on the question of the recognition of Huerta in Mexico. "We can command these people, this tight island, and its world-wide empire," Page wrote Wilson. "They see the time near at hand when we shall command the capital and the commerce of the world." [15] Given a period of peace, American supremacy was certain. The United States had more capable people, many times the territory of both England and Germany, and "more *potential* wealth than all Europe."

If the United States provided the leadership in "cleaning up the tropics under our . . . code of ethics," for the good of the people involved and without territorial annexation, this would permit imperial energies to be shifted from armed rivalry over the status quo, and thus avoid war. Page foresaw a new era of "sanitary reformation," an era that had begun, perhaps, with the American action in Cuba; an era based on "conquest for the sole benefit of the conquered." [16] The future, Page assured Wilson, belonged to the United States. In economic and political terms "we *are* [the] world." [17]

Wilson did not respond to Page's romantic concept of an imperialism of good intentions, but he did approve the suggestion by House that he embark on a "Great Adventure." With the support of British Foreign Secretary Sir Edward Grey and his secretary, Sir William Tyrrell, and with the permission of President Wilson, House sailed for Berlin to persuade Germany to abandon its naval program in exchange for a zone of influence in Persia and Asia Minor, and for the "hope" that Germany might gain a freer hand commercially in Central and South America. [18]

When House arrived in Berlin and presented his scheme to Admiral von Tirpitz, his confidence was shaken. He encountered the realities of the Anglo-German struggle and its relationship to the Alliance structure of Europe. Admiral von Tirpitz was unimpressed with House's description of Wilson's "iron courage and inflexible will" as demonstrated in Mexico. When House suggested that Britain would have to crush Germany rather than permit a challenge to British naval supremacy, von Tirpitz replied that German naval and military strength were a deterrent to war. [19]

House wrote Wilson in alarm that the situation was "jingoism run stark mad." Only Wilsonian influence might avoid an "awful cataclysm." Germany was menaced by France and Russia who

were held back only by the British need for Germany as a barrier
against Russia. Britain, on the other hand, could not permit a
German challenge to its naval supremacy.[20] The Kaiser, House
believed, was less prejudiced and belligerent. He had expressed
greater interest in House's scheme for a community of interest
with the United States and Great Britain against the Russians and
the French. But he also refused to abandon Germany's reliance
on a naval program for protection and commercial expansion.[21]

House suggested to the British that the capital-investing countries might reach a tentative understanding to encourage investments at reasonable rates and development programs under favorable terms. That agreement should be coupled with a consensus
on conditions whereby loans would be made safe. He thought
that the elimination of "usurious" interest rates and concessions
that undermined weak and indebted countries would reduce the
causes of friction and stabilize conditions in recipient countries.[22] German participation might be secured by the offer of a
share of Persian development. House also reported to Wilson that
Lord Grey thought it might be useful, though dangerous, to play
Germany and Russia off against each other in the Middle East.[23]
Lord Tyrrell suggested that the United States develop such a plan
for cooperation in the Western Hemisphere and then approach
the Central and South American republics through Jusserand as
"representative of a Latin power."[24] These discussions were
interrupted by the assassination of Archduke Franz Ferdinand on
June 28, 1914.

With its last-minute efforts to develop a system of cooperative
empire to stabilize Europe checked, the United States renewed
the effort to organize the Western Hemisphere. Wilson's earlier
attempts to control Central America and Mexico had not produced stability, and Robert Lansing, counselor for the State
Department, finally suggested that the President's appeals for
Pan-American cooperation were contradictory to his insistence
on the right of unilateral intervention. Lansing tried in June,
1914, to provide a consistent basis for Wilson's appeals for
hemispheric solidarity and the primacy of American investments.
Something had to be done, he told Bryan, to avoid the charge of
"insincerity and inconsistency" about the relationship between
the United States and Latin America. The attacks had become
too frequent and contained too much substance.[25]

Lansing pointed out that the Monroe Doctrine had not been
developed to preserve Latin American integrity, but rather to

protect the national interests of the United States. Intervention by the United States in the affairs of other American states was an assertion of the primacy of the United States in the Western Hemisphere—a direct contradiction of the principle of national equality and Pan-Americanism. Pan-Americanism, Lansing wrote, was founded on the legal fiction of national equality: the Monroe Doctrine was founded on the reality of the superior power of the United States to compel submission when its national safety was menaced.

A new condition had developed with the gradual domination of undeveloped countries by foreign investors. The scramble for markets and investments was now closely tied to political domination, Lansing concluded, and resulted in control as complete as if occupation had occurred. United States intervention against foreign investments violated the assumptions of Pan-Americanism and could only be justified in behalf of the national interest of the United States. Lansing argued for a formal extension of the Monroe Doctrine to include a prohibition against European financial control as part of the unilateral policy of the United States. [26]

House countered with an alternative approach closer to the rhetoric of the Mobile address. He sought to expand Wilson's theme of hemispheric cooperation because he doubted the ability of the United States to honor a unilateral assumption of a political and economic protectorate for Latin America in the face of South American hostility and suspicion. Suspicion might be allayed by making the preservation of peace and "tranquility" a multilateral responsibility. That would benefit the United States "no less materially than morally." Underlying this approach, and also related to his overtures toward European cooperation, was the idea that a general Pan-American pact would also involve the British possesssions in the hemisphere and increase Anglo-American cooperation. As Charles Seymour has commented, the British presence in Latin America could not be ignored and the imperial power of Great Britain was necessary for any feasible plan of international cooperation. [27]

Wilson seemed to want the best of both approaches. Wilson asserted the unilateral right of the United States to maintain order in Central America and Mexico, to pursue (under the Monroe Doctrine) political and economic intervention as defined both in his Mobile address and in Lansing's memorandum. At the same time, Wilson defined his political and economic objectives in terms of the civilizing and liberating mission of the United States in the "interest of the peoples of the two continents." In this way he could use cooperation with, and pressure on, Latin American countries to secure the objectives he defined for the United States. [28]

The outbreak of violence in Europe in July, 1914, spread rapidly along the fuses of the alliance structure, and quickly revealed to the United States the extent to which American interests were involved. Europeans began to liquidate their holdings (totalling about $2.5 million) in American stocks and bonds, an action that staggered the New York Stock Exchange. When the London Exchange closed on July 31, it triggered a panic in Wall Street. The New York Exchange closed and only reopened on a limited basis in November. New York bankers resorted to an illegal embargo on gold exports to halt the flight of gold to Europe. The banking structure was saved from public panic by the hasty action of the Federal Reserve Board to distribute emergency currency from the United States Treasury. [29]

American trade suffered an even greater blow. Only nine American passenger ships and six freighters were in active service on the transatlantic and transpacific routes, [30] and the war quickly deprived the United States of access to European shipping facilities. Americans looked forward to British involvement in the war on the grounds that the Royal Navy would sweep the seas of German raiders and permit the United States to regain its Eastern European grain markets. [31] Even with British participation, however, the war made American shipments to belligerent ports hazardous. The president of the New York Chamber of Commerce protested, on August 13, 1914, that "Europe has placed an embargo on the commerce of the world." [32] The United States had harvested a record wheat crop, and American warehouses overflowed as exports to Germany dropped from 2.637 million bushels in July to none in August. Belligerent powers had absorbed 48 percent of the American cotton crop in 1913, and Germany alone had purchased 18 percent. The 1914 crop was 20 percent higher, and the war thus threatened economic ruin to the South and posed the danger of a rebellion against Wilson's leadership.

Wilson fought a rearguard action against demands for government price supports. He resorted to the creation of a pool of private capital to be loaned (at high interest rates) to cotton

farmers.[33]   In the interim he made an appeal to every American
to buy a bale of cotton, Wilson himself setting the example.[34]
Such gestures did not solve the cotton crisis or halt the paralysis
developing in the copper, steel, textile, and petroleum industries.
United States Steel, for example, cut back to 30 percent of
capacity.[35]   With the loss of customs revenues on which the
government depended for the bulk of its income, moreover, the
United States faced the necessity of major tax revisions.[36]

Under the impetus of the tremendous wartime dislocation,
American trade began to undergo a reorientation. New York
bankers feared the threat to American credit abroad more than
they did the risk of a flight of gold, and hence formed a gold
pool to guarantee foreign payments. Exports to Europe began to
revive under the protection of the British fleet. European capital
began to seek safety in the United States with the encouragement
of the guarantee of gold payments. The Federal Reserve System
also helped make New York the new banking depository for
Europe, and neutral and belligerent capital started to shift from
London to New York.[37]

American trade began to revive in late August and September,
1914, with shipments of food supplies, munitions, textiles, and
metals for armaments. Those items went largely to the Allies and
neutral countries. Other traditional exports, however, such as
cotton, iron and steel, agricultural implements, wood products
and tobacco suffered a considerable decrease in volume. Non-
European markets for American goods had been financed in the
past by European capital, and once the flow of credit was cut off
those areas could no longer purchase American products. The
United States learned during the first year of the war that its
markets in South America, Africa, and Asia had sharply contracted as those areas lost the purchasing power formerly derived
from Europe.[38]

The disruption of trade patterns provided the United States
with a challenge and an opportunity in Latin America. The
United States had been the third largest exporter to Latin America in 1913, surpassed only by Great Britain and Germany. In the
decade before the war, the major share of American exports had
gone to Cuba, Brazil, and Mexico. Political instability and friction between the United States and Mexico reversed the trend in
that country, however, and American exports to Mexico dropped
from $61 million in 1911 to $54 million in 1913. The onset of

the war in 1914 caused a considerable decline in exports to South America with the greatest decline in Mexico, the least in Cuba.[39]

The dislocation of European trade channels and capital provided an opening for the United States. It re-enforced the concern of the Wilson Administration with drawing Latin America closer to the United States, but a system had to be created to permit the United States to take advantage of the opportunity. Walter Hines Page and Colonel House lost no time in trying to fill that need. Page had been an ardent advocate of the creation of an American system for Latin America, and he urged in 1913 the use of the fleets of the United States and Great Britain to "make the world understand that the time had come for orderliness, and for the honest development of backward, turbulent lands and peoples.[40]

Page, drawing his idea from Wilson's Mobile address in which the President defined European investments as exploitive and United States investments as liberating, maintained that the counterpart of the Wilson Doctrine was "Cuba-izing" when Latin Americans were as uncooperative as were the Mexicans at Vera Cruz.[41] With the beginning of the war in Europe, the time had come when American action was necessary if the United States was to fulfill its destiny of world leadership. Leadership could no longer be an inevitable product of the passage of time. If Germany won the war, the Monroe Doctrine would be destroyed and the United States would have to "get out of the sun." If England won, it would emerge stronger than ever, without major enemies and no longer needing the friendship of the United States. The United States had to act now to "play a part in the world whether we wish to or not."[42]

The contest, Page told Wilson on October 6, 1914, was between British power and position and German "ambition to rule the world by sheer military strength." A British victory would mean the limitation of German armament and the continued growth of a huge British navy. The alternatives for the United States were: first, to offer full American support to the British in return for a voice in the peace terms; or, second, to organize neutrals in Europe and South America as an independent pressure bloc.[43] Page considered a victorious British the lesser evil but felt that the United States had to act to secure leadership while the opportunity existed. Europe was moving toward bankruptcy by consuming its capital and destroying its property. The postwar world would see major economic and financial readjustments. Now was the time for the United States to expand its financial influence and capture South American trade. "There's no telling the enormous advantages we shall gain if we are wise."[44]

House had attempted to avoid the war by forming a British-German-American entente based on the development of underdeveloped areas. He now turned to the definition of an American system in the Western Hemisphere. He sought to improve the position of the United States and create a force that would give the United States bargaining power at the peace conference. He urged the necessity of "welding together" the hemisphere by creating a league of American states to guarantee security from aggression and to furnish the mechanism for the peaceful settlement of disputes. Such a league would serve to orient the hemisphere toward the United States. It could also establish a procedure for handling developments such as the Mexican revolution and could help to isolate Latin America from the European war. In opposition to Lansing's position on the Monroe Doctrine, House called for the transformation of the Doctrine into a multilateral agreement to secure peace and equality. That would provide political stability for the smaller states in the hemisphere and enable them to "maintain the promises they had made."[45]

Though the suggestions of Page had their sources in Wilson's own rhetoric, they carried too much of the tone of white pith helmets and Gordon at Khartoum. Wilson turned instead to House. Their discussions had, by the middle of December, produced a draft for a Pan-American pact. The proposal would bind Latin America to a "common and mutual" guarantee of territorial integrity, political independence, a republican form of government, the arbitration of disputes, arms control, and the isolation from assistance of "enemies of any signatory government."[46] Such an arrangement would serve several purposes. It would curb the threat of regional revolution in Central America and block the shipment of arms or the provision of financing to such countries as Mexico. The commitment to a republican form of government might provide, moreover, a substitute for unilateral intervention against governments that the United States did not consider representative. The pact might also serve to ease some of the Latin American hostility toward unilateral and arbitrary use of the Monroe Doctrine.

The formulation of such a plan was part of the broader

program of expansion in Latin America at the expense of Europe. In his second annual address to Congress, December 8, 1914, Wilson candidly discussed the opportunity for the economic penetration of Latin America. It was the duty and the opportunity of the United States, Wilson asserted, to replace the European importer and to interpose itself between Latin America and the markets of Europe. The United States should capture the business of supplying Europe with Latin American goods. In so doing America would be aiding humanity. As a first step, Wilson urged the construction of a government-operated merchant fleet. The Federal Government was obligated to "open these gates of trade and open them wide" before it was profitable or reasonable to ask private capital to enter.[47]

It soon became clear that the United States was not merely concerned with filling a wartime gap in normal trade, but wanted to replace Europe in exports and capital as far as was possible. A Department of Commerce bulletin, released 10 days after Wilson's speech, closely followed his distinction between good and bad trade. It described the "unfair" tactics by which German trade had grown in Latin America during the past decade and argued that Germany had not copied the "vast and wise investment" of Great Britain. The Germans had coordinated manufacturing, banking, and government in an over-all trade offensive. Unlike United States businessmen, who acted singly and unaided, the Germans acted in combination in behalf of national trade interests. German banks and consular agents gave preferential treatment to German businessmen and reserved important credits and information for Germans. Americans who aspired for the "rewards of the rich neutral markets," the report warned, had to "strengthen their position for the inevitable struggle."[48]

Wilson's strategy in promulgating the Pan-American treaty was based on having House secure unofficial commitments from Argentina, Brazil, and Chile before the United States became involved officially. The treaty would be presented to the rest of Latin America only after the four countries reached agreement and presented a united bloc.[49] But the ABC powers had prior experience in international cooperation with the United States and proved somewhat elusive and suspicious. They finally agreed in principle, however, to the transformation of the "onesided character of the Monroe Doctrine into a common policy."[50] As often happens with agreements in principle, it proved difficult to progress beyond that point.

The Pan-American treaty was an effort to establish a pattern of cooperation. Robert Lansing's memorandum had clarified the fundamental difference between the Monroe Doctrine and Pan-Americanism, but events in Mexico reinforced the President's propensity to reassert the "Wilson Doctrine" which meant that when necessary the United States would abandon international equality and mutuality and assert its dominance.

Venustiano Carranza, who took power in Mexico on August 22, 1914, after the fall of the Huerta regime, failed to comply with Wilson's demands to end political conflict by making peace with the Huertistas and the Catholic Church.[51] Even worse, the Constitutionalist coalition splintered into a struggle over power and over revolutionary objectives. Fighting resumed between Carranza, Emiliano Zapata, Pancho Villa, and Alvaro Obregón. But the pressures for further social change produced the first agrarian reform law, promulgated by Carranza on January 5, 1915.

As the regime of Porfirio Diaz came to an end, Mexico had been rapidly becoming a land of large American estates. Large areas were held by oil companies, mining syndicates such as the Hearst and Guggenheim interests, and United States Steel.[52] Mexican landowners and foreign interests had absorbed a large portion of village land. The new agrarian reform law nullified all "illegal alienation" of village lands since 1856, and provided the expropriation of land where villages needed land but lacked proof of former title. Though the measure was circumscribed by limitations and tied to the existing framework of property law in a manner providing for long litigation, it quickly proved an incentive for peasants to seize the land for themselves. Local authorities wooed peasant support by facilitating expropriation. On the other side, large landowners frequently refused to recognize the legality of the decree and fought back. The result was the spread of small agrarian wars.[53]

Wilson found it difficult to maintain a consistent attitude toward revolution. His first response to revolutions in Nicaragua and Mexico had accorded with his early idea that revolutions were caused by bandits seeking power or loot. When Wilson had treated the Constitutionalists as bandit chieftains, to be bought with support or coerced with threats, the result was growing hostility toward the United States and armed resistance. The "Wilson Doctrine," as Page called the imposition by the United States of its definition of acceptable political behavior, also led to expressions of hostility and anxiety throughout South America. *La Prensa* of Lima, Peru, commented on September 13, 1913, that "the United States today controls Cuba, Porto Rico, [and] Panama. Tomorrow it is going to control Central America. It has commenced to control Mexico. Who says that it will not continue further?" To counter the trend, the editors made a plea for Latin Americans to come to the support of Mexico.[54]

When Wilson found that his "bandit" definition was unworkable without recourse to war, he was forced to support Carranza in April, 1914. He then asserted that the Mexican Revolution was a peasant movement for agrarian reform and that liberty was "attained by forces working below" rather than inherited only through 300 years of Anglo-Saxon civilization. Next, Wilson tried to understand Mexico by comparing it with revolutionary France,[55] though he earlier expressed distrust of the French Revolution and the "discontent of the pauperized and oppressed," and of democracy "bred by discontent and founded on revolution.[56] He tempered his newfound sympathy for the Mexican peasants with the belief that the United States had to establish order, define policy, and retain the right of "insisting that they take help when help is needed." [57]

Wilson was adamant about the right of the United States to guide the revolution in Mexico. His prescription seemed to be restricted to political reconciliation rather than the unfolding of revolutionary decisions through conflict. The idea of change from below was discarded, and Wilson concluded that an improvement in the condition of the people could come only through an imposition of order and stability. That would permit economic growth in which all, presumably, would share.[58] In this manner Wilson transferred his program for the resolution of social conflict in the United States to the Mexican situation.

Wilson ignored the assertions of the peon and his spokesmen that the land had been stolen through the absorption of the village *ejido* (communal land) into haciendas and foreign concessions. Wilson may have accepted the idea that land reform was essential, but it had to be on an Anglo-Saxon rather than a Mexican model. No distinction seemed to exist, in Wilson's thinking, between United States intervention and Mexican self-determination. He considered the legitimate objectives of both nations to be identical. Intervention thus became no more than a means to expedite self-determination.

Thus it was that on January 8, 1915, Wilson was able to make

a strong statement in behalf of the right of Mexicans to pursue
their own revolution and to determine their own form of government. Attempting to answer American demands for a military
campaign, and at the same time ease Latin fears of American
aggression,[59] Wilson proclaimed:

> It is none of my business, and it is none of your business, how they go
> about the business. The country is theirs, the Government is theirs. The
> Liberty, if they can get it . . . is theirs. And so far as my influence goes
> while I am President, nobody shall interfere with them.

Mexico, Wilson promised, shall have as much freedom in its own
affairs as the United States.[60]

Nevertheless, this sweeping pledge did not preclude American
interference.[61] Wilson's statement must be understood in terms
of his own role as interpreter of Mexican liberty, and his determination to judge the leaders of Mexico and to interpose the United
States between the people of Mexico and any policies or politicians of which he disapproved. Wilson withdrew and restored de
facto recognition to meet the fluctuation in the tides of battle
between November, 1914 and February, 1915. When the expropriation edict of January 6, 1915, took effect, General Obregón
appealed for peasant and labor support by calling for further
social reform. He condemned foreign exploitation and intervention, and thereby again aroused Washington to threaten the use
of force.

Secretary Bryan criticized Obregón's use of agrarian and labor
battalions and his "incitement" against foreigners. It may be
necessary, he wrote to Wilson, to "speak more emphatically than
we have done." Lansing suggested that Carranza and Obregón be
held responsible for any injuries to foreign lives and property
arising from their "inciting hatred of foreigners, and their interrupting traffic and communication."[62] Wilson acted on this
advice by calling on Secretary of the Navy Josephus Daniels to
dispatch ships with long-range guns to Vera Cruz.[63]

Within a month of his nonintervention statement, Wilson had
dispatched a confidential agent to Mexico with instructions to
weigh the strength of the contending factions, to judge their
programs, and to estimate the "moral" situation. This would
enable Wilson to "check what is futile and promote what
promises genuine reform and settled peace."[64]   Then, on March
6, 1915, Wilson accused Carranza and Obregón of trying to incite
riots among the inhabitants of Mexico City. He called this "out-

lawry" on the part of a "factional leader," and threatened "such measures as are expedient" in defense of American lives and property.[65]   Past reactions to threats to American commercial interests in Mexico City were extended by the complaints of International Harvester that the port of Progreso in Yucatan had been closed, thus blocking the shipment of their harvest of sisal hemp for binder twine. Wilson, denying the priority of revolution over the rights of American interests in Mexico, refused to recognize Carranza's right to blockade Progreso "to the exclusion of our commerce," and threatened naval force to break the blockade.[66]   The concept of the right of revolution might have existed in theory, but in practice it was hostile to the protection of American interests. Carranza, successful in his campaign for Mexico City, sent a conciliatory note to Wilson denying American charges of danger to foreign lives and property.[67]

As relations between Wilson and Carranza deteriorated, Lansing recommended caution. He warned the United States ought to prepare for any military intervention by seeking the cooperation of Argentina, Brazil and Chile. Unilateral action would only intensify Mexican resistance and produce an "unfavorable impression" in Latin America. There was a considerable element in the United States that advocated permanent control over Mexico, and if the United States had to resort to force it might not be able to stop short of annexation. Annexation of Mexico would seriously jeopardize relations with South America.

He suggested instead, as did House,[68]   that the ABC powers be called upon to accomplish the purposes of intervention without risking the consequences. The disadvantage of that proposal, however, was that it would limit the freedom of action of the United States It would set a precedent for joint action which would embarrass the United States in the future, and would substitute international policy for the national policy of the Monroe Doctrine.[69]   Wilson again faced the conflicting suggestions of Lansing, who had urged strengthening the unilateral nature of the Monroe Doctrine, and of House, who urged making the Monroe Doctrine multilateral.

Wilson believed he could ease the dilemma by finding someone in Mexico who would cooperate with the United States. In discussing the note threatening Mexico with naval attack, Bryan commented to Wilson that the Administration's position was really a kindness to Carranza, "as it was to Huerta." Carranza would probably not take offense; but, if he did, "we can assure

Villa and Zapata of our purposes." Then, if force had to be used, it could be restricted "within the smallest possible limit as at Vera Cruz."[70]

Wilson first considered Pancho Villa,[71] and next the counter-revolutionary conservative, Eduardo Iturbide,[72] in seeking a reliable Mexican ally. Finally, on June 2, 1915, he issued a statement declaring that it was his duty to select a man who could win, and whom he could support in his efforts at unifying the conflicting political factions. If that failed, Wilson added, he would support his choice in establishing a government.[73] When Wilson received word that Carranza might recognize the necessity of accepting American "interference," he expressed the feeling that "it was possible we were not using all the influences we might use in Mexico" to let Carranza know, unofficially, that the United States might recognize him. Carranza had to refrain from insisting on "establishing his own dominion" without making a "genuine effort to unite all groups and parties."[74] Wilson had made the transition from a belief in self-determination to insistence on a government of national unity.

Carranza rejected this overture, expressing perplexity that the United States should insist on conditions that would negate the possibility of revolutionary change. He asked, instead, that the United States remain neutral in order to allow him to finish his work.[75] Wilson replied, "I have never known of a man more impossible to deal with on human principles than this man Carranza."[76]

Finding no ally in Mexico, Wilson turned to the suggestion for ABC mediation. In January, 1915, House had gone so far as to suggest the ABC nations and the United States form a commission government for Mexico.[77] The conditions for Pan-American mediation, however, involved domination by the United States and a program prepared by Wilson.[78] Lansing provided the framework in a note to Wilson on July 5, 1915. The hostile factions, he said, had to be "harmonized" if responsible government was to be obtained in Mexico. The United States should insist that the factional leaders must retire and abandon all influence in Mexican politics. An invitation would be issued to the groups that complied to meet in conference (through their "lesser chiefs") to organize a coalition provisional government. The United States would then take action to insure the stability and permanency of that government.[79]

This was, in essence, the policy devised against Huerta, and

Wilson regarded it as an "excellent solution." He thought the ABC powers should be present in the event Carranza refused to cooperate. The revolutionary leaders, Wilson bragged, could be "used and controlled, provided one knew how to play these men as they are." [80] This was the Anglo-Saxon and the Burkean speaking, presupposing insight into the nature of men and the revolutionary situation. That assumption was Wilson's great weakness.

While the discussion proceeded, Lansing suggested that aid be given to Pancho Villa. He should be allowed to export meat to the United States to earn revenue. Lansing thought it inadvisable to leave Carranza as the only functioning leader, and hence argued that Villa should be allowed to keep his arms until the compromise was reached. [81] Carranza's growing strength in Mexico, however, led Wilson and Lansing to consider his recognition at the same time they were promising Villa they would never recognize Carranza. [82]

On August 5 and 6, 1915, Lansing informed the Latin American delegates of the program they were to approve. The three rival leaders had to be eliminated in behalf of a "constitutional successor to Madero." If the Mexicans refused to cooperate, the conferees would then select their own regime and give it recognition and support. [83] At the same time that briefing was taking place, however, the United States, in search of a strong man, was in the process of deciding to switch support back to Carranza.

Notes and References

1. For a discussion of the relative positions of the United States, Great Britain, and Germany in Latin America, see J. F. Normano, *The Struggle for South America: Economy and Ideology* (Houghton Mifflin Co., 1931), 22-23.
2. See Lester B. Shippee, "Germany and the Spanish-American War," *American Historical Review*, XXX (July 1925), 754-777; Samuel Flagg Bemis, *A Diplomatic History of the United States* (Henry Holt and Co., 1955), 477-487, 465-467, 521-523.
3. Alfred Vagts. "Hopes and Fears of an American-German War, 1870-1915," *Political Science Quarterly*, LIV (December 1939), 527; ibid., LV (March 1940), 53-76.
4. American dependency on, and satisfaction with, British naval supremacy is discussed by Edward H. Buehrig in *Woodrow Wilson and the Balance of Power* (Indiana University Press, 1955), 15-17. See also Howard Kennedy Beale, *Theodore Roosevelt and the Rise of America*

to World Power (The Johns Hopkins Press. 1956), 81-170, for the rise of the "Anglo-American entente."

5. Beale, *Theodore Roosevelt*, 95, 145.
6. Ibid., 147.
7. Alfred Thayer Mahan, *The Problem of Asia* (Harper and Bros., 1900), 179-181, 186-187.
8. Theodore Roosevelt in *Sewanee Review*, II (May, 1894), 358-360.
9. Theodore Roosevelt to Henry White, March 20, 1896, White Mss., courtesy of Howard Kennedy Beale.
10. Beale, *Theodore Roosevelt*, 23-54. This provides a good description of Roosevelt's concept of the spread of civilization through Anglo-Saxon imperialism. For Wilson's concept of the American obligation to spread the blessings of Anglo-Saxon guidance, see Chapter II, supra. Though Wilson did not advocate territorial annexations as belligerently as did Roosevelt, and spoke less readily of the use of force, he shared with Roosevelt the essential assumptions of the civilizing mission of Anglo-Saxons in general and the United States in particular, of opposition to European competition in the Western Hemisphere, and of the moral righteousness of American expansionism and the intellectual inferiority of those who disagreed.
11. House Diary, January 22, 1913.
12. James Speyer was a New York banker with German and American ties. He was also vice-president of the B. & O. Railway and member of the Executive Committee of the National Civic Federation. He was a supporter of Roosevelt in 1904 and a friend of Colonel House. Before the development of hostility toward Germany he seemed to have ready access with his views to the Administration. See *Who's Who in America, 1918-1919*, 2551; Henry F. Pringle, *Theodore Roosevelt*, (Blue Ribbon Books, 1913), 357; James Speyer to Colonel House, March 12, 1914, House Mss.; Speyer memorandum enclosed in John Bassett Moore to Woodrow Wilson, May 3, 1913, WW Mss.
13. House Diary, May 9, 1913.
14. Page to House, June 1913, in Seymour, *Intimate Papers*, I, 240-241.
15. Page to Wilson, September 10, 1913, WW Mss.
16. Page to House, August 28, 1913; Page memorandum, August, 1913; both cited in Hendrick, *Page*, I, 270-273.
17. Page to Wilson, March 2, 1914, WW Mss.
18. House Diary, July 3, 1913; December 2, 1913; December 12, 1913; and April 9, 1914; Wilson to House, April 28, 1914, WW Mss.
19. House Diary, May 27, 1914.
20. House to Wilson, May 29, 1914, WW Mss.
21. House Diary, June 1, 1914.
22. House to Wilson, June 26, 1914, WW Mss.
23. House Diary, June 17, 1914.
24. House to Wilson, July 4, 1914, WW Mss.

25. Lansing to Bryan, June 16, 1914, *Lansing Papers*, II, 459-460.

26. Lansing memorandum, June 11, 1914, ibid., II, 460-465.

27. Seymour, *Intimate Papers*, I, 191.

28. During the occupation of Vera Cruz, Wilson commented: "The American Flag . . . is henceforth to stand for self-possession, for dignity, for the assertion of the right of one nation to serve the other nations of the world. . . . So it seems to me that it is my privilege and right as the temporary representative of a great Nation that does what it pleases with its own affairs to say that we please to do justice and assert the rights of mankind wherever this flag is unfurled." *New Democracy*, I, 134.
   "My dream is . . . that America will come into the full light of the day when all shall know that she puts human rights above all other rights and that her flag is the flag not only of America but of humanity." "Address at Independence Hall," Philadelphia, July 4, 1914, ibid., 147.

29. Arthur S. Link, *Wilson: The Struggle for Neutrality 1914-1915*, (Princeton University Press, 1960), 76-81; Alexander D. Noyes, *The War Period of American Finance, 1908-1925* (G. P. Putnam's Sons, 1926), 51-61, 69-87; *New York Times*, August 3, 4, and 5, 1914.

30. Link, *Struggle for Neutrality*, 82.

31. *New York Times*, August 4, 1914.

32. Seth Low in *Annual Report of the New York Chamber of Commerce, 1914-1915*, Part I, 48, cited in Noyes, *War Period*, 68.

33. Noyes, *War Period*, 63-67; for the political revolt see Link, *Struggle for Neutrality*, 91-102.

34. *New York Times*, September 25, 1914; *New York Financial Chronicle*, October 3, 1914.

35. Noyes, *War Period*, 66-69.

36. See Wilson's "Special address to Congress," September 4, 1914, *New Democracy*, I, 160-163; Cordell Hull, *The Memoirs of Cordell Hull* (Macmillan, 1948), I, 76; Link, *Struggle for Neutrality*, 102-103.

37. United States Treasury, *Annual Report, 1914* (Washington: G.P.O., 1915), 4-7, 71-74; New York Evening Post, December 31, 1914. See Noyes, *War Period*, 81-91; speech by Jacob H. Schiff, August 13, 1914, *Annual Report of the New York Chamber of Commerce, 1914-1915*, I, 54-55.

38. For an extended discussion of this development and a statistical analysis, see Edwin J. Clapp, *Economic Aspects of the War* (Yale University Press, 1915), 209-220; see also *New York Times*, August 5, 1915.

39. See "Exports of Selected U. S. Merchandise: 1790 to 1957," *Historical Statistics of the United States: Colonial Times to the Present* (Washington: G.P.O., 1960), 654; "United States Exports to South America," ibid., 550.

40. Page memorandum, August 25, 1913, Hendrick, *Page*, I, 195-196.
41. Page to Colonel House, April 27, 1914, ibid., 230.
42. Page to Colonel House, September 22, 1914; October 11, 1914, ibid., 334-335, 341-343.
43. Page to Wilson, October 6, 1914, WW Mss.
44. Page to Arthur W. Page, November 6, 1914, Hendrick, *Page*, I, 345.
45. House Diary, November 25, 1914.
46. Ibid., November 30, 1914; December 16, 1914.
47. "Second Annual Address to Congress," December 8, 1914, *New Democracy*, I, 216-219.
48. *German Banking in Latin America*, Department of Commerce Bulletin No. 90, 63rd Congress, 2nd Session, December 18, 1914.
49. House Diary, December 29, 1914.
50. Ibid., December 19, 1914, December 29, 1914; Colonel House to Wilson, January 21, 1915, WW Mss.
51. Secretary Bryan to Vice Consul Silliman, July 23, 1914, *Foreign Relations, 1914*, 568-569; Isidro Eabila to J. Silliman, July 27, 1914, ibid., 575; Bryan to Silliman, July 31, 1914, ibid., 577.
52. For a discussion of the extent of American holdings in Mexico, see J. Fred Rippy, *The United States and Mexico*, (Alfred A. Knopf, 1926), 311-319.
53. For the decree of 1915, see Nathan L. Whetten, *Rural Mexico* (University of Chicago Press, 1948), 114-116. See also Frank Tannenbaum, *Mexico: The Struggle for Peace and Bread* (Alfred A. Knopf, 1950), 58-59; and Elyer N. Simpson, *The Ejido: Mexico's Way Out* (University of North Carolina Press, 1937), 54-62.
54. *La Prensa*, Lima, September 3, 1913, in WW Mss.
55. Samuel G. Blythe, "Mexico: The Record of a Conversation with President Wilson," *Saturday Evening Post*, CLXXXVI (May 23, 1914), 3-4.
56. See Chapter II, supra.
57. Blythe, "Mexico," ibid.
58. Ibid.
59. "Saxon ambition dismembers Panama, agitates Nicaragua, and overturns Mexico . . . . Will they not be able to make a declaration in the future limiting the amount of European capital which can be invested in each republic or determine the numerical importance of the current of immigration. Thus successful, they could impose on free peoples a hard tutelage." Americo Lubo, Argentinian Deputy, cited in Francisco Garcia Calderon, *Latin America: Its Rise and Progress* (T. F. Unwin, 1913), 280. Hiram Bingham, in "The Monroe Doctrine: An Obsolete Shibboleth," *Atlantic Monthly*, CXI (June, 1913), 721-734, describes how Argentina, Brazil, and Chile had formed the ABC agreement to seek mediation of disputes and offered mediation in Mexico with "the definite object of opposing encroachments of

the United States . . . to counteract the interference and intervention of the United States," 228. F. G. Calderon, Peruvian diplomat and publicist, described the ABC "treaty" as an effort to seek "equilibrium between the United States and Latin America," Calderon, *Latin America*, 349.

60. *New York Times*, January 9, 1915.
61. Arthur S. Link maintains that Wilson was "sincere" but found it difficult to hold his position. The question is not his sincerity but just what it was that his position really meant.
62. Bryan to Wilson, March 6, 1915, *Foreign Relations, The Lansing Papers* (Washington: G.P.O., 1940), II, 528.
63. Wilson to Bryan, March 6, 1915, ibid., 529.
64. Wilson to Duval West, February 5, 1915, WW Mss.
65. Bryan to Special Agent Silliman, May 6, 1915, *Foreign Relations, 1915*, 659-661.
66. Wilson to Bryan, May 12, 1915, *Lansing Papers*, II, 531.
67. Carranza to Wilson, March 9, 1915, *Foreign Relations, 1915*, 666-668.
68. House pointed out the dangers of unilateral intervention and suggested that they might be avoided by bringing in the ABC powers. This would also help his plan to make the Monroe Doctrine multilateral.
69. Lansing to Bryan, March 8, 1915, *Lansing Papers*, II, 529.
70. Bryan to Wilson, March 13, 1915, WW Mss.
71. *New York Times*, April 20, 1915.
72. See Link, *Struggle for Neutrality*, 471-475; Eduardo Iturbide was supported by refugees, former Huertista generals, anti-revolutionary Maderistas, Roman Catholic bishops. Leon Canova, Chandler Anderson of the State Department, and Secretary of the Interior Franklin K. Lane. Leon Canova proposed a scheme that Wilson later adopted for the Hoover program in Russia. Canova suggested that Wilson proclaim that the United States would save Mexico from starvation and, while providing food relief, take charge of the outstanding political problems such as the restoration of the rights of the Church and the return of all property "illegally confiscated" since February 1913, ibid., 473-474.
73. *New York Times*, June 3, 1915; Wilson to Lansing, June 2, June 3, 1915, *Lansing Papers*, II, 532-535.
74. Wilson to Lansing, June 17, 1915, ibid., II, 535.
75. Special Agent Silliman to Lansing, June 22, 1915, *Foreign Relations, 1915*, 718-719.
76. Wilson to Lansing, July 2, 1915, Lansing Mss.
77. House Diary, January 25, 1915.
78. J. S. Normano, in *The Struggle for South America*, 97-116, makes the significant distinction between "continentalism," which he traces

back to Alexander Hamilton and defines as multilateral cooperation based on a community of interest and the concept of distinction from Europe, and Pan-Americanism, which he defines as a policy of the United States attempting to draw Latin America to it in an effort to secure markets. "Continentalism was an idealistic movement of the first quarter of the nineteenth century . . .a direct descendant of the spirit of the French Revolution transplanted on American soil. . . . Official Pan-Americanism sprang from the needs of the new-born industry of the United States." Blaine, he said, conceived of Pan-Americanism as an "economic instrument which he adorned with the plumage of continentalism, thus attempting to rival the ideological fresco of Latin and Hispano-Americanism."

79. Lansing to Wilson, July 5, 1915, *Lansing Papers*, II, 538-539.
80. Wilson to Lansing, July 8, 1915, cited in Link, *Struggle for Neutrality*, 482-483.
81. Lansing to Wilson, August 6, 1915, August 9, 1915, *Lansing Papers*, II, 545-548.
82. Wilson to Lansing, August 11, 1915, *Lansing Papers*, II, 549; Lansing to Wilson, September 12, 1915, ibid., 550-552; Link, *Struggle for Neutrality*, 487.
83. Lansing to Wilson, August 6, 1915, *Lansing Papers*, II, 543-544; *New York Times*, August 6, August 7, 1915.

6
STABILITY *VERSUS* CHANGE CONTROLLED BY OTHERS

THE NEED FOR A WORLD SYSTEM

Even before the ABC Conference, on July 11, 1915, Lansing had expressed concern over the progress of the war in Europe. He feared German plotting and activity in Central America and Mexico, and felt that the United States had to strengthen its position in the area. That could be done through the "cultivation of a Pan-American doctrine" and the establishment of friendly relations with Mexico through the recognition of Carranza as the strongest available figure.[1] Colonel House had written Wilson of the necessity of a quick settlement and the restoration of order in Mexico so that Wilson's prestige might be enhanced in Europe before the war there ended.[2] By August 11, Wilson agreed that it might be necessary to work with Carranza.

Lansing had the task of changing the instructions to the ABC delegates through the device of reviving Wilson's old plea in the name of the interests of the Mexican people and their need for revolution. He argued that leadership was a matter for Mexico to decide and, reversing the earlier American position, asserted that those who had supported Huerta and the antirevolutionary Maderistas were "not entitled to participate in the initial establishment of government in Mexico."[3] Only a week earlier, the delegates had been instructed to find a "constitutional successor to Madero." Wilson's instructions to Lansing were to swing the conference to de facto recognition of Carranza. They were to inform the other factions in Mexico that they might discuss the terms of submission to Carranza, but "that was all."[4] The Administration hoped that Carranza would see the necessity of instituting Wilson's program of reform, the protection of foreign interests, and recognition of "their just claims."[5] Lansing later commented that he appealed to the philosophical structure of the Latin mind, arguing abstractly the right of revolution, and concretely the dominant position of Carranza. His concluding argument stressed the need to give recognition and financial aid to Carranza in order to forestall German influence in a chaotic situation.[6]

The tactic of encouraging Villa and then abandoning him for Carranza won neither Carranza's compliance nor Villa's resignation. Carranza refused to accept the gift of recognition on Wilson's conditions of special consideration for foreign property claims. He refused to "consent to a discussion of the domestic affairs of the Republic by mediation or on the initiative of any foreign government whatever." Forced conciliation of the conflicting factions, he said, would rob his followers of the victory for which they had fought. It would undermine the power of the government by destroying Mexican confidence.[7]

Villa was embittered by Wilson's betrayal. He was isolated by a new arms embargo applied to all but Carranza. Encouraged, perhaps, by the extent to which "Mexicans were lynched and terrorized right and left north of the Rio Grande," Villa attacked a party of American engineers who were proceeding at Carranza's invitation to reopen some mines. Then he was reported to have initiated the raid on Columbus, New Mexico, on March 9, 1916.[8]

The military expedition dispatched under General Pershing was ordered to capture Villa and disperse his "bandits." Having settled the question of which leader represented the revolution, Wilson was able to apply his definition of bandit to Villa. Beginning operations under Carranza's tentative permission limited to immediate pursuit,[9] the expedition was enlarged until it began to resemble an invasion. By the middle of June, almost twelve thousand soldiers were committed to Mexican soil and had penetrated some three hundred miles beyond the border. They were fighting not only Villa but also government soldiers and civilians who felt their country had been invaded.[10] Just as with the Tampico affair, the professed purpose of catching the bandit Villa paled to insignificance before the main objective of settling the Mexican situation.

Carranza tried to obtain the withdrawal of American troops through promising a joint Mexican-American border patrol. Wilson was more concerned, however, with terminating the Mexican question. Carranza denounced the United States for acting in bad faith, and instructed his commanders to prevent further penetration of Mexico. Though the United States had recognized the Carranza government for tactical reasons, it was now acting in behalf of a higher law—that of bringing civilization to backward areas. Americans were confident that they were acting benevolently by helping people to self-government and stability who could not help themselves.

On June 18, 1916, Wilson ordered one hundred thousand National Guardsmen to protect the Mexican-American border, and sent warships to both coasts of Mexico.[11] But more clashes occurred between Mexican and American troops, and the skirmishes led to a significant battle when Americans attempted to move south for supplies. The Mexicans notified the American officers of their orders to prevent passage. The American commander, assuming typically that the Mexicans would not fight, ordered a charge. The result was an American defeat and the capture of twenty-three American Soldiers.[12]

Wilson responded in the name of his disinterested duty to civilization. He prepared a speech to Congress in which he disavowed any intention of "intervention." The action was instead caused by the "powerless" and "possibly unconstitutional" de facto regime in Mexico. He asked for power to clear Northern Mexico of "bandit gangs."[13] At the same time, Secretary of War Newton D. Baker called for an embargo on arms to Mexico to prevent any from falling into the hands of "enemies of the de facto government."[14] Carranza complained that Wilson demanded he maintain order while depriving him of the necessary weapons.[15]

In Washington the problem of guaranteeing stability in Mexico and placing it within the economic sphere of the United States was examined. William H. Murray of Oklahoma sent a memorandum to the President expressing the belief that the penetration and occupation of Mexico, south to a line from Tampico to the Pacific, would include 80 percent of Americans and foreigners in the country and 90 percent of all investment. Such action would reduce to a minimum the causes of enmity, and end controversy until Americans penetrated further south. Considering the psychology of "semi-barbarous people," he felt it would be a miracle if the United States got out of Mexico without a war. American interests would never be safe until the country was "cleaned up by force of arms." Murray felt that an occupation could be made permanent because the Mexicans would need such financing that the Mexican government would be willing to sell the territory to the United States. He argued against any commitment to refrain from acquiring Mexican territory.[16]

Walter Hines Page's idea of "Cuba-izing" Mexico received support from Edward N. Smith, an old friend of Lansing and an upstate New York newspaper publisher. In a letter to Lansing on November 11, 1916, Smith discussed the issue in the context of the problem of finding foreign markets for surplus American production. Mexico was a natural market, he pointed out, but the people were so poor it would take years for them to generate purchasing power. Sometimes, Smith wrote, he thought that there was no remedy except intervention "of the same character and spirit as Cuba."[17] Wilson realized, however, that the United States could not afford an increased military commitment in Mexico, nor could he impose a protectorate without further alienating the rest of Latin America.

The war in Europe was creating mounting problems, and American involvement appeared increasingly probable. Wilson attributed Mexican hostility to "poisonous" German propaganda designed to involve the United States in a war to divert its attention from the submarine campaign. He told Tumulty that it looked as though war with Germany was inevitable and he wished to conserve American strength for the greater struggle.[18] Lansing became increasingly hesitant to gratify an "intense desire . . . to make the Mexicans pay full measure for their misdeeds." The War Department informed him, he later wrote in his diary, that it would require a force of over four hundred thousand men to occupy and hold any considerable portion of Mexico, and the United States had only thirty-five thousand men available at that time.[19]

The alternative was negotiation. The discussions from September, 1916 to January 2, 1917 clarified the broader purposes of the Pershing expedition. American conditions for withdrawal involved a complete definition of Mexican-American relations. The United States insisted on a pledge to protect foreign lives and property—"adequate to enable Americans to resume operation of mines and other industries in which they may be interested." All property rights acquired in the past were to be validated and guaranteed. A mixed claims commission was to be created to consider claims of injury to person or property arising since November 20, 1910. Finally, there would have to be a provision for "freedom of conscience" and "religious toleration," and "every facility" for such agencies of the United States as wished to combat disease and "relieve the distress and starvation now prevailing in many sections of the Republic. [20]

Those conditions would, in effect, have forestalled efforts at land reform through expropriation, prevented the limitation of location and size of foreign land holdings, and blocked the revolutionary demands that subsoil rights revert to the State. They would also have thwarted the efforts by the revolutionaries to curb the power of the Catholic Church and the influence of American missionaries.

In the name of national sovereignty, the Mexican delegates insisted on the withdrawal of foreign troops before internal issues could be discussed. They argued that it was the presence of foreign forces in Mexico that had aroused the hostility of the Mexican people. This hostility required the commitment of a large number of Federalist troops, soldiers that could otherwise be used to maintain order. The American spokesmen rejected this postulate, arguing that the border raids were merely symptomatic of "abnormal conditions prevailing in Mexico," and that they had to discuss and deal with the "basic causes of the trouble." Safeguarding American lives and property was as important as securing the border.

The Mexicans attempted, in reply, to explain the purposes and policies of their new government, the changes it was trying to institute, and the efforts to extend civil government and reorganize taxation. The Americans held firm, however, to the position that Carranza could not fulfill his obligations; that the status of foreign property had to be arranged, taxes on mining installations determined in a "satisfactory" manner and American and British oil interests protected as preconditions to withdrawal. [21]

On November 18, 1916, Wilson issued an ultimatum that might usefully be called a corollary to the Mobile address. While avowing his desire to see Mexico "strong, independent, sovereign, and completely fulfilling her domestic . . . and international obligations," and declaring his desire to "strengthen the Carranza Government," Wilson announced that his patience had ended. Present conditions were intolerable and he demanded Mexico settle its relations with American investments. Wilson added that he desired to do nothing to hurt Mexico's sovereign pride, or to curtail its freedom of action in determining national policy. But if the Mexicans did not desire to cooperate, "if you feel that you want to cut yourselves off completely," this would "vitally affect" American policy toward Mexico. Secretary of the Interior Franklin K. Lane, one of the American negotiators, added that, though the United States had no desire to dictate terms, Mexico would have either to accept the benefit of American cooperation or be forced into isolation and the accompanying downfall of the Carranza regime. The United States would reserve the right to "deal with any hostile incursion into American territory as may be deemed advisable," but protection of the border was tied to protection of American lives and property within Mexico. [22]

The ultimatum was not to be construed as interventionism. Wilson firmly denounced dollar diplomacy which, he said, "compelled Mexico to give precedence to foreign interests over [her] own." He disavowed intervention as "the use of the power of the United States to establish internal order . . . without the invitation of Mexico and to determine the character and method of her political institutions." Wilson reaffirmed the right of every nation to "order its own institutions as it will," and denounced foreign aid conditioned on concessions which had placed the greater part of Mexican resources in the hands of foreign capitalists. Mexico needed financial support that did not involve "the sale of her liberties and the enslavement of her people." The United States, Wilson concluded, could establish permanent peace in Mexico only by "resolute and consistent adoption in action of the principles which underlie her own life. She must respect the liberties and self-government of the Mexicans as she would respect her own. [23]

The Mexicans obstinately refused to adopt proper measures for safeguarding their liberties and adequate self-government in a manner satisfactory to the United States, and the negotiations dragged on for months. By March, 1917 the pressures of the approaching American entry into the European war forced Wilson to withdraw troops from Mexico. The Zimmerman note led to the United States' decision on a "soft policy" and disengagement. [24]   Until the end, however, American commissioners condemned the "economic, financial, sanitary, and social conditions in Mexico." They denounced the constitution being written on the grounds that it would make "the position of foreigners . . . intolerable and open the door to confiscation of legally acquired property," and they continued their efforts to modify Mexican labor reforms, land reforms, tax principles, and expropriation policy in behalf of American interests. [25]

Even after withdrawal, the United States continued trying to shape developments within Mexico. Wilson expanded his definition of the Monroe Doctrine to permit the British to use whatever influence they had to secure the oil production of Mexico for the Allied cause. [26] The British Government joined the oil companies in supporting and financing the counterrevolutionary movement of General Pelaez, titleholder to the lands leased to the Mexican Eagle Petroleum Company, and "friend of the oil companies." [27]

Wilson had entered the White House convinced of the necessity of expanding American economic activities, and viewing Latin America as an area of primary importance in that connection. But revolution, nationalism, and distrust of the United States jeopardized the peace, stability and cooperation necessary to "harmonious" economic development. In his efforts to secure the conditions that he felt would facilitate answers to the problems, the President attempted to construct a viable system for Latin America. In the main, his efforts failed, perhaps because of his lack of insight into revolutionary situations and his inability to understand the nationalistic sentiments of other peoples. Wrapped in the righteous cloak of his sense of moral superiority and Anglo-Saxon political wisdom, and confident in the conviction that what was to the interest of the United States must work for the good of others, Wilson struggled to create an empire of good will only to generate disbelief and hostility.

Wilson appealed to the ABC nations in the name of a "hemispheric moral partnership" in which there would be no "claim of guardianship or thought of wards." All governments were to stand on a footing of genuine equality and unquestioned independence. This, he said, was "Pan-Americanism." And it would have none of the "spirit of Empire." [28] Another kind of Pan-Americanism was spreading, however, as Ecuadorian leaders circulated an appeal to join together against the imperialism and aggression of the United States. [29]

Lansing also dissented from Wilson's efforts at implementing American policy through appeals to mutuality. He sent Wilson a second memorandum on the Monroe Doctrine on November 24, 1915. American national interests were at stake and had to be secured by American actions. The national safety of the

United States was menaced by European financial influence in the Caribbean. The United States had to intervene to create "stable" and "honest" government. Stability and honesty, Lansing contended, depended on the creation of sufficient force to resist revolutions, and sufficient control over revenues and resource development to prevent official graft and "dishonest" grants of privileges to foreigners.

Because of the strategic importance of the Canal, furthermore, the United States was required to intervene and shape the character of government in the region. The policy should not be justified on the grounds of benefitting the populations of the area because "too many international crimes have been committed in the name of humanity." It should be pursued simply on the basis of the national interest of the United States. It was in accord with this policy, Lansing said, that the United States had acted in Cuba, Panama, Nicaragua, the Dominican Republic and Haiti, and reserved the right to act in the neighboring republics, the Danish West Indies, and "other colonial possessions," should the need arise. [30]

Wilson agreed that Lansing's blunt reasoning was "unanswerable," but he was not prepared to moot or drop his appeal to morality. He suggested that the memorandum should not be published, but instead be held in reserve for the "guidance and clarification" of Caribbean policy, and for informal discussion with the Latin American nations from time to time, "semiconfidentially, and for the sake of a frank understanding." [31]

Wilson's effort to create a system of Latin American collective security based on American policies was greeted with hostility and suspicion. From the beginning, for example, Chile objected to any commitment to mutual enforcement of the Monroe Doctrine or other definitions by the United States of what constituted political legitimacy. [32] With the Pershing expedition to Mexico serving as an illustration of Wilson's concern for national sovereignty, Argentina and Brazil drew back and by August 9, 1916, the three countries had begun to openly reject the proposed agreement under the impact of "intense feeling aroused by the crisis in Mexico." [33]

The *Mercurio* of Santiago, voice of the Chilean government, printed an editorial on July 4, 1916, denouncing the proposed Pan-American treaty as involving "vague and indeterminate powers of intervention in the entire continent." It distinguished between a "Pan-Americanism of concord and equality" and a

Pan-Americanism of "predominance." A treaty that would give
de facto preponderance to one part of the continent over the
other would tend to destroy true Pan-American fraternity.
Ambassador Fletcher warned that if the United States tried to
go on without Chile, it would "turn elsewhere for finance and
trade" and hostility toward the United States would increase
even more. [34]

Wilson attempted to draw Great Britain into the Pan-
-American agreement in order to create "influence which could
control the peace of the world." That effort failed. Britain
decided to wait for agreement among Latin American nations. [35]

Undersecretary of State Frank Polk informed House on
August 8 that the proposed pact seemed "dead for the moment." [36] It remained so until the United States entered World
War I. By that time, however, Wilson had changed his focus
and had begun to use his Pan-American project as the basis for
constructing a European-oriented system on the assumption
that the Allies had a greater community of interest than the
nations of the Western Hemisphere.

Though political Pan-Americanism suffered a defeat in Mexico, its economic counterpart flourished as the United States
labored to take advantage of the opportunity provided by the
European war. John Hays Hammond, a prominant Republican
and top-ranking mining engineer with major interests in Mexico, and associated with leading American financial groups,
analyzed the situation perceptively in July, 1915. The war had
interrupted European financing to Central and South America,
and it would be years before Europe could again become
banker and broker for the region. If the United States was to
realize its ambition to claim a large share of Latin American
commerce, it would have to assume the risk of financing Latin
America. But to do so, the capitalists would have to be assured
of the cooperation and encouragement of the government.
They would also have to be guaranteed against "discriminatory
laws and confiscation, especially in time of revolutionary move-
ments." Hammond urged the creation of a Pan-American supreme court, composed of jurists from the United States and
Latin America, to handle disputes over investments and commercial transactions. That was one way of removing such disputes from the "naturally prejudiced" jurisdiction of individual
governments.

Commercial relations required more than "professed" amity.

Since the South American nations regarded the Monroe Doctrine as "supererogation" by the United States, it was good business to restrict the application of the Doctrine to the Canal area and to "our sphere of influence in the Caribbean." Pan-Americanism should be established for the rest of South America. Such action would calm the suspicions that lingered about the Monroe Doctrine, and undercut the efforts of European trade rivals to exploit that distrust. Latin Americans had the impression, Hammond reported, that American businessmen were taking advantage of the situation to establish "monopolistic control." That attitude had to be dispelled, for if it was the United States could promote the development of common interests and draw the nations together.[37]

Two months before Hammond offered his analysis, the United States called a Pan-American Financial Conference to discuss the same problems. Representatives of government and capital met in Washington in May, 1915 to discuss the cooperation of government, finance, and manufacturing in order to assure the capture by the United States of a large share of the former European trade with Latin America. Paul Warburg, of Kuhn, Loeb and Company, and the Federal Reserve Board provided an overview of the situation. Europe had taken the lead in developing the Western Hemisphere, and European bankers had in the past been "our staunch friends and allies." It would be disloyal and unbecoming for the United States to profit from their misfortunes, but the growth and development of the United States, combined with the wartime disruption in Europe, created a "momentous turning point in our economic history." The growing strength of the United States and the weakening of Europe meant that "the New World must in the future lean less heavily on the Old."[38] Though the United States was not ready to replace Europe completely, it had to shoulder part of the burden so that the American nations would never again be so completely dependent on Great Britain.[39]

The primary instrument in assuming the financial responsibility in South American trade was the Federal Reserve System. Charles S. Hamlin of the Federal Reserve Board described how the system was relieving the United States from dependency on British financing by creating a flexible central banking system to organize rediscounting, to unify credit functions, and to permit the formation of a pool of capital for financing foreign

trade.[40]   The influx of gold from Europe combined with the
new reserve requirements of the Federal Reserve Act provided
a surplus of almost $734 million. With the protection provided
by the Federal Reserve System, loan capacity could be expanded to two or three billion dollars. That would change the
traditional pattern of absorbing the bulk of American capital at
home and allow much to be used for foreign investments.[41]

The spokesmen also discussed the interrelationship of financing and exporting. A permanent market for Latin American
bonds required the development of intimate business relations
with countries offering securities. According to Paul Warburg,
the United States could now finance its own imports and
exports, and also the trade of other nations, playing the role of
international banker that hitherto had been the function of
Great Britain. As trade increased, financial ties would become
even stronger. But to accomplish those grand results, bankers
would have to be imbued with a spirit of "liberality and
patriotism." They had to realize that it was for the financial
good of their country and the security of the hemisphere that
in the future "import and export transactions touching this
country should . . . be financed by ourselves." The Federal Reserve System marked the advent of American financial independence and, with its aid, the United States would become
banker to the hemisphere.[42]

Secretary of the Treasury William G. McAdoo argued that
the establishment of a network of branch banks or agencies in
the leading cities of Latin America was the first step in the
permanent enlargement of American trade and influence. Latin
America could thereby be refinanced with American capital
replacing European. The result would be a great increase in
American trade. He also urged support for the Administration's
program of building a government financed merchant fleet, and
suggested the creation of a fleet of convertible naval auxil-
iaries, capable of functioning as merchant ships in time of
peace and defending trade when the need arose. Such a fleet
might operate at a loss, but the need justified subsidization.[43]

Secretary of Commerce William G. Redfield elaborated on
the kind of accommodation that had to be made. He stressed
the need for cheap and direct cable communications to compete with those of Europe, and the necessity of subsidizing a
merchant marine to "take over shipping from Europe." He
urged that American commercial ideas and methods be re-

adjusted; instead of regarding Latin America as the dumping ground for surpluses unmarketed in the United States, American manufacturers ought to study the needs and tastes of Latin America and design production specifically for those consumers. It was also necessary to establish common business methods, commercial regulations, and standards of measurement. Such a program would unlock the growing surpluses of capital, facilitate the permanent change from debtor to creditor standing, and permit a "broader participation in the financial growth of Spanish America."[44]

Though most of the remainder of the proceedings involved a discussion of trade patterns of the European countries with which the United States would have to compete,[45] gestures toward "continentalism" were made by two of the speakers. Joseph E. Davies, Chairman of the Federal Trade Commission, described the "common heritage" that existed despite differences in "race and tongues and creeds." All the Americas, he pointed out, shared ancestors who had "all had the virtue and vigor of the pioneer" who sought "betterment for themselves and their children." Unable to find common aspects of contemporary culture, as other Pan-American speakers strained to do, Davies was content with having common ideals for which Bolivar, Rosas, and San Martin, and the founders of the United States had fought for, and on which all the hemispheric governments were founded.[46]

The tenuous nature of this appeal was indicated by the sole speaker representing Latin America, Dr. Francisco J. Peynado of the Dominican Republic. Peynado advised the United States of the necessity of an educational campaign to overcome the long-standing "habits and prejudices" against the United States. That was necessary if the United States was to entrench itself firmly enough to retain its position at the end of the war. He also advocated such programs as a Pan-American Postal Convention to establish uniform rates and common regulations as one means of tying the two continents more firmly together.[47]

President Wilson acted to implement the measures that were suggested. At the start of the war, he fought for a shipping bill to permit the government to purchase German ships seeking refuge in neutral ports. Opposition came from two sources: the shipping interests, who argued that the competition of a government corporation to purchase and operate shipping was socialistic; and those who feared the policy would involve the

United States in conflict with Great Britain. The British protested that the action would help Germany, and that the ships
would be used in trade with Germany. [48]

The British fleet shortly cleared the seas of German raiders
and Allied commerce was restored. By the beginning of September, 1914, there were adequate shipping facilities available
except to Germany and the ship purchase bill was forgotten. A
few months later the bill was revived as a weapon in the
struggle for the Americanization of Latin American trade. In
his second Annual Address, Wilson stressed the need for a
merchant fleet to bring the American flag to Latin American
waters and open the area to American goods—much as the
railroads had opened the American west to settlement and
industry. [49]

Wilson argued for a trade offensive in terms of moral righteousness designed to appeal to the spirit of liberality and
patriotism. "Half the world is on fire," he cried, and the whole
world looks to the United States to serve its economic need.
He challenged Republican opponents of a shipping bill to
"show their right to stand in the way of the release of American products to the rest of the world!" What right had this
"blind," "misguided," "ignorant" minority to "defy the Nation?" The country was "bursting its jacket and they are seeing
to it that the jacket is not only kept tight but is riveted with
steel." As for the opposition Democrats, Wilson threatened
those who broke the "solidarity of the team" with
punishment. [50]

Though the opposition arguments were largely based on the
fear that German ships would be used in trade with Germany,
it was apparent that Wilson was concerned primarily with
building a national fleet to capture Latin American trade. He
was willing to accept as consistent with his purposes amend-
ments to the effect that no belligerent ships would be purchased, and that the new shipping board would give major
attention to Latin America. [51] The following year Wilson argued the duty of the Western Hemisphere to draw together to
"redress the balance of economic loss and confusion" in Europe. The American states had "become conscious of a new
and more vital community of interest and moral partnership in
affairs." Though the United States had assumed the role of
guardian, without invitation, it had done so in a "true and
disinterested enthusiasm for the freedom of the Americas."

It had been difficult, Wilson admitted, to avoid provoking "serious misconceptions" about the motives of the United States, but hemispheric relations were now appearing in a new light. The spirit of the Monroe Doctrine remained intact, but Mexico was a "test case" to indicate the lack of "selfish purpose." The "moral," according to Wilson, was that the states of the hemisphere had a new community of interest, both economic and political. They were "spiritual partners with common sympathies and common ideals." It was to serve this new economic community of interest, Wilson explained, that he argued for a merchant fleet. It was part of the fight for American "commercial independence." It was not to be expected that the United States would be permitted to use the ships of other nations in rivalry with their own trade. The United States had to have its own merchant fleet, not only to enjoy economic independence, but to provide "independence" and "self-sufficiency" for the entire hemisphere.

Such a fleet would bind the hemisphere together, and alone could "weave the delicate fabric of sympathy, comprehension, confidence, and mutual independence in which we wish to clothe our policy of *America for the Americans*." [52]   At the end of his argument, the President acknowledged that his first assertion of a community of interest had been in anticipation of future developments rather than a statement of existing fact. But he used his candor to argue that the United States now had the chance to clear its docks and sidings of surplus goods, and to avail itself of the "unparalleled opportunity" of linking the Americas together in "bonds of mutual interest and service." The opportunity, he warned, might never return. [53]

As part of an effort to synthesize a sense of community, the Financial Conference called for an educational campaign. This was furthered during the Pan-American Scientific Congress held in Washington in January, 1915. Wilson explained that even friendship was based on the perception of common sympathies, interests, ideals and purposes. Science was an international language just as commerce. In each there was a universal purpose, a common plan of action. The Financial Conference had also indicated the need for governmental cooperation and for legal uniformity to open the flow of commerce, and that naturally led to the need for a community of political interest to enable the growth of a common material interest. If nations were politically suspicious of each other, trade would be more difficult. To remove such fears and suspicions of the Monroe Doctrine, Wilson asked adherence to his Pan-American treaty. He claimed its purpose was to prevent revolution, and to maintain international peace as well. If any American state was "constantly in ferment," it would jeopardize relations with others. Thus it was the mutual interest of all to assist each other in maintaining internal stability.[54]

Lansing spoke to the Scientific Conference about a "continental family," a group separate and apart from the rest of the world but united by common ideals and aspirations. This feeling was growing each year, he claimed, and had become a "potent influence over our political and commercial intercourse." Such consciousness of family ties was the essence of Pan-Americanism, and was in complete harmony with the Monroe Doctrine. Lansing faced a difficult task in reconciling Pan-Americanism with the Monroe Doctrine; but he tried to do so by defining the Monroe Doctrine as a national policy of the United States to be distinguished from Pan-Americanism, the international policy of the Americas. Though the motives were different, the ends were the same.

If cooperation was to be effective, Lansing continued, it had to be based on more intimate knowledge. "We must not only be neighbors, but friends," he urged, "not only friends but intimates." It was necessary to study each other's processes of thought. Commerce, industry, science, art, public and private law, government, and education had to be examined from the point of view of promoting mutual esteem and trust. Such mutual knowledge would unite the republics more closely in politics, in commerce, and in intellectual activities. While Europe was torn by nationalism and war, Pan-Americanism represented the idea of internationalism of which "America has become the guardian."[55]

It was through these efforts to stabilize Latin America and allay the hostility of the region, themselves part of promoting the expansion of American trade, that Wilson developed his concept of internationalism. It was an internationalism, as Lansing admitted, guarded and guided by the United States. Unable to rely simply on the Monroe Doctrine and moral rhetoric, Wilson turned to a form of international cooperation in which the states of Latin America would cooperate in building the kind of world the United States needed. The events and circumstances of the war in Europe led Wilson to project this concept as a community that would permit American interests to flourish throughout the world. It is from these roots that Wilson's concept of Collective Security blossomed forth.

Notes and References

1. Lansing, Private Diary, July 11, 1915, Lansing Mss.
2. House to Wilson, March 15, 1915, Seymour, *Intimate Papers*, I, 220. Arthur S. Link attributed the change in policy to Wilson's sudden willingness to accept the revolution on its own terms, in opposition to Lansing's "intervention policy." In support of this Link cites Wilson's restatement of his by now familiar "eighty-five percent of the Mexican population" speech on July 4, 1915, and his urging that a provisional government adopt a reform program before elections or the formulation of a constitution; Link, *Struggle for Neutrality*, 490-491.
3. "Continuation of the Conference on Mexican Affairs," August 11, 1915, State Department Papers, extensively cited in Link, *Struggle for Neutrality*, 491-492.
4. Wilson to Lansing, September 13, 1915, *Lansing Papers*, II, 522.
5. House Diary, September 23, 1915.
6. Lansing, Private Diary, October 10, 1915.
7. Cited in Samuel Guy Inman, *Intervention in Mexico*, (George H. Doran Co., 1919), 92. This view was set to verse in a revolutionary *corrida*:

> Si Carranza se casa con Villa,
> Y Zapata con General Obregón,
> Si Adelita se case conmigo,
> Pos se acabara la revolucion.

> If Carranza would marry Villa,
> And Zapata marry Obregón,
> If Adelita would only marry me,
> The revolution would be dead as a stone.

Cited in Todd Downing, *Mexican Earth* (Doubleday, Doran & Co., 1940), 247-248.
8. Ibid., 250. Downing raises questions about the identity of the raiders. George Marvin, editor of *World's Work*, commented:

"Before the army took over the job, the borderland was pa-
trolled by Rangers. Some of these rangers have degenerated into
common man-killers. There is no penalty for killihg, for no jury
along the border would ever convict a white man for shooting a
Mexican. . . . The killing of Mexicans that has been going on
through the borderland in these last four years is almost incred-
ible. . . . Reading the Secret Service records makes you feel almost as though there were an open game season on Mexicans."

Cited in Inman, *Intervention in Mexico*, 150-51.

9. Silliman to Lansing, March 15, 1916, *Foreign Relations, 1916*, 491.
10. See Link, *Woodrow Wilson and the Progressive Era*, 136-140; Cline,
    The United States and Mexico, 176-180.
11. *New York Times*, June 19, 1916.
12. Report by Captain Morey, June 21, 1916, *Foreign Relations, 1916*,
    596; *New York Times*, June 25, 1916; U. S. Army Report, October
    2, 1916, WW Mss. The account in Cline, *United States and Mexico*,
    has it that the Mexicans gave warning and then opened fire. The
    United States charge is not mentioned.
13. Draft address, June 1916, WW Mss.
14. Newton D. Baker to Wilson, June 18, 1916, WW Mss.
15. See, for example, Report of Captain Louis C. Richardson to Chief of
    Naval Operations, "Mexico—Tampico and Vicinity," March 11, 1919,
    WW Mss.
16. Wm. H. Murray to A. S. Burleson, June 28, 1916, Lansing Mss.
17. Edward N. Smith to Lansing, November 11, 1916, Lansing Mss.
18. Tumulty, *Woodrow Wilson*, 159.
19. Lansing, Private Diary, November 17, 1919.
20. Franklin K. Lane, George Gray, John R. Mott to Cabrera, Bonillas,
    and Pani, September 6, 1916, *Foreign Relations, 1917*, 920-921.
21. Report of Proceedings of Mexican Joint Commission, September 4,
    1916, *Foreign Relations, 1917*, 917; Mexican Joint Commission Re-
    port, October 25, 1916, ibid., 919.
22. Franklin K. Lane to Mexican Commissioners, November 21, 1916,
    ibid., 924-925.
23. Wilson, "The Mexican Problem Again: An Interview," *Ladies Home
    Journal*, October 1916, reprinted in *Selected Papers*, II, 212-217.
24. Lansing to Edward N. Smith, March 3, 1917, Lansing Mss.
25. United States Commissioners to Wilson, Janaury 3, 1917, *Foreign
    Relations, 1917*, 936-937.
26. Robert Lansing, *War Memoirs of Robert Lansing* (Bobbs-Merrill Co.,
    1935), 315.
27. Ibid., 315-317; Nearing, *Dollar Diplomacy*, 117-119.
28. Wilson, "Annual Message to Congress," December 7, 1915, *New
    Democracy*, I, 407-409.

29. Ambassador Elizalde to John Bassett Moore, October 15, 1934; John Bassett Moore to Borchard, October 16, 1934, Borchard File, John Bassett Moore Mss.

30. Lansing to Wilson, memorandum on Monroe Doctrine, November 24, 1915, *Lansing Papers*, II, 466-470.

31. Wilson to Lansing, November 29, 1915, ibid., 470.

32. Bryan to Wilson, March 8, 1915; April 3, 1915; April 21, 1915, ibid., 473, 476-478.

33. House Diary, August 8, 1916; August 9, 1916; Ambassador Fletcher to Lansing, August 9, 1916, *Lansing Papers*, II, 496.

34. *Lansing Papers*, II.

35. House Diary, February 20, 1916; February 21, 1916; March 5, 1916.

36. Frank Polk to Colonel House, August 8, 1916, House Mss.

37. John Hays Hammond, "Trade Relations with Central and South America as Affected by the War," *Annals of the American Academy*, LX (July 1915), 69-71. Hammond's activities ranged from insurrection against the Boers in the Witwatersrand gold fields to Guggenheim representative in Mexico and South America to candidate for Republican vice-presidential nomination in 1908. See Harvey O'Conner, *The Guggenheims* (Convici-Friede, 1937), passim; *Who's Who in America, 1918-1919* (A. N. Marquis & Co., 1919), 1172.

38. Paul M. Warburg in *Proceedings of the First Pan-American Financial Conference* (G.P.O., 1915), 172-173.

39. Ibid., 168.

40. Charles S. Hamlin, ibid., 158.

41. Frank A. Vanderlip, ibid., 140-141.

42. Paul M. Warburg, ibid., 168, 172-173.

43. William G. McAdoo, ibid., 9-14.

44. William C. Redfield, ibid., 129-132.

45. Ibid., 57-59.

46. Joseph E. Davies, ibid., 199-200.

47. Dr. Francisco J. Peynado, ibid., 136. By this time the Dominican Republic had become a financial and political protectorate with a popularly disliked government holding power only because the armed force of the United States stood between the President and the people. See Link, *Struggle for Neutrality*, 540-541.

48. Sir Cecil Spring-Rice to Lord Grey, August 25, 1914, in Stephen Swynn, ed., *The Letters and Friendships of Sir Cecil Spring-Rice* (Houghton Mifflin & Co., 1929), II, 219-220. See also, Link, *Struggle for Neutrality*, 86-91; *New York Times*, January 19, 22, 23, 1915; *New York World*, January 31, 1915.

49. Wilson, "Second Annual Address to Congress," December 8, 1914, *New Democracy*, I, 217-219, 210-220.

50. Wilson, "Jackson Day Address," January 8, 1915, ibid., 240-243.

51. *New York World*, February 3, 1915.

52. Emphasis added.
53. Wilson, "Third Annual Address to Congress," December 7, 1915, *New Democracy*, I, 406-418.
54. *New York Times*, January 7, 1916. For a discussion of South American fear of the economic expansion of the United States and the *"Yanqui centrista,"* as the Pan-American Union was called, see Normano, *Struggle for South America*, 116, 156.
55. Robert Lansing, "Address to the Pan-American Scientific Congress," *Daily Bulletin of the Pan-American Scientific Congress*, I (December 29, 1915, 11-12, Lansing Mss.

7
NEUTRALITY *VERSUS* COLLECTIVE SECURITY

Wilson saw the war as a special opportunity for the United States. He conceived of America as playing a special role, standing independent, aloof and prosperous until Europe turned to it for salvation. He asked for strict neutrality, "in fact as well as in name," to insulate the nation from the pressures of the war. "The effect of the war on the United States," he told Congress on August 19, 1914, "will depend upon what American citizens say and do." It was "entirely within our own choice what its effect upon us will be."[1] He believed that the United States enjoyed freedom of action, that it could control the impact of conflict in Europe.

Wilson had made it clear even earlier, on July 4, 1914, that he expected the world to turn to the United States for "those moral inspirations which lie at the basis of all freedom," and in which "all shall know . . . that her flag is the flag not only of America but of all humanity." He predicted the expansion of American trade and influence to "all quarters of the world" and, through the process, the spreading of "human liberty and the rights of man"[2]

The Wilson Doctrine was based on unilateral action to implement a self-assumed role as spokesman for world morality. "Shooting people into self-government," as Walter Hines Page described it, or "intervening in behalf of liberty" in the words of Wilson, was justified because it was the heritage and destiny of the United States to be the "justest, the most progressive, the most honorable, the most enlightened Nation in the world."[3] The American flag, Wilson said, was a "sort of floating charter" that "came down from Runnymede," a proclamation that Americans would "seek [their] own liberty." With the coming of industrial maturity and the shift of the national frontier to the world, Wilson explained on June 6, 1914, the flag had become an "instrument of civilization" to "serve humanity."[4]

Wilson designed his reforms to provide American business its "constitutional freedom," to permit a "boom of business . . . such as we have never witnessed in the United States."[5] This was the "great thing that lay in the future for the United States;" to expand its enterprise and influence in every country in the world.[6] As Page wrote so enthusiastically from London, it was only a matter of time until America's moral and economic potential would place it in a position of world leadership. "I was never so sure that command is ours," Page wrote on February 22, 1914, "and will fall into our hands more and more."[7] He dated the "passing of commercial supremacy to the United States" from the tariff reform act of 1913.[8]

Stability, order, security, and free access to markets were necessary, however, for the unfolding of the national destiny. To obtain those conditions, Page suggested joint action by the United States, Great Britain, and Germany to provide a "new era of security" in Latin America, to provide for "orderliness and peace and for the honest development of backward, turbulent lands and peoples."[9] House, who was more concerned than Wilson with conditions in Europe, had urged the joint exploitation of the underdeveloped areas of the world on the basis of mutual agreement and the open door. That would eliminate the imperial rivalries that promoted war and the disruption of trade.[10]

Wilson had been willing to reach an understanding with Great Britain in order to bolster American pre-eminence in the Monroe Doctrine area. Nevertheless, he tended to regard American economic and moral superiority as being sufficient to rely on the Open Door as the path to American expansion. In this respect he deviated but little from other key spokesmen for expansion. He shared the views of Alfred Thayer Mahan on the logic of American industrial capacity necessitating expansion to maintain full employment and prevent social and political crisis. He likewise advocated a merchant marine. Perhaps he placed greater emphasis on moral influence and example and less on naval force as the means of keeping the peace, but both men viewed an open door empire as the desirable alternative to colonial expansion.[11]

Willard Straight of the State Department and the House of Morgan likewise defined dollar diplomacy and the open door as vehicles of economic expansion. He presented the position of the United States in terms similar to those favored by Wilson. "Our export trade," Straight remarked, "is constantly increasing and foreign markets are becoming each year more and more necessary to our manufactures." Dollar diplomacy was designed to protect Americans engaged in foreign trade and to promote fresh endeavor and "by diplomatic action pave the way for those who have not yet been, but who will later be obliged to sell capital or goods abroad." In undeveloped areas a government seeking to secure a market must "either acquire territory or insist on equality of commercial opportunity." It must "either stake out its own claim, or induce other interested powers to preserve the open door." [12]

Though Straight labeled dollar diplomacy "a logical manifestation of our natural growth," and Wilson denounced the phrase as meaning unwarranted support for the acquisition of special privilege for private interests, both shared the same objectives—the expansion of American trade throughout the world, and the assistance in this of the government. Wilson combined the theory of expansion with a well-developed sense of moral and political righteousness. "There is no man more interested than I am in carrying the enterprise of American businessmen to every quarter of the globe," said Wilson. "I am willing to get anything for an American that money and enterprise can obtain except the suppression of the rights of other men. I will not help any man buy a power which he ought not to exercise over his fellow beings." [13] Such action was made easier because Wilson believed that the development of the rights of other men were served by the expansion of American influence.

Such was the outlook that prompted Wilson's neutrality proclamation. He pledged the United States would keep a free hand and show itself a nation "fit beyond others to exhibit the fine poise of undisturbed judgement, the dignity of self-control, the efficiency of dispassionate action; a nation that neither sits in judgement upon others nor is disturbed in her own counsels, and which keeps herself fit and free to do what is honest and disinterested and truly serviceable for the peace of the world." That program would produce happiness for Americans and a "great and lasting influence for peace." [14] It was dependent, however, on the ability to remain neutral and expand, to steer a course by which the United States might "remain sane" and keep her resources and strength intact "to offer rescue when the time should come." [15]

Wilson had already urged Congress to enact merchant marine legislation to enable the United States to assume the carrying of raw materials to the Central Powers. American harvests would "waste in the warehouses" or "rot in the fields," he said, unless American ships could carry American cargoes to the ports of the world. [16] Walter Hines Page, yet to be swept along with dictates of British necessity, judged that the war would revive American shipping. "It will probably help us politically and it will surely help us economically." [17] The war would result in the destruction of the balance of power, he wrote Wilson on August 9, and Europe would be bankrupted, but the United States would emerge "immensely stronger financially and politically." [18]

This glowing picture of opportunity did not take into account the fact that Britain had not yet retired from empire, that economic influence might flow in two directions, and that the war was an economic struggle for survival. As the United States soon learned, a choice would have to be made between economic expansion and political influence and the desire to remain neutral.

Tasker H. Bliss, commanding general of the United States Army, who became a member of the Supreme Allied War Council, later pointed out the new character of wars between "nations at arms." War had become industrial in its basis and dependent upon access to the resources and supplies necessary to satisfy an enormous and continuous demand. Nations could not any longer store up the necessities of war. The key to victory was the ability to disrupt the sources of supply. Blockade was the most effective, the most certain of all the available agencies of war. Wars were no longer merely struggles of armies in the field, the stylized "prize fight" following rules of the game, but wars against nations, fought with food, clothing and raw materials. The "prize fighters" had found that the fight was no longer for "a purse and half the gate money, but for life." [19]

In such a war, trade with neutrals had too great a strategic importance not to be conscripted. Success in maintaining a flourishing and independent neutral trade depended on the rules of the game that were adopted, and on the willingness and ability of neutrals to protect the rules from infringement. The essential point in the argument over international law did not concern the need for a clear and unambiguous definition (and thus minimizing friction), but rather the need of the United States for a definition that would allow an expanding commerce and the continuation of neutrality. That was what the United States attempted to secure from the belligerents through the Declaration of London of 1909.

The Declaration of London had been an effort to codify naval prize law and freedom of the seas.[20] Growing out of the second Hague Conference, it was an attempt to reach an agreement based on prevailing practice and a compromise between the claims of the naval powers, the land powers, and countries such as the United States that expected to remain neutral in the event of a European war. Generally, the Declaration provided that a belligerent had the right, if it had the power, to capture enemy ships, to prevent contraband from reaching the enemy in *any* ship, and, if capable, to blockade an enemy seacoast, stopping all commerce with that country.

A blockade required sufficient naval force before specific enemy ports to stop and search ships, and to escort them to port. Mines might be used as defensive weapons to protect one's own coast, but they had to be harmless if they came adrift. Neutral commerce might be interrupted only when it involved contraband of war demonstrably in transit to enemy territory, or conditional contraband in transit to enemy *armed forces.* Cargoes were divided into three categories. Absolute contraband consisted of direct materials of war, guns, munitions, military equipment and vehicles. Conditional contraband, materials which might be used either by the military or the civilian population, such as food, clothing, harness, horseshoes, barbed wire, railway materials, and fuel, might be stopped only if en route to the enemy army. The remaining items, such as cotton, wool, hides, rubber, and other raw materials, might be intercepted only if a legal blockade were declared and maintained. These items were considered but distantly related to warfare, though necessary to the civilian population. It also contributed an important part of the commerce of neutrals. When in transit between neutral ports, absolute contraband might be intercepted only when consigned to the enemy, and conditional contraband could not be touched.[21] These definitions were designed to protect, as much as possible, civilian populations and neutral trade.

From the standpoint of Wilson's objectives of maximum trade and neutrality, these rules were indispensable if the United States was to maintain control of the effect of the war upon itself, and if it was to remain neutral while absorbing trade disrupted by the war. Within two days after Britain's entrance into the war, Secretary of State Bryan circularized the belligerents urging them to accept the Declaration of London. Such action would prevent "grave misunderstandings which may arise as to the relations between belligerent and neutral powers." The German and Austro-Hungarian governments quickly agreed under the proviso of Allied reciprocity.[22]

The British did not intend to allow the United States to supply the Germans. The Order in Council of August 20, 1914, announced that they would abide by the Declaration, subject to certain "additions and modifications." Those caveats obliterated the distinction between absolute and conditional contraband by making the assumption that any consignment to Germany was destined for military use. That made all consignments to Germany subject to seizure. Trade between neutral ports would be governed by the doctrine of continuous voyage, which meant that goods moving between neutral ports would be seized if they were subsequently destined for the enemy. British suspicion would be sufficient grounds for such a determination. Final judgment and restitution, if any, was to be made by British prize courts. The British also added the concept of blockade on the high seas; proclaiming that ships touching at an Allied or enemy port were presumed to know of the existence of a blockade and thence were liable to seizure in midocean.[23]

The issue thus joined was not defined by abstractions of international law, but by the conflict between the British desire to control and limit (or eliminate) neutral trade to Germany and the American objective to remain neutral while taking advantage of new trade opportunities. The British modifications, if accepted by the United States, would permit the British, backed by naval supremacy, to control the flow of American goods to Europe. Such agreement would make a fiction of neutrality. Thus the British denial of American "freedom of trade" presented the United States with the choice of insisting on freedom of trade with both sides, at the expense of Anglo-American amity, or complying with British terms at the expense of loss of economic independence and neutrality.

The United States pressed for other agreements designed to promote noncommitment. Secretary of State Bryan opposed loans to belligerents, arguing that "money was the worst of contrabands, commanding everything else." Why, he asked, should dollars "going abroad and enlisting in the war" be more protected than individuals doing the same. Robert Lansing admitted that loans would be considered an expression of sympathy for the recipient; and added that, while loans were legal, they should not drag in government support and involvement behind them. [24] Bryan argued further that loans to belligerents would divert capital from America's "special obligation" in Central and South America. [25] The President accepted the Bryan argument and on August 15 announced that loans to belligerents were "inconsistent with neutrality." [26] He made a coordinated effort to provide an adequate American merchant fleet. On August 17, 1914, the Administration presented a bill to facilitate the purchase of foreign ships. The *New York World* was enthusiastic: "We have stricken shackles from our commerce which can never be restored." [27]

But the British quickly made it clear that they would act to maintain control of Atlantic trade. J. P. Morgan relayed to Wilson the British warning that any German ships purchased by the United States would be treated as enemy vessels and seized, even if sailing under an American flag. [28] In the face of American objections, the British softened this stand to permit purchase of German shipping if "the United States pledged that such ships would not be used in trade with Germany or with neutral ports accessible to German territory." [29] The British intention to control neutral trade with Germany was further revealed by a royal proclamation of September 21, 1914, which shifted raw materials such as copper, lead, iron ore, rubber and hides from the free list to the category of conditional contraband. This modification of the Declaration of London made such items liable to seizure when en route between neutral ports under the British assumption of the doctrine of continuous voyage. The British claimed the right to draw "inferences" concerning destination, and eliminated the distinction between civilian and military use of materials. [30]

Even before the news of that British action reached Washington, Lansing protested. His arguments about legality were brief and not particularly forceful, stressing that the British seizure of food cargoes was in opposition to the "traditional" policy of the United States. It was also inconsistent, he said, with the British position in 1885 during the Franco-Chinese War, and during the Boer War in which Britain had been a belligerent. He based his main argument on the economic effects of British policy on the United States. Lansing condemned the degree of control the British would have over American trade, creating "duties or incapacities" for the United States which the Central Powers might regard as evidence of "unfriendliness." The Order in Council allowed the British to "infer" the destination of conditional contraband regardless of the destination to which it was consigned. This struck at the basic right of neutrals to continue their industrial and commercial enterprises with a minimum of interference. To concede this, Lansing protested, would make neutral trade to neutral ports dependent on British permission. It would give the British the advantages of a blockade without the difficulties of maintaining it. Under such conditions the United States could not maintain its legitimate trade with neutrals or with the Central Powers.[31] Since neutrality involved not only rights for the neutrals but the obligation of treating both sides with equality, Lansing recognized that acceptance of British conditions would make neutrality impossible.

In opposition to Lansing's position, House and Page emphasized the needs of Anglo-American cooperation in "a war for civilization." House was concerned with the effect that a change in the balance of power would have on the United States. He had foreseen an era of Anglo-American cooperation in peaceful empire, and for months before the war had urged Wilson to play a leading role in the establishment of a new world system that would provide a safe outlet for investment under conditions of stability.[32] House now feared that a German victory would "change the course of our civilization and make the United States a military nation."[33] He desired a defeated Germany, but one not so completely crushed as to allow the rise of reactionary Russian militarism. It was to the interest of both the United States and Great Britain, he said, to have German integrity preserved, "shorn, however, of military and naval power."[34]

Page expressed the same position in more emotional terms. On September 15, 1914, he cabled his belief that Germany had to be crushed. "Civilization must be rescued . . . there's no chance of it till German militarism is dead."[35] Civilization clearly meant Anglo-Saxon pre-eminence, and hence a British defeat would jeopardize the "inheritance" of the United States. If Germany won, the Monroe Doctrine would be "shot in two," and the United States would lose its "place in the sun." If England won, it would be stronger than ever, possessing a more unified empire and less in need of the friendship of the United States.[36] Either eventuality pointed to the danger of straining Anglo-Saxon relations, and would jeopardize America's "righteous conquest of the markets of the world."

The House warning about the catastrophic effect of Lansing's argument on Anglo-American relations moved Wilson to tone down the note and agree to allow House to undertake private conversations with Lord Grey.[37] Page was instructed to warn the British that "a spirit of resentment" might develop over their interference with the rights of neutral commerce; but a formal protest was to be avoided.[38] Page replied that "world reconstruction" was dependent on German defeat, otherwise "life's not worth living and civilization a delusion." But a British victory would mean the end of German military strength, leaving no curb on British naval power or on the size of the Russian army, and the United States would have no influence on the peace settlement.

Such influence might be gained if America organized the neutrals in a campaign against "militarism" (which was understood to mean German militarism) that brought them into the war against Germany. If the United States did not follow that course, it might bargain directly with England. It could offer to participate in the embargo, helping to starve Germany, while supplying England with arms, ships, and volunteers. In exchange, the United States might receive a voice in the peace conditions.[39] Page advocated yielding to the British because the nature of war had changed. "Precedents have gone to the scrap heap." It was a war for civilization and American insistence on the Declaration of London would merely provoke a serious quarrel (or possibly war with the British), and the United States could not afford that outcome.[40]

Lansing continued to argue for the protection of commercial interests of the United States. The doctrine of continuous voyage, he reiterated, would allow the British to "declare a nation to be neutral and treat it as an enemy," thus gaining the rights of belligerency without the burdens.[41] House responded by expanding on his view of the necessity of maintaining the balance of power. Britain, he argued, could be persuaded to cooperate in a limited peace if it was not alienated from the United States.[42]

Other reasons appeared for trying to maintain American influence with the Allies. The State Department had hoped that American interests in Asia might be stabilized and safeguarded from the effects of the war. The American chargé d'affaires in Peking, Edward T. Williams, reported that conspiracies, banditry, and favoritism jeopardized the newly proclaimed Chinese republic. He expressed a fear of Russian invasion through Mongolia,[43] and warned that the Chinese people were too ignorant to understand the meaning of a republic even though they were susceptible to being civilized through economic development.[44] Wilson's problems in Asia involved the earlier effort by Secretary of State Knox to promote American investments in China by neutralizing Japanese and Russian railroads.

His strategy had been based on promoting an American loan to China that would be used to purchase the rail lines. Then an Anglo-American group would finance and construct a new railroad. Russian and Japanese opposition, culminating in the Russo-Japanese Treaty of 1912, ended that effort. American bankers led by Edward H. Harriman had planned to promote the industrialization of Manchuria, but the Panic of 1907 kept them from raising sufficient capital, and they had turned to the internationalization of the loan through a consortium. Russia and Japan made their participation contingent, however, upon the recognition of their special rights and interests in Mongolia and Manchuria.[45]

President Wilson encountered the problem of the consortium loan to China immediately on taking office. Six years of effort on the part of a coalition of American financiers and State Department people to establish American financial priority in China and Manchuria had about collapsed. The efforts of the United States to secure a favored position were caught between the Japanese and Russian efforts at consolidating their position in Manchuria and mounting opposition in China. Great Britain did not provide the support on which the United States had depended and the American group lost control over the loan conditions. The maneuvering among the powers involved had precipitated revolution against the Manchu government, and the financial crisis which resulted allowed members of the consortium to greatly expand their demands on China.[46]   By January, 1913, State Department advisors argued that Russia and France were trying to use the loan to gain control in China and were winning the support of the British. Though China was in urgent need of the funds, the French were reported to be insisting that the loan be first applied to pay the damages to foreigners resulting from the outbreak of the Revolution in May, 1912.[47] Efforts were also being made by the French and the British to prevent other powers from participating in the financing of China.[48]   The American ambassador to Peking described the consortium maneuvering over the supervision of Chinese taxes as motivated by a desire to force the Germans and Americans out while extending the Triple Entente to China.[49] And the ambassador to France, Myron T. Herrick, suggested that the United States should abandon the consortium. That maneuver would give China a free hand and perhaps open the way for the United States to handle the loan independently.[50]

The American group was faced with the defection of Kuhn, Loeb and Company over Russian participation in the consortium. Financial reports indicated that the international market could not handle the large amount of Chinese bonds, and the American market contracted as a result of the Mexican situation. As a result of adverse financial and diplomatic conditions and a growing controversy over the recognition of the new Chinese Republic, the American group was determined to withdraw from the loan.[51]

An important element in the Democratic campaign of 1912 had been condemnation of the "money trust" exposed by the Pujo Committee. The financiers composing the American group, Harriman, Morgan, Kuhn, Loeb and Company, George Baker, and Frank Vanderlip, were identified with this "money trust." The new Administration did not have a predisposition to be sympathetic to the web of maneuvering in China. Within a few days after Wilson took office, representatives of the American group appeared in Washington to demand stringent conditions as the price of their participation in the loan, among which was the pledge of the Government that it would use force to compel China to live up to the contract.[52]

Wilson considered the dangers of participation to be great. The State Department had received warning from its embassy in Peking that Sun Yat-sen would lead a revolt against the government he had helped to install if the loan was concluded on the proposed conditions.[53] On March 19, 1913, therefore, Wilson notified the American embassies that the United States would no longer participate in the consortium. Instead, it would pursue an independent effort to expand trade and investment. The loan conditions jeopardized the independence of China and threatened to generate resentment against the United States. There was also the danger that America might have to intervene to safeguard the loan. The United States was sympathetic, Wilson said, to the aspirations of the Chinese people and wished to participate generously in opening up "the almost untouched and perhaps unrivaled resources of China." To achieve that end, Wilson promised to urge and support legislation giving American businessmen the banking facilities they needed to overcome their competitive disadvantage.[54]

Wilson naturally defined his move as a repudiation of Dollar Diplomacy. *The New York Times* praised the policy as the essence of Dollar Diplomacy. It pointed out that Knox had hoped to secure advantages for American trade through the original consortium. The other powers had tried to use the consortium to promote their advantage at the expense of the United States. Wilson's repudiation of this was his duty in order to promote the expansion of American trade and commerce. The amendment of American banking laws, and the favor the United States would win from the Chinese, would secure greater advantages than those provided by the consortium.[55]

Wilson's China policy produced results in the form of special offers from the Chinese Government to American financiers and concessionaires. Wilson favored industrial loans rather than railroad financing or loans to provincial governments because he felt that kind of financing was less likely to require intervention. [56] Unilateral action through the Open Door seemed to be working. Then the war in Europe threatened to jeopardize the improvement. The State Department hoped American interests in Asia could be stabilized and safeguarded from the effects of the war, and Bryan and Lansing considered the possibility of "neutralizing China" by persuading the belligerents to respect the neutrality of Chinese territory and thereby preserve the existing relationship of foreign rights and interests for the duration of the war. The preservation of the status quo, Lansing wrote, was "most important to American interests."[57]

The efforts failed. [58] The British acquiesced in the Japanese occupation of Kiaochow. The American chargé in Peking feared that was a prelude to Japanese occupation of South Manchuria and Fukien, [59] where the United States was interested in industrial development. Japanese troops began occupying the railroad and mines on the Shantung Peninsula in September, 1914, and it appeared that the status quo would be destroyed.[60]

Bryan reminded the Japanese of the Root-Takahira Note of 1908 and expressed the hope that they would consult on that basis before taking further measures to restore order. [61] But even he was aware of the slight chance of safeguarding American interests without British support.

The need for such support affected the opposition to Lansing's arguments against British curtailment of neutral rights. Page threatened to resign as Ambassador to Great Britain if Lansing prevailed. He accepted the British position that their "modifications" of the Declaration of London were necessary to win the war. [62] Page pointed out further advantages of cooperation with the British. They were not confiscating American cargoes, merely seizing them and reimbursing American shippers; hence there was little financial loss for the Americans. He argued that long-term American interests could be safeguarded and advanced only through Anglo-Saxon cooperation. The temporary advantage of freedom of trade was not worth the revival of past hatred and distrust. The insistence on neutral rights was "playing into the hands of the Germans." Where, Page asked, was the "neutrality of this kind of action?"[63]

American opinion was divided. Exporters of food, copper, oil, and cotton appealed to the government for protection of their trade. [64] Cotton growers and cotton politicians had panicked in August and September, and were heatedly demanding access to overseas markets. [65] Financiers such as J. P. Morgan, Henry L. Higginson, Thomas Lamont and Frank A. Vanderlip showed a strong inclination to work with the British system and finance the expansion of trade with the Allies. They opposed neutrality as conceived of by Wilson, and they opposed the Bryan policy on loans. [66]

British pressure mounted after they denied the United States the right of transferring German ships to the American flag. The British Navy captured the Standard Oil tanker, *George Washington* (formerly the German *Brindilla*), en route to Egypt with a cargo of illuminating oil. [67] The Admiralty ordered British underwriters to refrain from issuing war insurance on free list cotton destined to neutral ports unless shippers complied with British regulations. American insurance companies, closely affiliated with the British, followed British precedent. The United States War Risk Insurance Bureau had been created to underwrite cargoes sailing in American ships, but the insurance on the carrying trade in foreign ships depended on British approval. [68] American cargoes and ships were being held in British ports. Prize court proceedings and claims for damages were greatly delayed, and even ships that had left for Great Britain before the war began were being interfered with. [69]

Then the British offered to permit American trade with neutrals and with the British Empire if the ships first called at British ports and obtained clearance. The alternative seemed to be the disruption of American trade and on October 16, 1914, the State Department offered a compromise proposal. The note again urged the adoption of the Declaration of London, but also suggested that the British follow such agreement with an Order in Council expanding the contraband lists, and another order explaining that when the British Government was "convinced" a neutral port was being used to transmit supplies to the enemy, it would declare that port to have acquired enemy character insofar as contraband was concerned. [70] This would allow the British to adopt the doctrine of continuous voyage for an expanded contraband list and seal off trade with Germany without interferring with United States "approved" trade with neutrals. Wilson supported this proposal as a means of resolving the conflict with a minimum of friction and at the same time maintaining the fiction of an agreement on the Declaration of London. The latter would avoid a hostile reaction at home. [71]

Lord Grey rejected the subterfuge on the grounds that the Declaration of London specifically prohibited the addition of such items as rubber and iron to the contraband list. It was impossible to accept the Declaration while violating it so directly. He proposed the adoption of an amended Declaration that added nickel ore, iron ore, copper, lead and oils to the absolute list, and such items as food, grain, clothing, fuel, and hides to the conditional list. That move would be coupled with another amendment providing for the interception of conditional contraband on British determination that the ultimate destination was Germany. Lord Grey announced that the British would follow that line and asked only that the United States refrain from public protest. [72]

The British policy deprived the United States of the opportunity to pretend that its insistence on neutral rights had been vindicated. Ambassador Page argued that "the large facts were": British military necessity, the lack of direct American commerce with Germany, the fact that commerce with neutrals on the North Sea relied on British sufferance in any event, and that claims for damages could be collected after the war. The British were going to maintain their position, and acceptance of the proposal would allow the United States to comply while placing the blame on the British. But "if we assume that we are working under normal conditions" and argue the questions publicly, the result would be a break with the British. No substantial advantage would be gained, and it would result in the destruction of "such good will as is now left in the world."[73]

The United States fully capitulated on October 22, 1914, with a request that the original suggestion for the adoption of the Declaration of London be withdrawn.[74] That meant that there were no accepted criteria of international law. Lord Grey understood that the United States would stop its formal protests over the broad issues and reserve the right to protest and file claims for monetary damages in any particular case where American rights were violated.[75] In effect, American acceptance of the British policy reserved the right to claim damages after the war. On the basis of the new understanding, the British promptly released American ships.[76]

The United States continued to argue over details but did not challenge the broader pattern of British policy. Functional neutrality and economic independence began to dissolve.[77] The result was the evolution of a closer economic relationship with the Allies at the expense of German trade. Germany's warfare against the flow of war materials finally brought the United States into the war. Wilson was thus forced to abandon the idea that the United States could pursue an independent course while seeking trade abroad. He had to come to terms with the Allies, and his strategy for maintaining American predominance in that situation led to the League of Nations. Wilson had learned that American access to Asian trade and European markets could not be secured unilaterally any more than in Latin America. Collective security or Anglo-American cooperation was essential.

Notes and References

1. Woodrow Wilson, "Neutrality Address to the Senate," August 19, 1914, *New Democracy*, I, 157-158.
2. Wilson, "Address at Independence Hall," Philadelphia, July 4, 1914, ibid., p. 144, 147.
3. Wilson, "Address at the Unveiling of the Statue to the Memory of Commodore John Barry", May 16, 1914, ibid., 108-110.
4. Wilson, "Annapolis Address," June 5, 1914, ibid., 127-128.
5. Wilson, "Address to Virginia Editorial Association," June 25, 1914, ibid., 137.
6. Wilson, "Independence Hall," ibid., 143.
7. Page to Wilson, February 22, 1914, WW Mss.
8. Page to Wilson, September 12, 1913, ibid.

9. Page, memorandum to Colonel House, August 25, 1913, House Mss.
10. See Chapter VI, supra.
11. For a relevant discussion of Mahan's views on expansionism, see Walter LeFeber, "A Note on the 'Mercantilistic Imperialism' of Alfred Thayer Mahan," *Mississippi Valley Historical Review*, XLVIII (March 1962), 674-685.
12. Willard Straight, "China's Loan Negotiations," in George H. Blakeslee, *Recent Developments in China* (F. C. Stechert, Co., 1913), 121-122.
13. Wilson, "Independence Hall," July 4, 1914, *New Democracy*, I, 143.
14. Wilson, "Neutrality Address to Congress," August 19, 1914, ibid., 158-159.
15. See Wilson to House, August 25, 1914, House Mss.; "The great economic tide of the century flows our way. We shall have the big world questions to decide presently," Page to Wilson, October 25, 1913, WW Mss.; Wilson to Frank E. Foremus, September 4, 1914, WW Mss.; Wilson to House, August 25, 1914, House Mss.
16. *New York World*, August 1, 1914; *New York Times*, August 4, 1914.
17. Page memorandum, August 2, 1914, cited in Hendrick, *Page*, I, 301, 302.
18. Page to Wilson, August 9, 1914, WW Mss.
19. Tasker Howard Bliss, Report on the Supreme War Council, February 6, 1920, *Foreign Relations, Lansing Papers*, II, 220-222 (hereafter cited as *Lansing Papers*). See also Edwin J. Clapp, *Economic Aspects of the War* (Yale University Press, 1915). "From the very beginning this war went beyond the limit of military and naval actions. It became an 'economic war,' namely a process of interrupting the flow of commerce between neutrals and belligerents and even between neutrals themselves.... But an economic war ... is also a war against neutrals." Clapp, 4.
20. See H. C. Allen, *Great Britain and the United States* (St. Martin's Press, 1955), 621-625. The ambivalent position of the United States, torn between the interests of a rising world trading power and dependency on British naval power is discussed in Howard K. Beale's *Theodore Roosevelt and the Rise of America to World Power*, 348-349.
21. For the text of the Declaration of London, see *Foreign Relations, 1909*, 318-333; for commentary see Samuel Flagg Bemis, *A Diplomatic History of the United States* (Holt, Rinehart and Winston, Inc., 1965) 596-597; Edgar Burlington, *Neutrality, Its History, Economics and Law* (Columbia University Press, 1936), IV, preface; and A. W. Ward and G. P. Gooch, *The Cambridge History of British Foreign Policy, 1783-1919* (Cambridge University Press, 1923), III, 349-355, 429-435.

22. For official correspondence see *Foreign Relations, 1914, Supplement*, August 6 to August 22, 1914, 216-218.

23. For text of Order in Council of August 20, 1914, and covering letter, see Page to Bryan, August 26, 1914, ibid., 218-220.

24. Bryan to Wilson, August 10, 1914, *Lansing Papers*, I, 131. Arthur S. Link calls this Bryan's unrealistic policy. Lansing, Link says, had indicated that loans were not illegal or unneutral but "had seemed to support" Bryan's position. Actually Bryan quotes Lansing's arguments against loans, not on legality but on policy; see Link, *Struggle for Neutrality*, 62-63.

25. William Jennings Bryan, "No Loans to Belligerents," *The Commoner*, XIV (September, 1914), 2; cited in Link, ibid., 63. Link indicates, "in fairness to Bryan," that there was another motive behind the desire to maintain neutrality, the assumption that Germany would need the loans while the Allies would not, Link, ibid., 64.

26. *New York Times*, August 16, 1914; Bryan to J. P. Morgan and Co., August 15, 1914, *Foreign Relations, 1914, Supplement*, 580.

27. *New York World*, August 18, 1914.

28. J. P. Morgan to Wilson, August 21, 1914, WW Mss.; *Lansing Papers*, I, 100.

29. Lansing to Wilson, August 24, 1914, ibid., 101-102.

30. Text in Page to Secretary of State, September 30, 1914, *Foreign Relations, 1914, Supplement*, 236.

31. Lansing to Page, September 26, 1914, ibid., 225-232.

32. House to Wilson, May 29, 1914; June 1, 1914; June 26, 1914; WW Mss.

33. House Diary, August 30, 1914.

34. Ibid., August 6, 1914.

35. Page to House, September 15, 1914, Seymour, *House*, I, 33.

36. Page to House, September 22, 1914, Hendrick, *Page*, I, 334.

37. House Diary, September 27, September 28, 1914.

38. Lansing to Page, September 28, 1914, *Foreign Relations, 1914, Supplement*, 232.

39. Page to Wilson, October 6, 1914, WW Mss.; Hendrick, *Page*, III, 172-176.,

40. Page to Bryan (for Wilson), October 15, 1914, *Foreign Relations, 1914, Supplement*, 248-249.

41. Lansing to Page, October 15, 1914, *Lansing Papers*, I, 253-255.

42. House Diary, September 28, 1914; House to Page, October 3, 1914, House Mss.

43. Chargé d'Affaires E. T. Williams to Bryan, March 11, 1913, *Foreign Relations*, 1913, 94-95.

44. Chargé E. T. Williams to Bryan, March 18, 1913, ibid., 96-98.

45. Pauline Tompkins, *American-Russian Relations in the Far East* (Mac-

millan Co., 1949), 16-28; see also C. Walter Young, *Japan's Special Position in Manchuria* (The Johns Hopkins Press, 1931).

46. This whole episode is thoroughly examined in Charles Vevier, *The United States and China 1906-1913* (Rutgers University Press, 1955). See particularly pages 192-211.

47. American Minister Calhoun to Secretary of State, January 12, 1913, *Foreign Relations, 1913*, 146.

48. British Foreign Office to U. S. Embassy, memorandum, January 7, 1913; Ambassador (to France) Herrick to Secretary of State, January 26, 1913; Calhoun to Secretary of State, January 27, 1913; ibid., 145, 149-150.

49. Calhoun to Secretary of State, January 30, 1913; February 5, 1913; February 9, 1913; February 17, 1913; Ambassador (to Russia) Guild to Secretary of State, February 15, 1913; Calhoun to Knox, February 21, 1913; ibid., 151-152, 155, 158-159, 163.

50. Ambassador Herrick to Knox, March 8, 1913, ibid., 168.

51. Vevier, *The United States and China*, 200-208.

52. Ibid., 208.

53. Sun Yat-sen, Manifesto, May 6, 1912; Calhoun to Knox, February 21, 1913, ibid., 123, 163.

54. Acting Secretary of State Alvey A. Ades to Paris, London, Berlin, St. Petersburg, Tokyo, March 19, 1913, ibid., 170-171.

55. *New York Times*, "Wilson, Dollar Diplomacy and China," March 21, 1913.

56. Chargé E. T. Williams to Bryan, July 11, 1913, *Foreign Relations, 1913*, 183-186; Minister Reinsch to Bryan, February 6, 1914; December 19, 1913; ibid., 62-63, 98.

57. Lansing, memorandum, August 7, 1914, *Lansing Papers*, I, 1-2.

58. Bryan to Wilson, August 8, 1914, WW Mss.

59. Chargé d'Affaires MacMurray to Bryan, August 11, 1914, *Foreign Relations, 1914, Supplement*, 166; Page to Bryan, August 11, 1914, ibid., 167-168; Ambassador (to Japan) Guthrie to Bryan, August 15 1914, ibid., 180-181. Chargé MacMurray to Bryan, August 13, 1914, ibid., 167.

60. Chargé MacMurray to Bryan, September 28, 1914; September 29, 1914, ibid., 181.

61. Bryan to Ambassador Guthrie, August 19, 1914, ibid., 172. It is interesting to note that the United States would not act on the German request to utilize its good offices (having taken charge of German affairs) to prevent the spread of hostilities to the African colonies and to maintain the status quo there; see correspondence in *Foreign Relations, 1914, Supplement*, 77, 80, 106-107, 112.

62. Page to House, October 22, 1914, in Hendrick, *Page*, I, 382-383.

63. Ibid., 380-383.

64. See representative correspondence from Kansas City Board of Trade, Wichita Mill and Elevator Co., Copper Country Commercial Club, Governor of Montana, Silver City Chamber of Commerce, American Mining Congress, Galveston Cotton Exchange, etc., in *Foreign Relations, 1914, Supplement*, 271-287. See also Baker, *Life*, IV, 204-205; and correspondence in August and September, 1914, WW Mss.

65. Link, *Struggle for Neutrality*, 91-102.

66. Special Committee on Investigation of Munitions Industry, *Report on the Adequacy of Existing Legislation*, United States Senate, 74th Congress, 2nd Session, 1936, Part VI, 9-19; Link, *Struggle for Neutrality*, 12.

67. Lansing to Wilson, October 20, 1914; Wilson to Lansing, October 22, 1914; *Lansing Papers*, I, 106.

68. For description see Harris Irby Cotton Co. to Senator Gore, October 23, 1914, *Foreign Relations, 1914, Supplement*, 288; Lansing to Page, October 24, 1914, ibid., 289.

69. Correspondence from American shippers to State Department, *Foreign Relations, 1914, Supplement*, 304-318.

70. Lansing to Page, October 15, 1914, ibid., 249-250.

71. Wilson to Page, October 15, 1914, ibid., 242-243.

72. Page to Bryan, October 19, 1914, ibid., 253-254; Lord Grey to Cecil Spring-Rice, October 17, 1914, ibid., 254-255.

73. Page to Bryan, October 21, 1914, ibid., 256. Page threatened to resign unless Lansing's position was modified; see Hendrick, *Page*, III 186-187.

74. Lansing to Page, October 22, 1914, *Foreign Relations, 1914, Supplement*, 257-258.

75. Page to Bryan, October 23, 1914, ibid., 258.

76. Page to Wilson, October 28, 1914, WW Mss.

77. Link comments that Lansing and Wilson acquiesced to the British system "in order to be neutral." Adherence to the Declaration of London, he wrote, would have helped Germany and thus was "unneutral." The United States could not have been "substantially neutral" and not recognize the British right, born of power and necessity, to stop trade with Germany; Link, *Struggle for Neutrality*, 126-127. Lansing rejected this interpretation in his diary entry for May 3, 1915: "One belligerent strikes at his enemy and thereby deprives neutral nations of their rights; and the other belligerent strikes back in a way that deprives neutrals of other rights. Thus neutral rights of trade are ground to powder between the upper and nether millstones." The alternatives, according to Lansing, were "useless protest, war, or patience with payment to come at the end of the war." The third alternative was reserved for the British, the second for the Germans.

8
SECURITY THROUGH NUMBERS

COOPERATION TO SAFEGUARD A TRADE EMPIRE

Having conceded its basic position of neutral rights, the United States found itself increasingly tied to British regulations. Assured of American cooperation, the British proceeded to add key items on the free list to the contraband list, arguing "the special considerations of the present war." They proclaimed the doctrine of continuous voyage for entire countries (instead of specific importers) by announcing that when the British were satisfied that Germany was receiving supplies from any neutral nation, any conditional contraband destined to that nation would be treated as though it was going directly to the German army. [1] Since the United States had agreed not to insist on the principles of the Declaration of London, protest was limited to details, technicalities, and claims for postwar payment. No immediate action was required of the British, nor was there any consideration of the rights of other neutrals or any recognition of possible trade obligation to Germany. Thus the United States could work with the British system and avoid any serious or fundamental confrontation with the British while maintaining the formality and fiction of a neutral posture.

Without the support of the United States, neutrals were forced to agree to refrain from exporting to Germany in order to receive American goods. Once the arrangement was worked out, the British allowed American exports to flow freely to the Allies and approved neutrals. With a growing market in war materials now available, the loss of German markets did not remain an important economic consideration. [2] On a private basis the British negotiated agreements with American producers, offering them a guaranteed market for copper, meat, and oil in exchange for their refusal to sell to Germany. [3]

On December 6, 1914, the British proposed a "working agreement," under which the United States, without public declaration, would lend support to the British undeclared blockade of Germany by inducing American shippers to stop shipments of copper. In exchange, the British would grant permits for the exportation to the United States from the British Empire of

146

rubber, hides, jute, lead, and various alloys and ores used in steelmaking. The United States would have to guarantee that none of the manufactured products using the materials would be re-exported to Britain's enemies or to neutral countries from which the British had not obtained satisfactory guarantees.[4] In return for raw materials and an Allied market the United States would act as an unofficial agent for the British blockade. The United States replied that there did not "appear any insurmountable obstacle."[5] Until final agreement was reached on December 23, 1914, the British maintained pressure by withholding raw materials from the United States.[6]

The American restriction on war loans was likewise modified. On October 20, 1914, Willard Straight urged the acceptance of French and Russian Treasury notes as a means of extending credit. Lansing commented to Wilson that, though the form was different, there was no doubt that such a transaction would be a loan.[7] Samuel Roberts of the National City Bank also urged the extension of short term credits, arguing that "otherwise the trade will go to Australia, Canada, Argentina, and elsewhere."[8] Lansing informed Wilson that American trade with the Allies was of such magnitude that the cash credit of the European governments was rapidly being depleted. If the United States did not accept European Treasury notes, the purchases would be made elsewhere.[9] Wilson, having yielded on the trade pattern, began to draw distinctions between bank credits and public loans. "As trade with belligerents is legitimate and proper it is desirable that obstacles such as interference with the arrangement of credits or easy methods of exchange should be removed." Wilson preferred that the matter not be submitted to the government for an opinion, but that Lansing give out this information as an "individual expression."[10] That was done on October 23, 1914.

The existence of the earlier pronouncement that war loans were contrary to the "true spirit of neutrality," was embarrassing to Lansing. His legalistic mind did not permit him to make Wilson's moralistic leaps. Nevertheless, he was entrusted with the job of changing the Administration's position without appearing to abandon Wilsonian principle. By January, 1915, he had devised the technique of using a public statement that discussed distinctions between "general loans" and "credit loans" without mentioning the earlier prohibitions. In March and August of 1915 the issue was raised before the public when the Morgan group and Secretary of the Treasury William G. McAdoo declared that extension of credit was imperative to American trade, "to the avoidance of depression and general unrest and suffering among workers." [11] Lansing released a statement in September 1915 asserting that the "practical reasons" for the ban on loans had disappeared. The United States had more capital than it could use, public sentiment had crystallized and would be unaffected by loans, and the economic situation was critical. Loans were necessary in order to finance American trade. The problem, he explained to Wilson, was to find some means of "harmonizing our policy so unconditionally announced, with the flotation of general loans." [12]

By the end of 1914, according to Ray Stannard Baker, the traffic in war materials with the Allies had become "deeply entrenched in America's economic organization, and the possibility of keeping out of the war by the diplomacy of neutrality . . . had reached the vanishing point." By October, "perhaps earlier, our case was lost." [13] Though limited protests were made, and claims were filed for damages, the over-all pattern of British control of trade was not challenged, nor was the understanding that the United States would not trade with the Central Powers to any significant extent. As Lansing wrote in January, 1915, "I cannot believe . . . that this correspondence [with the British] will in any way affect the friendly relations between the two countries." The whole thing, he said, was a matter of "mutual trust." He was sure that the United States will "come at least half way." [14] He "did all he could," he later wrote of this period, "to prolong the disputes by preparing, or having prepared, long and detailed replies, and introducing technical and controversial matters in the hope that before the extended interchange of arguments came to an end something would happen to change the current of American public opinion, or to make the American people perceive that German absolutism was a menace to their liberties and to democratic institutions everywhere." [15]

Wilson had abandoned the substance of an independent economic role for the United States. The United States was no longer above the struggle, supplying markets and becoming peacemaker and banker to the world. In response to German protests against the new definitions of naval warfare, and requests to clarify America's action in the defense of neutrality, [16] the United States replied only that it reserved the right to protest in its own behalf in "each case in which those rights and duties so defined . . . are violated." [17] A more direct challenge came from

Harvard University Professor Hugo Munsterberg, spokesman for pro-German sentiment, who protested to Wilson in November, 1914, against what he considered American acceptance of British violations of neutrality. He condemned changing the definition of contraband, the destruction of United States mail on Dutch ships, and the doctrine of continuous voyage. He argued that in permitting these new interpretations the United States was practically supporting the "starvation policy" of the Allies. [18]

Wilson needed an answer to these criticisms, for he admitted to Lansing that "the case they make out is *prima facie* very plausible indeed." [19] Lansing responded with a reply based on a personal attack on Munsterberg as a German agent. He argued that the United States had to enforce the neutrality laws impartially without considering the advantage or disadvantage that might accrue to a particular side. If one side had superiority in naval or geographic location, "the rules of neutrality could not be varied so as to favor the less fortunate." The United States must consider belligerents to be "on equal footing and to possess equal opportunities in the conduct of the war." [20] Lansing's argument contradicted his earlier argument in favor of the abandonment of the Declaration of London on the grounds that it would be unneutral not to recognize British necessity and superior sea power. That implied a recognition of *unequal* footing and *unequal* opportunities and acted to support that lack of equality.

The matter of contraband was disposed of by Lansing through a statement that the Declaration of London was not in force, and the United States had to be governed by international law. Since there was no general agreement on contraband, the recourse remaining to a neutral was that of sending notes of protest. [21] The weakness of relying on the "right of protest" as practiced by the United States was that it did not take into consideration the effects of a few seizures of ships, for which the British might pay, or the threat of seizures, on a much greater number of shippers who refrained from taking the risk. [22] The United States might claim damages in specific instances but this permitted the whole pattern of trade to be regulated by the British by agreement or intimidation.

Secretary Bryan remained unreconciled to the policy of allowing Britain to control American trade with neutrals and eliminate its trade with Germany. He protested to Wilson over the extent to which the United States had departed from neutrality as originally defined by Wilson. Not only had American exports suffered, especially cotton, but "delicate questions" were constantly arising concerning neutrality which threatened not only to disturb relations with belligerents, but to upset domestic political conditions. [23] Bryan's protests to Great Britain had constantly been softened by Lansing and Wilson. [24] Notes were modified to appear "amicable and not defiant," [25] and Wilson even made a statement to the press that the United States did not intend to force the issue. [26]

As American neutrality increasingly became subordinated to Anglo-American cooperation it found itself subjected to mounting pressures. Wilson had been concerned with building up a merchant fleet to help expand American trade. One method of doing this appeared to be the purchase of interned German ships. The British refused to allow German ships to be transferred to American registry. On January 23, 1915, Wilson warned the British against interference with the former German ship *Dacia*, then loading with American cotton for Germany. Wilson promised that the ship would be used only for neutral trade and warned that "America must have ships." If such ships could not be used, he threatened the construction of an American merchant fleet which would compete with the British after the war. If the British allowed the use of German ships then the United States would cooperate with British regulations and friction and hostile sentiment would be avoided. [27] A confrontation was averted when the French, on Ambassador Page's advice, seized the *Dacia*. [28] Eventually the issue of British control of American merchant shipping was superseded by the dispute over German submarine warfare.

It was not surprising that the American relationship to the British created a German reaction. Ambassador Gerard wrote from Berlin of the resentment developing over American compliance with British efforts at throttling legitimately neutral trade, and over the failure of the United States to insist on observance of the Declaration of London. [29] As early as November, 1914, Colonel House warned Wilson that Germany would never forgive the United States for the attitude it was taking. The United States ought to strengthen itself while it had the chance. [30] Wilson responded that Europe would be exhausted after the war and posed no threat. Even if Germany won it would be in no condition to threaten the United States for some time. [31] Robert Lansing warned Colonel House in December, 1915, that the

United States would have no friends when the war was over "unless we gradually favor one side or the other." [32]

German protests increased as the United States refused to join the Scandinavians in opposition to the British use of mines in the North Sea, even though Lansing termed this mine warfare "the most reprehensible and utterly indefensible method employed in naval warfare." [33] The Germans, faced with British command of the seas and the heavy tide of war materials flowing across the Atlantic, turned to the use of the submarine as a weapon against maritime commerce. [34]

On February 4, 1915, the German Government declared a war zone around Great Britain in which enemy merchant ships would be destroyed "even if it may not be possible always to save their crews and passengers." Neutral ships would be exposed to danger because of the British use of neutral flags to disguise their own shipping. [35] Using the same argument with which the British had justified their policies, the Germans now defended the new policy as justified by necessity. [36]

As a consequence of the increasingly one-sided supply line, the Germans launched an attack in the one area in which the United States was vulnerable. The German government argued that the British had abolished the distinction between absolute and relative or conditional contraband, seizing noncontraband German property on neutral ships in violation of British agreements. The British had declared the North Sea a war zone and closed it to neutral shipping in violation of international law. The purpose of that was to throttle the economic life in Germany and doom the population to starvation. When neutrals acquiesce to such policies they abandon the status of neutrality. Great Britain had justified her actions by pleading "vital interests" to the satisfaction of neutrals. Now the Germans had to consider abandoning the Declaration of London and retaliate in defense of their own "vital interests." [37]

Lansing's first reaction to the German position was a proposal to denounce the German threat to destroy neutral ships as a "wanton act unparalleled in naval warfare." [38] When the full text of the German note arrived a few days later, Lansing saw sufficient merit in the German position to find the advisability of protest "open to question." [39] Wilson responded by warning the Germans he would hold them to "strict accountability" for any American ships or American lives lost. He denied that the United States was open to criticism for unneutral action because it had

not consented to, or acquiesced in, any measures "which operate
to restrict neutral trade." [40]

In justification of Wilson's defense, the State Department
warned the British, at the same time, that the British ship
Lusitania was flying the American flag to avoid attack. The
United States said it would reserve "for future consideration the
legality and propriety of the deceptive use of the flag of a neutral
power . . . ." [41]

Germany offered to withdraw its proclamation if Great Britain
abided by the Declaration of London, or if it allowed food to
enter Germany. Ambassador Gerard suggested that Congress embargo arms unless England consented to this. [42] German Ambassador von Bernstorff went so far as to say that Germany would
accept an American organization to supervise the distribution of
food to civilians. [43] He also reported to Wilson that British
merchant ships were being armed with naval guns and had orders
to ram or shell submarines surfacing for visit and search. Under
these circumstances British merchant ships could no longer be
regarded as undefended and exempt from attack without warning. In view of the admission that armed British ships used
neutral flags so that neutrality or belligerence could no longer be
recognized on sight, and search and seizure was not possible
because submarines attempting to do so would be subject to
destruction, it was felt that the circumstances justified attack on
all merchant ships in the war zone. [44]

Lansing commented to Wilson on the German notes. The
situation was growing more delicate and a disaster was possible
that "will inflame public opinion." He regarded the German
proposals to withdraw the war zone restrictions in exchange for
an American supervised distribution of food in Germany as
depriving the British of their excuse for a food blockade. The
British effort at starving the German civilian population would
arouse moral indignation and encourage sympathy for Germany
in the United States. Lansing suggested that the United States act
on von Bernstorff's suggestion. If not, "we would approach a
serious crisis." [45] The contrary point of view was expressed by
Ambassador Page who cabled from London that American supervision of food distribution in Germany might be an "unneutral
act." It might appear that the United States was trying to
"compel" the British. [46] Lansing expressed the American dilemma. The German position had merit. Berlin had observed the
provisions of the Declaration of London while London had not

hesitated to violate it. But what did the Germans expect neutrals to do? American markets were open to all, and it was not the business of the United States to curb arms sales to Britain because Germany was unable to avail itself of them. Lansing rejected, he said, the German suggestion that neutrals retaliate against the British by prohibiting trade in contraband. Americans should not stop all their trade because of the loss of part. "Our merchants would be the sufferers." Though the British had been the major violators of international law, German policy was the greatest menace to neutrals. It was directed against all commerce, indiscriminately. Lansing rejected the German argument that submarines were vulnerable to attack by armed merchantmen because a submarine could surface "at a safe distance" and "require [a] boat to be sent from the vessel stopped." [47] He did not attempt to define what a safe distance would be from a ship mounting naval guns and with instructions to ram submarines.

The question of compromise was resolved by the British. In a memorandum dated February 19, 1915, Ambassador Cecil Spring-Rice informed the United States that since the Germans had proclaimed their new method of warfare on commerce, the British "must now hold themselves free to use a self-defensive armament" in anticipation of attacks. [48] Lord Grey sent a clarification of this on the next day. Since the Germans threatened to sink merchant ships on sight, the British would have to protect themselves by flying neutral flags. The United States could not ask the British to forego the means for escaping destruction. [49] Lord Grey justified the food blockade in the same manner. Since the Germans had now declared a war zone blockade of Britain, the British were justified in blockading food shipments to Germany. Thus, the British measures that had caused the German change in policy were now justified by that policy change. Walter Hines Page added the final note. Since the Germans had sunk a food ship early in the war and now proclaimed a blockade, the arrangement for compromise suggested by the United States was "absolutely cut off." [50]

On March 1, 1915, the British announced a total blockade of Germany as retaliation for the German use of the submarine. They denounced the use of the submarine as illegal because it could not be used for visit and search, it could not take prizes, it could not discriminate between neutral and enemy ships and it could not provide for the safety of crew or passengers. [51] On the same day the Germans expressed substantial agreement to the proposals of the United States. They offered to modify their use of mines and to limit attacks on merchant ships to those necessary to enforce search and seizure. That would be done if the British would refrain from the use of neutral markings and allow supervised food shipments to Germany. [52] The British quickly rejected the German suggestions and announced that neutral ships going to the continent would be apprehended though not confiscated. Ambassador Page commented to Wilson that the British measures would bring the war to its final stage. In view of the position of paramount power that the British would hold at the end of the war, the United States should limit itself to "friendly inquiry as to how the proposed reprisal could be carried out" and give notice that it would wait till after the war to take up cases of damage to commerce. [53]

The United States expressed its capitulation to British policy on March 5. The message contained reservations about the doubtful legality of the British methods of handling neutral ships and of blockade policy in general, but it concluded with the recognition that the submarine may have rendered the more traditional forms of blockade impossible. [54] The substantive issue was buried, as Page and Lansing had both suggested, in a maze of legalistic quibbling to be straightened out after the war.

The next week the British announced their new procedure toward neutral shipping. Merchant ships were forbidden to go to any continental port without British approval. All goods would have to be discharged in Great Britain unless the shipper obtained a permit to go to a neutral or allied port. Cargoes would be restored to their owners if they were noncontraband or were not requisitioned by the British Government. Cargoes leaving Germany would be seized and sold, unless requisitioned. The proceeds of all such sales might be paid to the owners after the war was terminated. [55] This new policy was not accepted without grumbling. Lansing complained to Wilson that Britain had no right to menace neutral trade with Germany in retaliation for German disturbance of neutral trade with Britain. He denied the legality of the blockade, claiming it violated all accepted forms. With so much discretion in the hands of British prize courts the British could exercise great control over trade, taking what they wanted. The British accumulation of prize sale proceeds would be kept until the end of the war and would give Britain "a handle to force neutrals to comply with the suggestions of Great Britain." No neutral nation could enter into this sort of bargain. It would be unneutral and highly offensive to the countries at war with Great Britain. [56]

Ambassador Page fulfilled his usual role by explaining American self-interest in continued cooperation with the British. This new form of blockade was really better than the old. The British use of moving cruisers instead of anchored warships (as specified in the Declaration of London) was legitimated, Page indicated, because the submarine made a stationary blockade too dangerous. The British measures were designed to "leave [the] fullest opportunity to favor neutral trade and especially American trade." The only practical difference the new Order in Council would make would be that it shut off cotton and food to Germany. Since most food shipments had already stopped and since the British were prepared to buy American cotton, the new measures were of little consequence to the United States. American trade with the Allies was growing rapidly. The British wanted to cause Americans a minimum of inconvenience, but felt that American proposals for compromise with the Germans were "remote" and "impracticable." Since the United States had not insisted on its objections to British policy at an earlier date, the British would consider protests at this time as made for domestic political effect. The British received American protests with courtesy, ignored them, settled American shipping claims with generosity while greatly increasing their orders of war materials. The Americans ought, therefore, to concentrate on concrete claims of damage instead of protesting violations of general rules of warfare. The German blockade was a failure, Page concluded. Its chief effect was to provoke a British blockade which was effective. [57]

Lansing advised Wilson that the United States had the choice of accepting the British blockade or threatening to withhold arms shipment unless the blockade was modified or lifted. If the United States accepted British policy, it would be in direct violation of the rights, duties, and obligations of neutrals. But it would insure Anglo-American friendship and the further growth of American trade with the Allies. [58] There was little for America to lose—except nonbelligerent status.

Wilson discarded Lansing's warning of illegality and, instead, drafted a note to the British acknowledging that changing conditions of warfare justified the new type of blockade. He assumed, he said, that the British measures would not hinder American trade with the Northern European neutrals. [59] Lansing replied

once more that the British measures were illegal, but he urged
that the United States leave matters of principle to a postwar
discussion. [60] He had no desire to press the issue to the point of
rupture with the British, but merely wanted to record a protest.
This would avoid popular resentment at home, deprive the Republicans of an issue, and establish an American claim for damages after the war. The United States would maintain the position of "guardian of neutrality." The British would admit the
legal correctness of the American position after the war. The
United States should assert its rights in such a way as to avoid
forcing the employment of "drastic measures to compel their
recognition." The idea, Lansing said, was to "file a *caveat*, to
permit their violation under protest, deferring settlement until
[peace] had been restored." [61] In an interview held the next day
with Samuel K. Ratcliffe, a London journalist, Lansing assured
the British that the caveat was merely directed toward protecting
postwar rights of neutrals and included "no hint" of anything
being done at the present. [62]

Secretary Bryan conceded that new methods of warfare might
require new forms of blockade, but felt that the United States
could not consent to British interference with shipments of
noncontraband through neutral countries. [63] President Wilson
replied by putting the question into the context of American
policy. Inconsistencies in international law or between British
statements were not to the point. This was *"something they are
going to do"* regardless of American protests. The United States
should ask that "the path of legitimate trade be left open [with
neutrals] and that the British be held to account for injuries after
the war." [64] Wilson cut off argument by casting his note in the
form of a statement and interpretation not calling for a reply. [65]

Ambassador von Bernstorff protested the failure of the United
States to comply with neutral obligations. He argued that the
one-sided arms trade of the United States with the Allies was
unneutral. The right to participate in the arms trade during
wartime stemmed from the assumption that many sources of
supply would be available and that a curtailment of such trade
would damage a neutral's economy. This circumstance did not
exist during the current war. Von Bernstorff tactlessly used
Wilson's words against him by quoting the President's argument
of 1914 for lifting the American embargo on arms to Mexico

because Huerta had access to imported arms while Carranza had not. Wilson then referred to the "true spirit of neutrality as compared with mere paper neutrality." [66]

The consequences of the American position were revealed almost immediately when the Germans sank the S. S. *Falaba*, and an American citizen was killed. [67] Lansing informed Wilson that the attack was legal if preceded by warning. If not, the United States should demand that Americans on belligerent ships be entitled to search and seizure. This would compel the United States to denounce the sinking of merchant ships and, inevitably, the German war zone plan. [68] Bryan protested that the doctrine of "contributory negligence" had some bearing. The United States could hardly insist that an American presence rendered British ships immune from attack. [69]

As far as Lansing was concerned, the arguments about legality were wearing thin. The United States had accepted the British contention that changing conditions justified changing methods of warfare. The United States could not make a case for accepting this argument for the British while refusing it for the Germans. On April 2 he sent a memorandum to Bryan pointing out more substantial considerations. The only commerce between the United States and Germany was a negligible trickle smuggled through neutral ports. The United States traded freely with the Allies, on the other hand, in all munitions of war and military supplies. In case of American involvement in the war the commercial situation would change but little. If the United States entered the war it could not send an army to Europe, Lansing believed, and its fleet would contribute little to British naval strength. All the United States might gain from belligerency would be the seizure of $100 million in interned German shipping. It might suffer from civil discord at home. The advantages to Germany might outweigh the disadvantages. [70]

Though Wilson was uneasy about the situation, he stated that the sinking was in violation of the rules of international law, and that the United States had to insist on "the lives of our citizens not being put into danger by illegal acts." [71] This meant that Wilson was characterizing the use of the submarine against merchant ships as illegal. Lansing proposed a "strong, vigorous" note to dispel any German contempt for weakness though the consequences "may be most momentous." In accord with Wilson's decision, Lansing insisted Americans had the right to travel anywhere in any kind of ship without being subject to torpedo attack without warning. [72]

Bryan continued to object. The United States could not accuse the Germans of misconduct without knowing whether or not the *Dacia* had been warned. Even more, could an American "assume for his own advantage unnecessary risks and thus involve his country in international complication?" Germany had had no knowledge of the presence of an American and had warned the United States of its intended action. What claim could the United States rightfully make for "an unintended loss which ordinary diligence would have avoided?" [73] Wilson rejected Bryan's qualms and proceeded to widen his attack on the German position. He denied the German argument that British armed shipping necessitated attack without warning and argued that the presence of some armed ships did not justify the assumption that all were armed. [74] Germany could not change the rules or essential principles of international law no matter how radical the change in the practical conditions of warfare. He protested the use of the submarine as a weapon because it could not be used with the old safeguards of search, visit, and provision for the safety of passengers. Wilson urged an emphatic protest against the use of the submarine, appealing to humanity, fair play, and the rights of neutrals. The whole note, he said, should be "put on very high ground." [75]

Bryan argued that the American position was one-sided. It might inflame German feeling and possibly provoke a war. Though Germany had seemed willing to negotiate, the British refused and Bryan feared that the "denunciation of one and silence as to the other" would be construed as partiality. He urged, instead, an appeal for mediation of the war. [76] Wilson rejected such an appeal as "futile," and probably "offensive" (to the Allies.) "We would lose such influence as we have for peace." [77]

The position of the United States became increasingly difficult. Each decision seemed to make neutrality more perilous and uneasy. Each decision seemed to make the situation more tense. Each incident undermined the ground on which the Americans stood. The Germans, after issuing warning, sank the British liner *Lusitania* on May 1, 1915. This resulted in the loss of almost 1200 noncombatants, including 128 Americans. Bryan maintained that the Germans had a right to prevent contraband from reaching the Allies, and that a contraband ship should not rely on women and children as a shield. [78] Lansing replied that if the United States took this position it would be an admission that the Administration had failed in its duty by permitting Americans to sail on a belligerent ship in a war zone without trying to prevent them. By its silence the government had allowed hundreds of passengers to "believe that their government approved and would stand behind them." If Bryan's view was valid, the United States should have declared so at the time it protested the war zone. An admission at this time that travellers should not have taken the risk would "cause general condemnation and indignant criticism." [79] By having kept silent the government gave the impression that the German warning might be ignored. [80]

Wilson felt that Lansing's argument was "unanswerable." Even if Bryan's position had validity, "It is now too late to take it." [81] Wilson then resorted to the "very high ground," and read a statement to the Cabinet on May 11, 1915, in which he said he had warned Germany that she would bé held to strict accountability for American lives and denounced the use of submarines as an "inevitable violation of many sacred principles of justice and humanity." Americans had a right to travel on the high seas, Wilson affirmed, and their government would protect that right. [82]

Wilson still hoped to avoid participation in the war, allowing the British to protect American interests by defeating the Germans. His statement, however, served to place the United States in the position of accepting the British food blockade while rejecting German efforts at cutting off war materials to Britain. Senator William J. Stone of Missouri, Democratic leader and Wilsonian stalwart, raised the issue that the Administration preferred to avoid. When Lansing argued that the loss of lives to German submarines was more important than loss of property, Stone referred to the effects on Germany of the food blockade, the death of German babies because the British would not allow the shipment of condensed milk. Lansing assured Wilson, however, that Stone would stay in line, though not with enthusiasm. [83]

Austrian Ambassador Konstantin T. Dumba urged negotiation of the submarine issue and suggested it would be easier to do so if Germany could say she expected the United States to "insist in the same spirit upon freedom of trade with neutrals." Lansing

replied that this would embarrass the United States and make it
more difficult to deal with the Allies. Germany "ought to assume" that the United States would live up to the position taken
in defense of neutral rights. [84] Wilson also refused to protest to
the British, insisting that Anglo-American relations were "none
of [Germany's] business." [85] When Colonel House tried to get
the Germans to suggest a proposal to the British calling off
submarine warfare in exchange for food being allowed to pass to
neutral ports, Wilson responded with anger that there was no
connection between British and German violations of American
rights. [86] As Wilson wrote Bryan, "Germany always misses the
central point, that England's violation of neutral rights is different from Germany's violation of the rights of humanity." [87]
Bryan, unable to reconcile himself to a position he considered
one-sided, unnecessary, and likely to provoke war, resigned on
June 7, 1915. As a replacement House suggested Lansing, who
did not have "too many ideas of his own" and who would be
"guided" entirely by Wilson, without unnecessary argument. [88]

In a policy memorandum dated July 11, 1915, Lansing defined his views on Germany. The German government was "utterly hostile to all nations with democratic institutions," and
threatened democracy throughout the world. Of particular danger were German plots and influence in Mexico, Haiti, San
Domingo, and "probably elsewhere" in Latin America. German
penetration there might be in preparation for a war with the
United States after the Allies were defeated. In the meantime,
the submarine issue had to be temporarily settled because Americans were too divided on the merits of the war. Pan-Americanism
might be built up with the "object of alienating American Republics from European influence, especially the German influence." In the event that it appeared that the war would end in a
German victory, or a draw, the United States would have to
participate. [89]

Lansing believed that it was better to wait "until the indignation of the great bulk of the American people could be sufficient-
ly aroused to force their representatives to vote for war with
substantial unanimity." [90] Lansing commented in his memoirs
that the education of the American people to the "evil nature of
the German Government's aims and the menace of those aims to
our national safety" was a long slow process lasting almost two
years. [91]

German economic competition with the United States had

been a matter of growing concern. Aside from the turn of the century rivalry in the Pacific, there was a rivalry for markets within Europe. In January, 1913, *The New York Times* had carried a special article on German competition in agriculture, pointing out that the German yield per acre was almost double that of the United States because of the intensive use of fertilizer. The wheat yield was 32½ bushels an acre compared with about 13 in the United States. From 1891 to 1912 German exports had increased by 143 percent while the United States increase was 105 percent. [92] By the beginning of the century the Germans had begun an intensified campaign of overseas investment and trade on an organized and coordinated basis. Under unofficial governmental leadership, German banking, commerce and manufacturing tended to cooperate and promote an efficiency with which the United States was not yet ready to compete. [93]

Perhaps of greatest concern to the United States was the German role in Latin America. The Department of Commerce Bulletin of December 18, 1914, defined the German threat to American interests in that area. During the past decade Germany had expanded its activities at the expense of the British. Unlike other American competitors in Latin America, German manufacturers, traders, financiers and consular officials had coordinated their activities to become effective rivals of the United States. [94] The United States had been able to contain British rivalry in the Monroe Doctrine area, winning from them a recognition of American pre-eminence in Mexico and Central America. The United States could maneuver the British into curbing their efforts at securing oil reserves. [95] Germany was not so cooperative. The United States had feared German support for revolution in Central America and the exportation of German arms to Huerta in Mexico. Lansing feared that the growing involvement of America with the British war effort would drive Germany into greater rivalry with the United States. He told House on July 30, 1915, that the United States should not jeopardize its relationship with the Allies because "our friendship with Germany is a matter of the past." [96]

The new Secretary of State drafted a note for Germany which focused on a condemning of the use of submarines as weapons against merchant ships and rejecting the argument that search and seizure was impractical. [97] Germany offered to allow marked American ships without contraband safe passage, asking only that

Americans not be "hired" by the British as passengers to protect their ships. [98] Wilson insisted, however, that it was not only a question of the rights of Americans to cross the seas, but the "rights of neutrals everywhere." [99]

Both Wilson and House shared Lansing's view that an Allied victory was necessary to protect the postwar interests of the United States. At the start of the war in Europe, Wilson and House had discussed the necessity of a limited German defeat. Defeat was necessary to eliminate Germany as a future American rival and opponent. The defeat had to be limited to prevent the development of a Russian threat. [100] House and Wilson had then believed that a posture of neutrality would mean a strong America, able to define peace conditions for an exhausted Europe. House urged that America had to arm itself to prevent a victorious and expansionist Germany from penetrating Central and South America. Wilson opposed arming at the time because he felt that even as a victor Germany would not have the strength to be an immediate threat to the United States. There would be time to arm later if necessary. [101]

As the war progressed the position of nonbelligerent cooperation with Great Britain became increasingly untenable. The independent position Wilson had called for faded in the face of British control of the seas. By the spring of 1915 the United States found that the British were curbing American trade to the Northern neutrals by buying up such cargoes and re-exporting them to Britain. [102] The American expectation of exerting control over the conditions of peace also faded as the United States began to learn that elements of a peace settlement were being arranged without American participation, and that the United States was becoming committed by means of its support for the Allies to something beyond its control and definition.

The idea of a limited Allied victory receded in the face of growing Allied objectives and commitments. In October, 1914, Colonel House had gone to Europe on a peace mission, assuming that peace would be based on frustration of German aspirations. He believed that territorial realignments would be followed by arms control and mutual guarantees of territorial integrity to stabilize the new situation. [103] Stability was the most important need for the United States if it was to pursue its own economic objectives. Ambassador Page informed House, however, that Russia "won't talk till she has Constantinople," and England would insist on maintaining her naval strength—making it impossible to refuse a postwar army to Germany. [104] Wilson acknowledged at this time that though Germany was "not alone responsible for the war," the German government had to be "profoundly changed." Furthermore, Austria-Hungary had to be broken up for the "welfare of Europe." It would not greatly hurt the interests of the United States to have France, Russia, or Great Britain dictate the terms of peace. [105]

By January and February, House reported to Wilson that the Allies rejected any peace settlements short of outright German defeat. House thought overtures to Germany might prove useful to demonstrate "how utterly unreliable and treacherous the Germans were by exposing their false pretences of peace to the world." [106] On February 9, 1914, House reported to Wilson something of Allied plans for territorial expansion and their interest in involving the United States in some sort of general guarantee of postwar peace. [107] It was almost as important to the United States as it was to the Allies to have the settlement "laid upon the right foundations," he wrote a few days later. If the war did not end militarism (which House defined as a German phenomenon), the "future is full of trouble for [us.]" If Germany were willing to agree to Allied terms, he said, he would continue his peace feelers; if not, he would abandon his efforts for fear of losing the "sympathetic interest" of the Allies. Though Lord Grey might be willing to settle for minimum terms, others were making demands for the division of the German Empire. [108] In May, 1915, the Administration began to receive reports of Allied promises to Italy and Rumania of portions of the Austro-Hungarian empire as the price of participation. [109] House found that though the popular sentiment was "for peace," the French "ruling class . . . do not desire peace," and their great demands put peace "out of sight." [110]

The pressures on the United States mounted rapidly. German efforts at providing safe conduct for ships carrying noncontraband were rejected with Wilson's insistence on visit and search, even though he had acknowledged the impossibility of this being done by submarines. The significance of Britain arming merchant ships and of using neutral flags was indicated by the case of the *Baralong*, a British "Q Boat" disguised as a merchant ship and flying an American flag. The *Baralong* used this cover to approach German submarines that were waiting for the merchant ship to be evacuated. The *Baralong* opened fire at a range of one hundred yards, sinking the submarine immediately. The crew of the *Baralong* shot at German sailors struggling in the water. ¹¹¹

Wilson's insistence on visit and search was, in effect, a demand that Germany eliminate the submarine as a weapon against Britain's munitions lifeline. House wrote to Wilson on June 16, 1915, that the war was one of munitions rather than men and that the British were dependent on American supplies for victory. "I need not tell you that if the Allies fail to win, it must necessarily mean a reversal of our entire policy." ¹¹²

This statement was the key to the shifting position of the United States in its negotiations with Germany over submarine warfare. ¹¹³ The Germans attempted to find a compromise position whereby modifications could be made in submarine warfare in exchange for the lifting of the British blockade, or the promise of the United States to restrict its shipments of contraband. Wilson continued to insist on the cessation of German attacks on neutral ships carrying contraband "under any circumstances." He insisted that such ships could not be sunk but had to be taken to port. ¹¹⁴ When the Germans attempted a settlement by promising adequate warning, Wilson insisted that this was not enough. "Mere warning on a stormy sea, mere putting of passengers and crew into open boats might be as brutal as giving them no warning at all." There had to be full provision for the safety of noncombatants, perhaps to the point of towing the lifeboats close to shore. ¹¹⁵

Wilson's position was undercut when British merchant ships appeared carrying naval cannon. Lansing complained to Wilson that this made it difficult for the United States to demand that the submarines give warning. Under international law any armed merchant ship lost its civilian status and had to be regarded as a ship of war subject to attack and destruction. ¹¹⁶ In accord with this argument the United States detained the British merchant ship *Marion* when it appeared at Norfolk with a heavy gun mounted on her deck. Wilson had the ship released on the promise that the gun would not be used for offense. ¹¹⁷

In February, 1916, Lansing found the solution to the problem by developing the argument that naval ordnance on a merchant ship was not really an offensive weapon until used for attack. Submarines were thus required to wait for specific evidence of hostility (namely an attack on the submarine) before firing. Americans should not be warned against travelling on such armed ships, he added, to avoid the implication that "the Government was admitting a practice which may embarrass it later, or approving a principle (German attack on armed ships) for which it cannot stand." [118]

Lansing recorded his difficulties in his private diary on January 9, 1916. "We are not yet ready to meet the submarine issue squarely. Our people are not aroused to a sufficient pitch of indignation at the barbarism of the Germans." He felt that the arguments against the shipment of war supplies to the Allies and against the British blockade of neutral ports had a "plausibility" that still appealed to many. Congress would not favor drastic action and "would be resentful of the President should he act without their authorization." If Germany won, however, it would then turn on the United States. It was better to be "one of many enemies than to be in the future alone against a victorious Germany." [119]

Notes and References

1. Order in Council, October 29, 1914, *Foreign Relations, 1914, Supplement*, 261-263.
2. See Clapp, *Economic Aspects of the War*, 27-36; Marion C. Sinev, *The Allied Blockade of Germany*, 1914-1916 (University of Michigan Press, 1957), 33-59, 75-122.
3. Examples of such agreements are reprinted in Clapp, *Economic Aspects of the War*, 322, 324-325; see also David Lloyd-George, *The War Memoirs of David Lloyd-George* (Ivor Nicholson and Watson 1933-1936), II, 664-665.
4. See Page to Bryan, December 6, 1914, *Foreign Relations, 1914, Supplement*, 356-358; for correspondence on Allied embargo of raw materials to the United States see ibid., 418-428.
5. Bryan to Page, December 9, 1914, ibid., 9.
6. Ibid., December 23, 1914, 430.
7. Lansing to Wilson, October 20, 1914, WW Mss.
8. Samuel McRoberts to Lansing, October 23, 1914, *Lansing Papers*, I, 136-137.
9. Lansing memorandum to Wilson, October 23, 1914, ibid., 139-140.
10. Lansing memorandum on conversation with Wilson, October 23, 1914, ibid., 140. A report of the change in position was sent to Willard Straight and R. L. Farnham of the National City Bank.
11. J. P. Morgan to Lansing, March 25, 1915, McAdoo to Lansing,

August 23, 1915 (enclosing letter from James B. Forgan of First
National Bank of Chicago), *Lansing Papers*, I 141-142; Lansing to
McAdoo, August 26, 1915, ibid., 144. For an examination of the
position of the Morgan group, see Special Commitee . . . Munitions
Industry, *Report*, VI, 9-63; V, 164-174.

12. Lansing to Wilson, September 6, 1915, WW Mss.; *Lansing Papers*, I,
144-147. Link describes this shift as "learning to accept the most
important economic consequence of neutrality . . . the development
of a large war trade between the United States and Allied Nations,"
Link, *Struggle for Neutrality*, 133. Considering the circumstances it
might be more meaningful to define this as the economic consequences of the abandonment of functional neutrality through dependency on Allied trade. Link's comment has plausibility only if neutrality becomes defined by Wilson's policy, just as morality is so
defined.

13. Baker, *Life*, V, 181.

14. Lansing to Sir Charles Fitzpatrick, January 9, 1915, Lansing Mss.

15. Robert Lansing, *War Memoirs of Robert Lansing* (Bobbs-Merrill Co.,
1935), 112.

16. Memorandum of the German Foreign Office relative to the position
of England and France touching on the London Maritime Declaration, October 10, 1914, *Foreign Relations, 1914, Supplement*,
263-265; Memorandum of the Austro-Hungarian Foreign Office
. . . ibid., 267.

17. Lansing to Ambassador Gerard, October 24, 1914, ibid., 259.

18. Professor Hugo Munsterberg to Wilson, November 19, 1914, *Lansing
Papers*, I, 162-165.

19. Wilson to Lansing, December 1, 1914, ibid., 161.

20. Lansing to Wilson, November 19, 1914, ibid., 167-169.

21. See correspondence from cotton, oil, and copper exporters to the
State Department, *Foreign Relations, 1914, Supplement*, 285-301.
Exports changed as follows:

Year	To Allies	To Central Powers
1914	$ 824,860,237	$169,289,775
1915	1,991,747,493	1,878,153
1916	3,214,480,547	1,159,653

Based on statistical analysis in Special Committee . . . on Munitions
Industry, *Report*, V, 113.

22. Bryan to Wilson, December 1, 1914, *Lansing Papers*, I, 10-16. For
examples of neutral protests see statement of the Swedish Foreign
Minister that "neutral rights were being destroyed, lawful commerce
imperiled, the freedom of the seas and the inalienable right of
neutrals to use the highways common to all have also been curtailed
and circumscribed through the pretension to compel neutral vessels to

take certain routes and call at certain ports without just cause being given by the neutrals." Minister Wallenberg to the German, French, British, and Russian Ministers, November 12, 1914, *Foreign Relations, 1914, Supplement*, 360-361.

23. House Diary, December 18, 1914; see also Link, *Struggle for Neutrality*, 172-173, for description.

24. House warned the British of the protest note of December 26 and urged release of ships and cargoes to forestall complications; House Diary, December 18, 1914. When the British threatened to seize the *Dacia*, Ambassador Page suggested to Lord Grey that the French do it instead to avoid an increase in anti-British sentiment; Hendrick, *Page*, I, 394.

25. See Wilson to Bryan, January 14, 1915, *Lansing Papers*, I, 266; Lansing to Sir Charles Fitzpatrick, January 9, 1915, Lansing Mss.

26. *New York Times*, December 30, 1914.

27. Bryan to Page, January 23, 1915, *Foreign Relations, 1915, Supplement*, 694-697.

28. *New York Times*, August 5, 1915, August 7, 1915; Hendrick, *Page*, I, 394.

29. Ambassador Gerard to House, November 1914, House Mss.; Gerard to Bryan, December 4, 1914, *Foreign Relations, 1914, Supplement*, 578.

30. House Diary, November 8, 1914.

31. Ibid., November 9, 1914.

32. Lansing to House, December 3, 1915, *Lansing Papers*, I, 89.

33. Lansing to Bryan, February 18, 1915, *Lansing Papers*, I, 37-38.

34. "America had not raised her voice in protest and has taken little or no action against England's closing of the North Sea to neutral shipping. What will America say if Germany declares submarine war on all the enemy's merchant ships? Why not? England wants to starve us. We can play the same game. We can bottle her up and torpedo every English or Allied ship which nears any harbor in Great Britain." Admiral von Tirpitz, *New York World*, December 23, 1914. For the German debate on the use of the submarine, the possible effects on neutrals, and the military and economic consequences, see Link, *Struggle for Neutrality*, 312-321.

35. *New York Times*, February 7, 1915.

36. German memorandum, February 4, 1915, *Foreign Relations, 1915, Supplement*, 96-97.

37 Ibid.

38. Lansing, Draft Note, February 6, 1915, WW Mss.

39. Lansing to Wilson, February 7, 1915, WW Mss.

40. Bryan to Ambassador Gerard, February 10, 1915, *Foreign Relations, 1915, Supplement*, 98-99.

41. Bryan to Page, February 10, 1915, ibid., 100-101.

42. Ambassador Gerard to Bryan, February 12, 1915, ibid., 102.

43. Ambassador von Bernstorff to Bryan, February 13, 1915, ibid., 104-105.
44. Ambassador von Bernstorff to Bryan, February 15, 1915, *Foreign Relations, 1915, Supplement*, 104-105.
45. Lansing to Wilson, February 15, 1915, *Lansing Papers*, I, 353-354.
46. Ambassador Page to Bryan, February 17, 1915, *Foreign Relations, 1915, Supplement*, 111.
47. Lansing to Wilson, February 18, 1915, *Lansing Papers*, I, 354-356; German note to Ambassador Gerard to Bryan, February 17, 1915, *Foreign Relations, 1915, Supplement*, 112-115.
48. Cecil Spring-Rice to Bryan, memorandum, February 19, 1915, *Foreign Relations, 1915, Supplement*, 116-117.
49. Page to Bryan, memorandum, February 19, 1915, ibid., 117-118.
50. Page to Bryan, February 20, 1915, ibid., 118-119.
51. *Note verbale*, Cecil Spring-Rice to Bryan, March 1, 1915, ibid., 127-128. Link points out that the British welcomed the submarine decree; it was not a threat to their commerce and would serve to involve Germany in serious difficulties with the United States; Link, *Struggle for Neutrality*, 335.
52. Ambassador Gerard to Bryan, March 1, 1915, *Foreign Relations, 1915, Supplement*, 129-130.
53. Page to Bryan and Wilson, March 3, 1915, WW Mss.
54. Lansing Draft Telegram, *Lansing Papers*, I, 272; Wilson to Bryan, March 4, 1915, ibid., 273. Bryan to Page, March 5, 1915, *Foreign Relations, 1915, Supplement*, 132-133.
55. Transmitted in Page to Bryan, March 15, 1915, ibid., 143-145.
56. Text of Order in Council with Lansing's comments, March 15, 1915, *Lansing Papers*, I, 273-275.
57. Page to Bryan, March 21, 1915, *Foreign Relations, 1915, Supplement*, 146-147.
58. See Lansing's comments, page 71, supra. The Joint Neutrality Board reported that the British blockade was "a grave violation of neutral rights," and that under the Prussian-American Treaty of 1828, the United States had an obligation to keep the channels of German-American trade open; see James B. Scott et al. to Lansing, March 18, 1915, Anderson Mss., cited in Link, *Struggle for Neutrality*, 343.
59. Wilson to Bryan, March 19, 1915, *Lansing Papers*, I, 277: text in *Lansing Papers*, I, 278-279; Wilson to Bryan, March 22, 1915, ibid., 281. Link assumes Wilson "may have been totally naive about the legal aspects of the problem," or trying to force the British to allow noncontraband trade with neutrals; Link, 342. Lansing had pointed out the problems of legality to Wilson which he chose to ignore. It seems more reasonable to conclude that, having adopted the practice of conforming to the British position, Wilson was prepared to continue with the tactic suggested by Page and described by Lansing, that

of keeping the argument going over technicalities and details while ignoring the main issue.

60. Lansing memorandum, March 22, 1915, *Lansing Papers*, I, 282-283.
61. Ibid., 290-291.
62. Lansing memorandum on interview with Ratcliffe, March 25, 1915, ibid., 291-292.
63. Bryan to Wilson, March 23, 1915, ibid., 287-288.
64. Wilson to Bryan, March 24, 1915, ibid., 293.
65. Wilson to Lansing, March 28, 1915, ibid., 293; For the text of note see Bryan to Page, March 30, 1915, *Foreign Relations, 1915, Supplement*, 152-156.
66. Von Bernstorff to Bryan, April 4, 1915, ibid., 157-158. Link misinterprets Wilson's comment, understanding it to demand an "embargo on the export of arms to the parties to a conflict;" Link, *Struggle for Neutrality*, 352. Actually Wilson was asking for the embargo to be lifted because of its unequal effect. Von Bernstorff argued the same principle, not that neutrals could not sell arms, but that the unequal effect of the arms sale violated the spirit of neutrality.
67. According to German studies, the *Falaba* attempted to escape after being warned, and fired on the submarine. British accounts complain that the sinking was done in a brutal manner; Link, *Struggle for Neutrality*, 359. More important, however, was the fact that the United States did not know the circumstances of the sinking.
68. Lansing to Bryan, April 2, 1915, *Lansing Papers*, I, 355-356.
69. Bryan to Wilson, April 2, 1915, ibid., 366.
70. Lansing memorandum, February 15, 1915, ibid., 367-368.
71. Wilson to Bryan, April 3, 1915, ibid., 368.
72. Lansing memorandum to Bryan, April 5, 1915, ibid., 369; Draft Instructions . . . ibid., 370-371.
73. Bryan to Wilson, April 6, 1915, *Lansing Papers*, I, 372-373, 376. Bryan's position was supported by Special Adviser Chandler P. Anderson who felt that if the sinking was in fact illegal (without warning) Germany's liability was still limited to monetary damages; April 5, 1915, WW Mss.
74. Wilson to Bryan, April 6, 1915, *Lansing Papers*, I, 372-373.
75. Wilson to Bryan, April 22, 1915, ibid., 377-378.
76. Bryan to Wilson, April 23, 1915, ibid., 378-380. The submarine campaign was launched at the time of the Russian invasion of Austrian Galicia. Italy was on the verge of joining the Allies. German mobilization in the East meant the weakening of the Western offensive. In this context it was vital to deprive the British of munitions imported from the United States; see Charles Seymour, *House*, I, 365-366.
77. Wilson to Bryan, April 28, 1915, *Lansing Papers*, I, 380.

78. Bryan to Wilson, May 9, 1915, ibid., 386. The *Lusitania* cargo manifest revealed brass, copper, food, and large quantities of guns, rifles, and ammunition; see Assistant Secretary of the Treasury Peters to Lansing, May 8, 1915, ibid., 385-386.

79. Lansing to Bryan, May 9, 1915, ibid., 387-388.

80. Lansing memorandum on *Lusitania*, May 10, 1915, ibid., 390.

81. Wilson to Bryan, May 9, 1915, ibid., 392.

82. Wilson's Draft Note, May 11, 1915, ibid., 395-398.

83. Lansing to Wilson, December 31, 1915, ibid., 221.

84. Lansing to Wilson, May 17, 1915, ibid., 308-310.

85. Wilson to Lansing, May 20, 1915, ibid., 410; Wilson to Bryan, May 20, 1915, ibid., 411.

86. Wilson to House, May 20, 1915, Baker Collection; see also Link, *Struggle for Neutrality*, 393.

87. Wilson to Bryan, June 2, 1915, *Lansing Papers*, I, 220.

88. House to Wilson, June 16, 1915, WW Mss.

89. Lansing Memorandum on Consideration and Outlook or Policies, July 11, 1915, Lansing Mss.; see also Lansing, *War Memoirs*, 19-23.

90. Lansing, *War Memoirs*, 28.

91. Ibid., 25.

92. *New York Times*, January 19, 1913.

93. Henry Cord Meyer, "German Economic Relations with Southeastern Europe 1870-1914," *American Historical Review*, LVII (October 1951), 81-83.

94. Department of Commerce Bulletin, *Banking and Credit in Argentina, Brazil, Chile and Peru*, 63rd Congress, 3rd Session, Senate Document No. 659, December 18, 1914.

95. See Peter A. R. Calvert, "The Murray Contract: An Episode in International Finance and Diplomacy," *Pacific Historical Review*, XXV (May 1966), 203-224.

96. Lansing to House, July 30, 1915, Seymour, *House*, II, 70.

97. Lansing to Ambassador Gerard, June 9, 1915, *Foreign Relations, 1915, Supplement*, 436-438.

98. Ambassador Gerard to Lansing, July 3, 1915, July 5, 1915, ibid., 459-462.

99. Wilson to Lansing, July 13, 1915, *Lansing Papers*, I, 455-456.

100. House to Wilson, August 22, 1914, WW Mss.

101. Seymour, *House*, I, 297-298.

102. See following correspondence: Bryan to Page, May 21, 1915, *Foreign Relations, 1915, Supplement*, 505; Consul General to London Robert P. Skinner to Ambassador Page, June 11, 1915, ibid., 449; Skinner to Lansing, June 20, 1915, ibid., 455-456, describing the increase in British exports to neutrals with which the United States was not permitted to trade, and the cutting off of British raw materials to the United States and increase of manufactures; Skinner to Lansing, June 28, 1915, ibid., 466-467, describing the use of

blockade to advance British trade to neutrals at the expense of American trade; Skinner to Lansing, July 9, 1915, ibid., 479-480; ("While the articles under report cannot be shipped from the United States to neutral European countries . . . these same articles are being exported from Great Britain itself in enormously increased quantities.")

103. House to Ambassador Page, October 3, 1914, House Mss.

104. Page to House, December 22, 1914, cited in Hendrick, *Page*, I, 418.

105. Wilson, Interview with H. B. Brougham, December 14, 1914, cited in F. Frazier Bond, *Mr. Miller of "The Times"*, (Scribners, 1931), 142-143.

106. House Diary, January 13, January 25, 1915.

107. House to Wilson, February 9, 1915, WW Mss.

108. House to Wilson, February 23, 1915, WW Mss.

109. House to Wilson, May 27, 1915, WW Mss.; Page to Lansing, May 7, 1915, Lansing Mss.; Laurence Evans, "United States Policy and the Syrian Mandate, 1917-1922," unpublished Ph.D. dissertation, The Johns Hopkins University, 1957, 5; Ambassador Sharp in Paris reported the contents of the secret treaty giving Slavic territory from the Austro-Hungarian Empire to buy Rumanian support; Sharp to Lansing, May 1, 1915, *Foreign Relations, 1915, Supplement*, 31.

110. House to Wilson, March 14, 1915, WW Mss.

111. Ambassador Page to Lansing, August 26, 1915, August 29, 1915, *Foreign Relations, 1915, Supplement*, 527-529.

112. House to Wilson, June 16, 1915, WW Mss.; Seymour, *House*, I, 468-469.

113. A good account of the negotiations between the United States and Germany, indicating the area of German efforts at compromise, and the rigidity of the United States concerning any overture to the British, is to be found in Link, *Struggle for Neutrality*, 368-455, 551-587, 645-681. See also Charles Callan Tansill, *America Goes to War* (Little, Brown, and Co., 1938), passim.

114. Lansing to Gerard, June 24, 1915, *Foreign Relations, 1915, Supplement*, 450-453.

115. Lansing to Wilson, August 26, 1915, *Lansing Papers*, I, 471-472; Wilson to Lansing, August 27, 1915, ibid., 473; House to Wilson, September 26, 1915, ibid., 478.

116. Lansing to Wilson, September 12, 1915, ibid., 330-331.

117. Wilson to Lansing, September 13, 1915, ibid., 331-332.

118. Lansing, Secret memorandum to Representative Flood, House Committee on Foreign Affairs, ibid., 349-350.

119. Lansing Diary, January 9, 1916.

9
FROM FRONTIER TO
COLLECTIVE SECURITY

The United States hoped to maintain a posture of selective neutrality but came to learn that such a position was untenable. It could not enter and control world frontiers on its own terms. Other powers had their own purposes and policies, and even destinies, to fulfill, and they opposed Wilson's concept of a new order. The drive of the United States for the righteous conquest of the markets of the world was disrupted by the instabilities of nationalism, revolution, and war. Even America's Anglo-Saxon partner insisted in pursuing its own interests and well-being at the expense of American objectives.

Wilson had hoped for a limited Allied victory but the game of war was played for higher stakes. He had hoped to be able to pursue an independent course in wartime trade but was caught between German demands for nonpartisan neutrality and the British ability to manipulate American trade. The British approved the formation of the Netherlands Overseas Trust in December, 1914, to "enable the unmolested conveyance from overseas of merchandise which has been declared contraband." [1] Americans learned by mid-1915 that the British were using their blockade power to force American shippers to operate through the Trust, and that American goods seized under the British blockade were being reconsigned to the Trust for reshipment to Europe. The Trust operated in conjunction with the British Government under an arrangement whereby seized cargoes could be re-exported under Trust auspices. [2] Ambassador Reinsch reported from China that the British were using such devices to "squeeze out" American trade in favor of their own merchants. [3]

Colonel House attempted to protect American trading aspirations by appealing to the principle of freedom of the seas. He went to Germany in an effort to secure support for that axiom by expressing the hope that Germany and the United States might work together in order to limit the effects British naval power might have on the postwar world. [4] According to Charles Seymour, the scheme was designed to curb British expansion of controls which would eventually mean the destruction of independent American trade. House suggested that since the British were being hurt by the submarine and the Germans needed food, both sides might be willing to return to the original definition of contraband and end both blockades. Germany could then receive food, and Britain's trade with its empire would be secured against submarine attack. Under such an arrangement the United States would gain its primary objective of being able to trade with as much freedom as in peace time. [5]

Germany indicated its willingness to accept the proposals. House was surprised by this because he believed that Britain would receive the greater benefit. He promised the Germans he would "help them in the big thing later on." [6] The British, however, refused to abandon their efforts to dictate the conditions of trade. Sir Edward Grey scoffed at such a commitment. If Germany means that its commerce is free during wartime, "while she remains free to make war upon other nations at will, it is not a fair proposition." Britain would approve a new arrangement only if Germany entered into some "League of Nations," which would provide mutual security. The sea was free during peace time. [7] Britain would not commit itself to an unhedged principle of freedom of the seas. For those who entered a mutual alliance of cooperation with Britain, there might be an agreement on terms. For those in conflict with the British system, there would be no freedom of the seas.

The United States would have to join a closer relationship with the Allies to cope with British trade policies, to gain a voice in the conduct of wartime trade and warfare on the seas, and to have a role in arranging the postwar conditions of trade. It would have to earn its influence through participation in the war. By December, 1915, Wilson called for the expansion of the regular army from 108,000 men to 142,843, and he asked for a naval construction program to build ten battleships, six battle cruisers, ten scout-destroyers, fifty destroyers, fifteen submarines, eighty-five coastal submarines, and miscellaneous other ships within five years. He also called for the construction of a "great" merchant marine. Without the independence so provided, he argued, "the whole question of our political unity and self-determination is very seriously clouded and complicated indeed." But such an armada of ships would permit the development of a "true and effective American policy." [8]

Wilson was furious about the effects of the British blockade on American trade, the British blacklist of noncooperative American

businessmen, and the various Allied restrictions on trade with
neutrals. He considered asking Congress for authorization to
prohibit loans to the Allies and to place export restrictions on
trade. And Congress did delegate authority for him to inaugurate
drastic retaliatory measures. "Let us build a navy bigger than hers
[Britain]," Wilson remarked to House, "and do what we
please." [9] Even the perennial Anglophile, Walter Hines Page,
erupted in a communication to House. "We don't owe them a
thing. There's no obligation . . . we've set her an example of
efficiency, an example of freedom of opportunity. The future is
ours, and she may follow us and profit by it." Americans were
"sixty percent of the Anglo-Saxons in the world. If there be any
obligation to please, the obligation is on her to please us." [10]

The Administration was not prepared, however, to translate its
anger into action. Belief in the necessity of Anglo-Saxon cooperation was too strong. American interests could be redeemed after
the war. Lansing later wrote that he was prolonging discussion
with the British and avoiding a rigid stand because he expected
early American participation in the war; and, as a belligerent, he
did not want his hands tied by a position the United States might
take as a neutral. The United States had to be prepared to use the
same tactics against other neutrals which it now protested against
to the British. "That reason," he wrote, "was never lost sight of"
during the controversy over trade. Everything was "submerged in
verbosity." It was done, Lansing admitted, with deliberate purpose. It insured the continuance of the controversies and left the
question unsettled. Such procedure was necessary in order to
leave the United States free to act and "even act illegally when it
entered the war." [11]

American economic objectives were to be secured as the fruits
of cooperation in the war, and of the five-year program of naval
and merchant ship construction. Hostile action would upset the
assumptions on which Wilson and his administration were basing
their policies. A break with Britain would have been
unthinkable.

Page soon recovered from his unusual outburst. He pointed
out to Lansing, early in 1916, the need for a decisive victory in
Europe. If the war ended in a draw, Europe would remain
committed to armaments. The Allies were turning to the United
States, he said, to break the stalemate. But he warned, once
more, of secret treaties through which the Allies were planning to
"retain certain large advantages and privileges" after the war.

Japan would use such agreements to "set up a sort of Monroe Doctrine behind which she will exploit China and dominate the Pacific." England was too heavily committed in Europe to intervene. Only American support for Britain and a decisive defeat of Germany would enable the "aggressive ambitions of both Germany and Japan" to be halted. Otherwise they will "smash our legal structure in their assault on democratic civilization." Wilson remarked that Page's analysis had force and should be considered on its own merits. The arguments, he said, were "evident enough and of considerable weight." [12]

The danger to American interests in the Pacific appeared to have substance when the United States learned of German overtures to the Japanese. The German Foreign Office offered the Japanese postwar possession of Kiaochow Bay and the German islands in the Pacific as well as loans to help develop Japan's military and economic position in exchange for a separate peace. The Japanese communicated the German overtures to the Allies in a bid for better terms. [13] That served to point up Page's contention that the United States would not be able to secure its interests in the Far East from the sidelines.

American relations with Latin America continued in a state of disarray, but Wilson increasingly dealt with that problem by blaming the Germans. Germany's "poisonous propaganda" was responsible for the terrible condition of affairs in Mexico, Wilson explained to Joseph R. Tumulty in mid-1916. Germany wanted to force the United States into war with Mexico to divert American attention from the war in Europe. It began to look, Wilson said, as if a war with Germany was inevitable. [14] House went so far as to suggest that British participation in the Pan-American Pact might help stabilize the situation, [15] but the problems were not so easily controlled. Chile and Brazil became increasingly suspicious of American intentions, and the Ambassador to Chile warned House in August 1916 that Chile would turn elsewhere if the United States tried to impose its system without Chilean approval. [16] Nicaraguan politics, once seemingly settled by Knox, also began dissolving in factionalism and the United States grappled with the problem of arranging elections. [17]

The United States found, more and more, that it was unable to control trade conditions in Latin America by itself. The Federal Trade Commission issued a report in 1916 warning of Latin American competition from England, France, and Germany. Each country had pooled its commercial and financial forces and presented a united front. That strategy had elevated Germany, in particular, into a formidable rival. "If American interests are to succeed," the report warned, "they must develop a like solidarity against rival nations." [18] As Wilson's dream of a Pan-American alliance faded he shifted to a broader conception of alliance to stabilize not only Latin America but the world. He concluded, according to Ray Stannard Baker, that American "isolation" was henceforth impossible.

"We are the participants," he proclaimed before the League to Enforce Peace on May 27, 1916, "whether we would or not, in the life of the world . . . We are partners with the rest." The United States either had to turn to some form of international cooperation "in which America could lead," or arm itself as a great military power. [19] A few days before, Wilson privately concluded that the United States must either make a "decided move for peace" or else take steps to protect itself from Allied attacks on trade. "We must act, and act at once, in one direction or another." He then drafted a proposal for a "universal association of nations" to maintain security of the seas for all nations, and to prevent wars begun either in violation of treaties or without warning and disclosure of causes. [20]

Wilson found it difficult to face the implications of the basic decisions he had made. That is understandable, for he had told House in August, 1915, that "it would be calamity to the world . . . if we should be drawn actively into the conflict and so deprived of all disinterested influence over the settlement." It is not surprising that he explored the possibility of convincing England to rescind its blockade order and depend, instead, on an extended contraband list to implement its policy of depriving Germany of the materials it needed. [21]

Lansing had at that time suggested to Wilson that something had to be done. The United States was losing influence on both belligerents. "It would take but little to eliminate us entirely in the final settlement." He believed that the United States had lost all hope of influence with Germany. It could regain the friendship and confidence of the Allies, however, if it severed diplomatic relations with Germany. The United States would then be in a position to exert influence for a "generous peace," and that would restore the good will of Germany. Even if Germany should win, the United States as a participant would be included in the general peace settlement with the Allies and not be dealt with separately by a victorious Germany. American usefulness in the restoration of peace might even be increased if it participated in the war. [22] Wilson responded to this formulation with a note of appreciation and the comment that it ran "along very much the same lines" as his own thought. [23]

Wilson deliberated and floundered, tossed by British and German pressures. He bemoaned the "labyrinth" in which he was caught. [24] He condemned Germany and her "militaristic system" and leaned more and more toward Lansing's position that participation in the war was the only way out. [25] Wilson had once appealed to the American people in behalf of the manifest duty of the United States to remain "studiously neutral;" it was necessary, he had explained in December, 1915, for some member of the great family of nations to "keep the processes of peace alive, if only to prevent collective ruin and breakdown" of the world's industrial system. [26]

American cooperation with the British system during the war generated new economic conditions that made neutrality increasingly difficult. The first part of May, 1916, brought what Secretary of the Treasury William G. McAdoo called the greatest era of prosperity in the nation's history. The great economic growth might be made permanent if the United States could take advantage of the new opportunities. Surplus capital was accumulating and would enable the United States to undertake an investment program in Europe, the Orient, and South America. After the war Europe would be burdened with "an almost insupportable load of debt," heavy taxes, lack of skilled workmen, and the destruction of productive facilities. A great potential for American economic expansion existed in rebuilding Europe and penetrating South and Central America and Asia. [27]

Wilson outlined a similar vision of economic opportunity for the United States in July, 1916. America had to finance the world to an important degree, and those "who finance the world must understand it and rule it with their spirits and with their minds." [28] America had to sell the goods that would make the world "more comfortable and more happy, and convert them to the principles of America." [29] Wilson's dream was of an American world empire of righteousness and trade, based on that world's recognizing the implicit goodness of the United States and the liberating and uplifting effect of American wishes and American cargoes. It had been threatened by ugly reality in the form of war, nationalism, revolution, and the conflicting interests of the other powers. His happy future was predicated on peace, tranquility, stability, and belief in American virtue. And, just as the effort to create these conditions led to intervention and military occupation in Latin America, so it led to involvement in world war. Intervention was necessary in order to gain the influence and power required to reshape the world to fit the dream.

The United States, Wilson explained on July 10, 1916, was going to have to meet the competition for world trade and either "make . . . peaceful conquest of the markets of the world, or . . . be prevented for evermore of boasting of the business ability of America." Its horizons were now as "wide as the world itself." With the support of the Department of Commerce, the Federal Trade Commission, the Bureau of Foreign and Domestic Commerce; with the development of trade associations to share information; with a tariff commission to guide the use of flexible rates to further exports; and with the Webb-Pomerene Law permitting combinations in foreign trade, the United States was prepared to take its "place in the world of finance and commerce . . . upon a scale that she has never dreamed of." [30]

It remained, however, to come to terms with the nations of Europe and construct a system conducive to the continued growth of the United States and consistent with America's new "place in the world of finance and commerce." Whatever the earlier image of Germany as a rival, the Administration now recognized that Germany was an enemy, albeit so redefined in part through American policy. In January, 1916, Ambassador Gerard suggested to Lansing that it was perhaps best to accept the inevitable. [31] The United States might as well enter the war and secure Central America from German reprisals. Lansing acknowledged that American legislation favoring and protecting the development of an American dye and chemical industry gave Germany every reason for fear, for American industry was organizing in direct competition with Germany. [32]

German submarine warfare was harming American trade by sinking British ships. On December 30, 1915, when a German submarine had sunk the British ship *Persia*, Lansing, ever the lawyer, concerned himself once more with the consistency and legality of the American position. He warned the British and Italians that their persistent arming of merchant ships made it difficult, if not impossible, to insist that a submarine should expose itself to attack by coming to the surface and hailing vessels before an attack. He notified the Italian ambassador that a merchant ship carrying arms would have to be considered a vessel of war. [33] And, in a memorandum to Wilson, he admitted that he appreciated the German argument with regard to the danger of a submarine attacking an armed merchant ship. He wanted Germany and Austria to agree not to torpedo enemy vessels without providing for the safety of the passengers—provided the ships did not attempt escape. In exchange, the Allies should refrain from arming merchant ships. [34]

Wilson agreed that the proposal sounded reasonable. [35] Lansing sent the memorandum to the British first because, if the Germans should agree and the British refuse, it might stir adverse criticism and public resentment against the Allies. [36] The British refused the suggestions, and the British ambassador bluntly told Lansing that he expected the United States to denounce the principle of submarine warfare against commercial vessels, and expressed disappointment that the United States "failed to be the instrument to save British commerce from attack by Germany." [37]

In a private memorandum, Lansing reviewed his position; "we are not yet ready to meet the submarine issue squarely. Our people are not aroused to a sufficient pitch of indignation at the barbarism of the Germans." There was a "plausibility," he said, to the German argument that Americans shipped war supplies to the Allies while allowing neutral ports to be blockaded against goods to Germany. The argument had enough weight to "prevent our presenting a unified front against Germany." The time had not yet come for open hostility because the people were still divided and Congress would be resentful if the President acted without its authorization. But Germany was an enemy to "democracy in every form" and, if it defeated the British and French, it would turn to the United States as the "next obstacle to imperial rule over the world." [38]

Lansing's efforts to ease the American position by proposing modifications of submarine warfare were rejected by both sides. Page informed him that the British considered the proposal "wholly in favor of the Central Powers." Gerard reported that the Germans felt that any settlement without a disavowal of British practices or an admission of their illegality would not be acceptable. [39] Thus caught, the administration had to repudiate either the British or the German position. The House of Representatives was considering a resolution denouncing the arming of merchant ships. Lansing sent a secret memorandum to Henry D.

Flood of the House Committee on Foreign Affairs arguing against approval. He maintained that the German statement condemning armed merchant ships did not contain evidence that the British were placing offensive arms on their ships. There was a difference between offensive and defensive arms. This difference was defined by the use to which the arms were put. If the British merely used them to give warning and did not attack, "then the mere intention to destroy without an overt act" did not constitute an attack. He also opposed the idea of warning American passengers of the danger of traveling on Allied ships because it would imply that the Government acknowledged the practice and feared that this might embarrass them later. Such warning would diminish the freedom of action of the United States and it would weaken its rights rather than defend them. It would indicate favor for "this kind of inhuman warfare which the United States had denounced from the beginning." [40] This statement was untrue: Lansing had not always condemned the German use of submarines. His position seemed instead to be dictated by the British rejection of his suggestion that they remove such arms.

Lansing did prepare a memorandum expressing regret that the British had rejected his proposal to refrain from arming merchant ships. [41] But Wilson ordered Lansing not to sent the note, and suggested that the Administration be as noncommital as possible. To do otherwise might support the German arguments. The letter to the British should be "as colourless as possible." [42]

The Germans were not to be satisfied with such a position. The Foreign Office asserted that it had already modified submarine warfare to meet American wishes at the expense of considerable efficiency. The Americans had not responded with an adequate defense of freedom of the seas and the protection of neutral trade. The British continued actions that isolated Germany from legitimate commerce. Though there had been regrettable mistakes for which reparation had been made, the German Government had shown its good will by making concessions affecting the efficiency of submarine warfare while England conceded nothing. Germany expressed the expectation that America would "at least take energetic steps to establish real freedom of the seas." [43]

The United States had already abandoned the principle of freedom of the seas in exchange for Anglo-American cooperation. The issue of freedom of the seas was never again raised seriously. At the time, moreover, Gerard reported from Berlin that the Chancellor and the Foreign Secretary had come to the conclusion that the United States had a secret understanding with the British and that nothing more could be accomplished. [44] The Junkers were demanding unlimited submarine warfare under the pressure of Admiral von Tirpitz. [45] Within a month Gerard sent word that the food situation was becoming desperate. People were starving in some rural sections. Admiral von Tirpitz submitted his resignation in protest over the continued curtailment of submarine warfare. [46] By the end of May, Gerard warned Lansing that the submarine question was going to be raised once more, and that the "Pan-Germanists and Conservatives" would demand a "reckless U Boat war because we have done nothing against England." [47]

Wilson responded to the situation by elevating the war into a crusade. In a speech on May 27, 1916, before the League to Enforce Peace, Wilson called for the right of every people to "choose the sovereignty under which they shall live." The "small states had a right to enjoy the same respect for their sovereignty and for their territorial integrity that great and powerful nations expect." The world, he said, "has a right to be free from every disturbance of its peace that has its origin in aggression and disregard of the rights of peoples and nations." [48] Austria recognized in Wilson's rhetoric an attack on the Austro-Hungarian Empire. The Germans added that if the rights of small states, and the freedom to choose sovereignty, were to be discussed, then the Irish question, the Indian question, and the Boer question should be included. [49]

Walter Hines Page was once more urging the United States to join the Allies in order to secure British support against Japanese expansion in Asia. He did not believe, he wrote in February, 1916, that the United States would have to fire a gun or risk a man. It would gain the support of the British Empire, the British fleet, and all the Allies. The English-speaking nations would then be able to control the conditions of permanent peace and end the Japanese threat. [50]

Another indication of the need for better Anglo-Saxon cooperation was contained in the reports of Ambassador to Russia David R. Francis. The negotiations for a Russian-American commercial treaty had broken down because the Russians refused to sign until after the Allied Economic Conference scheduled for Paris. Francis warned that the British were taking control of

Russian trade, and transmitted a report from an agent of the
National City Bank expressing the belief that Russia had agreed
that all commercial or financial arrangements would be made
through London. [51]

Lansing responded by suggesting pressure on the British. He
recommended a note to the British protesting a long list of
violations of American rights of neutrality. The content of the
proposed note closely paralled the German position on the one-
sided nature of American trade. [52] Wilson rejected this proposal
as dangerous. The attempt to put pressure on Britain by raising
the neutrality issue might arouse public opinion and change the
whole face of foreign relations. Instead, Page could convey a
private message to London. "We had better stop there," Wilson
said. "Let us forget the campaign so far as matters of this sort
[are] concerned." [53] Lansing expressed doubts that "Page will
make the situation clear to the British as he should." It was hard
to forget the election campaign, he added, since the opposition
was so strongly critical of Administration policy. [54]

Ambassador Gerard continued to report growing hunger and
desperation in Germany. He warned that the National Liberals
and Conservatives were cooperating more effectively and were
growing increasingly vocal in their demands for resumption of
submarine warfare. [55] The German pressures to force the issue
between the United States and Great Britain were growing.
Lansing, in September, 1916, warned that the "pro-German"
press in the United States was denouncing the Administration as
"slaves of the British." Wilson, he felt, could not seem to make
up his mind. The President was becoming increasingly bitter of
the "British invasion of our rights" and would have denounced
the British if it had not been for the approaching elections.
Though Lansing attempted to explain the situation to Wilson, he
felt the President did not grasp the full significance of the war
and the "principles at issue." Lansing felt that Wilson wanted to
act as mediator and "to stand forth as the great neutral peacemaker." [56]

Wilson's original formulation had been that a neutral United
States would gain great economic advantages and the advantages
of moral leadership. Underlying this assumption was the belief
that American postwar goals required a limited German defeat.
As both sides resorted to commercial warfare and the United
States lost the ability to trade impartially with both sides, and
instead, became increasingly embroiled with the British commer-

cial structure, the prospects of advantages from wartime neutrality evaporated. If the United States wanted to preserve its access to world frontiers and gain support against its chief rivals in Latin America and Asia it appeared that the United States would have to join the Allies. The one alternative that appeared viable was a negotiated peace that would secure America's objectives.

Wilson did try once more to resolve his dilemma by negotiating a peace settlement. The suggestion was first made by House in October, 1915, when he proposed that the United States obtain assurances from one side that it would accept an American call for a peace conference. Then, if the other side rejected the call, the United States would intervene. Charles Seymour argues that Wilson was sure the Allies would cooperate because they would prefer the promise of a future international organization to preserve peace to an undefeated Germany that would remain a menace. Such an agreement would involve the German evacuation of invaded territories, an indemnity for Belgium, and the cession of Alsace-Lorraine to France. In return, "something might be found to satisfy German colonial aspirations." The United States by this time had knowledge of the secret treaties concluded among the Allies, and House hoped they would give up their "dream of conquest" in exchange for American aid. [57] This was an effort, according to Seymour, to reach peace on terms securing the avowed purposes of the Allies. [58] The implication of such overtures, however, was that the United States would have to go to war unless the Germans agreed to the conditions. [59]

By September, 1915, Wilson had to face up to the possibility of American participation in the war. It is true, as Arthur S. Link has pointed out, [60] that Wilson did not intend to support the British so overtly. During the first months of the war Wilson had attempted to define a viable neutral role for the United States. When the British refused to allow such a role, Wilson accepted the situation. His underlying assumptions concerning American needs did not allow for a German victory. Anglo-American cooperation was necessary to the fulfillment of American objectives in too many areas to permit that. An American refusal to accept the British position would help the German war effort while acceptance would help the British cause. Since the British had naval superiority, American neutrality would have in fact helped the Germans, and this was incompatable with Wilson's definition of American national interest. The course of American efforts at negotiation was not predicated on a position of neutrality but on the desire to obtain postwar Anglo-American cooperation on terms suitable to the needs of the United States.

House suggested to Wilson in September, 1915, that he ask the Allies to approve his demand for an end to hostilities in the name of neutral suffering. If the Allies understood his real purposes, House said, the President could be as severe in his public criticism of them as of the Germans. If both sides accepted the offer, then the United States "would have accomplished a master stroke of diplomacy." If the Central Powers refused, the United States could push its insistence to the point of war. If this happened then perhaps all neutrals might be carried into the war with the United States. [61] House explained to Lord Grey that peace would be established on terms acceptable to the Allies. When Grey would inform him that the time was "propitious" for this intervention, then House would propose it to the President. He would then proceed to Germany and threaten to throw the weight of the United States on the side of whoever accepted the proposal. He would not let the Germans know of his prior understanding with the Allies. [62]

The British still distrusted Wilson, not believing he would really enter the war. [63] Lord Bryce wrote House explaining the British intent to fight on to victory, [64] and Lord Grey warned that the British would not commit themselves without knowing the exact nature of the proposition and whether the United States would intervene. [65] Wilson responded with formal assurance that he would cooperate in a policy to bring about and maintain permanent peace among civilized nations. This was his first pledge to participate in a League of Nations to secure the conditions of a victorious peace for the Allies, and led him to make his May 27 speech before the League to Enforce Peace. [66]

Such guarantees were not adequate. The British and French distrusted each other, and Lord Grey added his belief that the time was not ripe. Any suggestion of peace before victory might lead to a moral debacle. [67] If the United States should proceed with its call for negotiations and the Allies refused, the implication of House's plan was that the United States would have to join Germany. Obviously this could not be allowed. In November, 1916, however, the United States was poised at the edge of war and another attempt seemed necessary. Wilson sent for

House and discussed a note to the belligerents demanding they end the war. If this were not done, he feared the United States would drift into the conflict. House replied that the Allies would consider it an unfriendly act because they were beginning to be successful after two years of war. Wilson believed, however, that the attempt had to be made before the United States went ahead and broke off diplomatic relations with Germany. [68]

The result, shown to House on November 27, 1916, was Wilson's famous "peace note" to the belligerents that urged them to state their terms of peace. House and Lansing opposed sending the note because both believed Britain would reject it. [69] Lansing argued simply that the United States would soon be involved. Furthermore, what if the Germans responded in a favorable spirit and the British did not! Suppose that the unacceptable answer comes from the belligerents "whom we can least afford to see defeated on account of our national interpretation of interests and on account of the future domination of the principles of liberty and democracy in the world—what then?" [70]

The Germans proceeded to make real Lansing's fears. They offered peace negotiations on the basis of the status quo on December 12, 1916. Wilson erupted that the German maneuver undermined his peace offer and placed him in the position of appearing to collaborate with the Germans. [71] Britain rejected Wilson's note. Lord Balfour explained that peace could not be durable if not based on the success of the Allied cause. The Allies refused negotiations or any exchange of views. Even Spain, considered by Lansing the most prominent of European neutrals, declined Wilson's request to associate itself with the United States in an effort to compromise the differences between the belligerents. [72]

Wilson did not respond to the German note. He turned, instead, to the Senate of the United States. He announced, on January 22, 1917, "that it was inconceivable that the people of the United States should play no part in that great enterprise." The war was the opportunity for which Americans had been preparing themselves throughout their history, the opportunity to "show mankind the way to liberty." He proclaimed the necessity of a peace settlement including the peoples of the New World. It was necessary to create a force to serve as the guarantor of any settlement.

Wilson called for a "peace without victory," a peace between equals. But equality, he said, had to be based on equality of rights. To that end he called for an independent Poland with an outlet to the sea, and acceptance of the principle of freedom of the seas, arms limitations, and a Monroe Doctrine for the world. He claimed that he was "perhaps the only person in high authority amongst all the peoples of the world who is at liberty to speak and hold nothing back." He was speaking, he said, for the silent mass of mankind. [73]

The Peace without Victory speech was designed to avoid the implications of the German acceptance of Wilson's note. It implied an attack on Austro-Hungarian interests and conveyed a promise to the British of a postwar system of cooperation and security. Lansing suggested that the Allies might misunderstand the call for Peace without Victory, but Wilson disagreed. He was appealing, he said, over the heads of governments who had shown their opposition to his personal intervention in the war. [74] Germany replied on January 31, 1917, by resuming unlimited submarine warfare. Wilson moved to war almost automatically while still talking of peace. By February 2, 1917, the United States had severed diplomatic relations with Germany.

Wilson tried to persuade the neutrals of Latin America to join the action even though Lansing warned that such a move was dangerous unless assured of success. Only Panama and Cuba responded to Wilson's appeal. Others, such as El Salvador, Honduras, Colombia, and Mexico were antagonistic. Revolt broke out in Costa Rica and Wilson told Lansing he would suppress it by force and stop such revolutions from occurring. [75] Wilson had counted on being able to unite Latin America behind him but had seriously miscalculated. The final blow came with the British exposure of the Zimmerman note. Germany had offered Mexico an alliance, and mention was made of Japanese participation. Wilson had regarded German competition in Latin America as a plot. That view was now greatly strengthened.

Wilson had hoped to avoid entering the war but found that the United States could not, in fact, play an independent role. His definition of American interests required Anglo-American cooperation. Without it the United States could not pursue its world frontiers of trade. Without it the United States could not count on a postwar world of safety and economic opportunity. Wilson's overtures for peace had been predicated on a settlement favorable to the Allies. When Germany rejected this and declared unlimited submarine warfare, the only method open for intercepting the American flow of supplies to the Allies, war had to follow. Wilson could not defend American trade aspirations without becoming a belligerent. [76] On April 2 Wilson asked the joint session of Congress to accept the status of belligerency.

Notes and References

1. Consul General at Rotterdam, Listoe to Bryan, December 21, 1914, *Foreign Relations, 1915, Supplement*, 268.
2. Minister to the Netherlands, Van Dyke to Bryan, January 9, 1915, ibid., 269; Wilbur J. Carr for Bryan to Consul General Skinner, May 24, 1915, ibid., 413-414; Skinner to Lansing, September 27, 1915, ibid., 556-557; Skinner to Lansing, September 16, 1915, ibid., 559-560. See also Ethel C. Phillips, "American Participation in Belligerent Commercial Controls, 1914-1917," *American Journal of International Law*, XXIV (March 1933), 675-693.
3. Minister Reinsch to Lansing, November 9, 1915, *Foreign Relations, 1915, Supplement*, 610-611; Reinsch to Lansing, November 30, 1915, Lansing to Page, December 18, 1915, ibid., 616-617, 641.
4. House to Wilson, March 20, 1915, WW Mss.; House Diary, March 19, 1915, March 23, 1915; House to Wilson, March 29, 1915, WW Mss.
5. Seymour, *House*, I, 405-410.
6. Seymour, *House*, I, 405-410; House to Wilson, March 27, 1915, ibid., 410-411.
7. Sir Edward Grey to House, April 24, 1915, ibid., 425.
8. Wilson, Third Annual Message to Congress, December 7, 1915, *New Democracy*, I, 412-418.
9. Charles Seymour, *American Diplomacy During the World War* (The Johns Hopkins Press, 1942), 77.
10. Page to House, September 7, 1915, Hendrick, *Page*, II, 28.
11. Robert Lansing, *War Memoirs of Robert Lansing* (Bobbs-Merrill Co., 1935), 128-134.
12. Page to Lansing, January 22, 1916; Wilson to Lansing, January 24, 1916, *Lansing Papers*, I, 306-308.
13. Frank W. Ikle, "Japanese-German Peace Negotiations During World War I," *American Historical Review*, LXXI, 1 (October, 1965), 63-65.
14. Joseph P. Tumulty, *Woodrow Wilson as I Knew Him* (Doubleday, Page & Co., 1921), 159.
15. House Diary, February 21, 1916; Seymour, *House*, I, 228-229.
16. Henry P. Fletcher to House, August 9, 1916; House Mss.; Seymour, *House*, I, 220-231.

17. President Diaz to Charge d'Affaires Guardia, July 26, 1916; statement of J. B. Wright, July 28, 1916; J. B. Wright to Frank Polk, August 2, 1916, Lansing Mss.

18. Federal Trade Commission, *Report on Trade and Tariffs in Brazil, Uruguay, Argentina, Chile, Bolivia and Peru* (G.P.O., 1916) 20-23.

19. Ray Stannard Baker, *Woodrow Wilson and World Settlement* (Doubleday, Page & Co., 1922) I, 243-249.

20. Wilson to House, May 16, 1916, cited in Seymour, *American Diplomacy*, 174-175.

21. Wilson to House, May 21, 1916, Wilson Mss.

22. Lansing to Wilson, "Consequences of War with Germany," August 4, 1915, *Lansing Papers*, I, 470-471.

23. Wilson to Lansing, August 26, 1915, ibid., 471.

24. Wilson to House, September 7, 1915, Seymour, *American Diplomacy*, 140.

25. Wilson to House, September 22, 1915, Seymour, *House*, II, 84.

26. Wilson, "Third Annual Address to Congress," December 7, 1915, *New Democracy*, I, 412-418.

27. William G. McAdoo, *Prosperity and the Future*, May 31, 1916, Senate Document 457, 64th Congress, 1st Session, 1916.

28. Wilson, "Fighting is the Slow Way to Peace," Address Before the Salesmanship Congress, Detroit. July 10, 1916, *New Democracy*, II, 229.

29. Ibid., 223; Wooarow Wilson, "Address at Shadow Lawn," September 23, 1916, *New Democracy*, II, 301-302.

30. Wilson, "Fighting is the Slow Way to Peace," ibid., 312-321.

31. Gerard to Lansing, January 3, 1916, *Lansing Papers*, I, 675.

32. Lansing to Gerard, January 11, 1916, ibid., 676.

33. Lansing to Wilson, January 2, 1916, ibid., 332-333; Lansing to Italian Ambassador, January 2, 1916, *Foreign Relations, 1916, Supplement*, 749.

34. Lansing to Wilson, January 17, 1916, *Lansing Papers*, I, 334.

35. Wilson to Lansing, January 10, 1916, ibid., 335.

36. Lansing to Wilson, January 17, 1916, ibid., 336.

37. Lansing to Wilson, January 27, 1916, ibid., 338.

38. Lansing, private memorandum, January 9, 1916, Lansing Mss.

39. Lansing to House, February 2, 1916, *Lansing Papers*, I, 339; Gerard to Lansing, January 29, 1916, *Foreign Relations, 1916*, 153.

40. Lansing to Representative Flood, March 3, 1916, *Lansing Papers*, I, 343; Lansing Memorandum on House Resolution No. 147, ibid., 344.

41. Lansing to Cecil Spring-Rice, draft note, March 31, 1916, ibid., 350.

42. Wilson to Lansing, March 30, 1916, ibid., 351; Wilson to Lansing, April 7, 1916, ibid., 351; Lansing to Cecil Spring-Rice, April 7, 1916, *Foreign Relations, 1916, Supplement*, 223.

43. German Foreign Office to German Embassy, January 10, 1916, *Lansing Papers*, I, 517.

44. Gerard to Lansing, February 29, 1916, *Lansing Papers*, I, 678.

45. Gerard to Lansing, February 16, 1916, ibid., 678.
46. Gerard to Lansing, March 7, 1916; March 14, 1916; March 20, 1916; ibid., 679-681.
47. Gerard to Lansing, May 17, 1916; May 24, 1916, May 30, 1916; ibid., 685-690.
48. Baker, *Woodrow Wilson and World Settlement*, 243-245; Max Beer, *The League on Trial* (Houghton Mifflin Co., 1933), 20-33.
49. Gerard to Lansing, June 7, 1916, *Lansing Papers*, I, 688.
50. Page to Lansing, February 17, 1916, ibid., 704.
51. David R. Francis to Lansing, May 2, 1916, ibid., II, 309-10.
52. Lansing to Wilson, September 22, 1916, ibid., I, 314.
53. Wilson to Lansing, September 29, 1916, ibid., 319.
54. Lansing to Wilson, October 2, 1916, ibid., 320.
55. Gerard to Lansing, June 21, 1916, *Lansing Papers*, 689; July 25, 1916, ibid., 691; August 8, 1916, ibid., 692; August 23, 1916, ibid., 695; January 3, 1917, ibid., 698; January 16, 1917, ibid., 699.
56. Lansing, private memorandum, September 1916, Lansing Mss.
57. Seymour, *American Diplomacy*, 140.
58. Seymour, *House*, II, 83.
59. Ibid., 84.
60. Arthur S. Link, *Wilson the Diplomatist* (The Johns Hopkins Press, 1957), 35-39.
61. Link, *Wilson the Diplomatist*, 85.
62. House to Sir Edward Grey, October 17, 1915, ibid., 90-91.
63. Seymour, *American Diplomacy*, 149.
64. Lord Bryce to House, November 26, 1915, Seymour, *House*, II, 110-111.
65. Wilson to House, January 9, 1916, cited in Seymour, *American Diplomacy*, 145.
66. Lansing, *War Memoirs*, 176-181.
67. Seymour, *American Diplomacy*, 148-149; Hendrick, *Page*, II, 282; Lord Edward Grey, *Twenty Five Years, 1892-1916* (Frederick A. Stokes, 1925), II, 128-132, 121, 129.
68. House Diary, November 14, 1916; November 15, 1916; Seymour, *House*, II, 390-392.
69. House to Wilson, November 30, 1916, Seymour, *House*, II, 394-395; Lansing, *War Memoirs*, 178.
70. Lansing to Wilson, December 10, 1916, ibid., 179.
71. Lansing, *War Memoirs*, 181-182.
72. Ibid., 191-193.
73. Woodrow Wilson, "Address to Senate," January 22, 1917, *New Democracy,* II, 407-414.
74. Lansing, *War Memoirs*, 193-196.
75. Ibid., 307-309.
76. Wilson to Matthew Hale, March 31, 1917, WW Mss.; Link, *Wilson the Diplomatist*, 87.

10
PAX AMERICANA

Wilson's statement in December, 1918, that Americans were the only disinterested people at the peace conference demands examination. It might be considered either an indication of extreme Wilsonian cynicism or his belief in the extreme naiveté of his audience. There is every indication, however, that Wilson was sincere—that he believed in what he said, no matter how it might contradict earlier statements. The Calvinist and the Anglo-Saxon in Wilson led him to the conviction that his voice was the voice of truth and righteousness, and that what he thought was good for his nation and his people was objectively and universally good. America was the nation of the elect. That which benefitted America benefitted the world. A desire for an expanding American system was not only to be beneficial to the United States but beneficial to the rest of the world. If one believed this then one might assume that one had no special interest but that which is right. Those who opposed Wilson's program could be regarded as being unrepresentative of the real aspirations of their own people. In this manner Wilson could attempt to manipulate and control Mexican affairs while at the same time insist that he was pursuing the principle of self-determination.

Wilson had started with the view that the United States was in danger of disintegration because of internal factional conflict. James Madison's prescription of balance and expansion needed revitalization. Wilson had learned from Frederick Jackson Turner of the effect on American stability of the closing of the territorial frontier. The old frontier had provided the United States with an imperial outlet for its surplus population, capital, and energies. It had bought opportunity for successive generations to share in the economic growth provided by the infusion of new resources. Now a new frontier had to be found for the capital and the products of an industrial society if the American system was to continue to function. Democracy, Wilson feared, would become an increasingly factionalizing force if it was no longer domesticated by economic growth. The people were no longer following wise leaders who could look after their best interests.

190

America might be compelled to confront itself and its own institutions. Wilson believed that the American people needed two things: a strong, centralized, moralistic leadership capable of unifying the nation, and an expanding share of world markets for trade and finance. This new frontier abroad would restore prosperity and stability and provide the lubricant necessary to ease internal friction. Wilson's efforts at creating the conditions necessary for American expansion in Latin America and Asia were jeopardized by the forces of nationalism and revolution, and by the competition of rival nations.

Revolution disrupted Wilson's attempts to secure an expanding sphere in Mexico and Central America. Wilson regarded this sphere of economic interest as necessary to the welfare of Latin America as well as the United States. Since revolution threatened commerce and damaged property, it was to be considered mere banditry. Any legitimate aspirations of depressed peasantry or workers were best served, in Wilson's view, by their integration into a growing economic system dominated by the United States rather than by social upheaval and a revolutionary reordering of institutions. Wilson's efforts at exercising "benevolent" guardianship through the use of force and pressure generated a spreading nationalistic reaction instead of an appreciation of his benign intentions. He sought to create some form of international organization to maintain order and prevent or isolate revolution. The British proved to be cooperative but the Germans, who were becoming formidable economic rivals, refuse to recognize American hegemony.

United States efforts to carve out an economic sphere in China were similarly disrupted by nationalism and revolution and the lack of international cooperation with American objectives. Russia and Japan were not willing to yield their own expansionist objectives. Here too Wilson learned that the United States could not act independently even though its pursuit of interest was combined with moral justifications.

War in Europe indicated even more sharply the destructive effects of international disorder and rivalry on American aspirations and interests. Wilson could not find a tidy world thankfully receiving the moral uplift and civilizing effect of American trade. Wilson hoped that the war would allow the United States a free hand in building its own economic empire while the major powers were otherwise occupied. He learned, however, that even here he could not pursue an independent role. Great Britain would not allow the United States to take advantage of the war to capture new markets at the expense of British interests.

In order for the United States to pursue "the righteous conquest of the markets of the world" a system of collective security based on Anglo-Saxon cooperation was required. Wilson needed help in curbing the competitive threat of Germany in Latin America and of Japan in the Pacific. He needed help in fighting economically disruptive revolutions. He wanted an international system that would ensure stability, suppress troublemakers and secure an open door for American trade.

It appears to be true that Wilson had not wanted to enter the war in Europe. He found, however, that he had to choose between the British and the Germans. The British would not allow the United States to be neutral and the Germans would not allow it to be nonbelligerently partisan. The broader benefits of Anglo-Saxon cooperation and the dangers of postwar German rivalry decided the issue. It may be true that Wilson did not want war; but the things he did want led him into war.

Even as Wilson entered the war, the image of the peace conditions he needed had begun to emerge. American economic expansion required collective security—a primarily Anglo-American alliance against hungry rivals for markets and against revolutionary disruption and war. It needed peace and stability, an open door for new trade and the protection of established interests including a closed American sphere in Latin America. The principle of freedom of the seas was expendable rhetoric if there was a suitable alliance in the form of a League of Nations. Last of all, Germany must not be permitted the strength to retaliate, nor should that country or Japan compete too vigorously. The Russian Revolution and the threat of Leninism were understood by Wilson in light of his Latin-American experiences.

If these were Wilson's primary considerations they were provided for in the Versailles Treaty and the League Convenant. From this aspect one may conclude that the peace was in fact Wilsonian. Similarly, the failure of that peace may be construed as the failure of Wilsonian liberalism. That particular combination of economic expansion, alliance, Anglo-Saxonism, and moralizing did not provide a viable approach in a world of revolution, nationalism, and revisionism.

Notes and References

1. Robert Lansing called the League of Nations a "Quintuple Alliance" in support of "international autocracy." See Robert Lansing, *The Peace Negotiations: A Personal Narrative* (Houghton Mifflin Co., 1921), 138-139.

BIBLIOGRAPHY

Manuscript Collection

The Papers of General Tasker Howard Bliss, Library of Congress.
The Papers of William Jennings Bryan, Library of Congress.
The Papers of Norman C. Davis, Library of Congress.
The Papers of Colonel Edward Mandell House, Yale University Library.
The Diary of Colonel Edward Mandell House, Yale University Library.
The Papers of Robert Lansing, Library of Congress.
The Papers of John Bassett Moore, Library of Congress.
Theodore Roosevelt Files, miscellaneous material courtesy of Howard Kennedy Beale.
The Papers of Woodrow Wilson, Library of Congress.

Public Documents

Annual Report of the New York Chamber of Commerce, 1914-1915.
Department of Commerce, *Banking and Credit in Argentina, Brazil, Chile and Peru*, 63rd Congress, 3rd Session, Senate Document No. 659, December 18, 1914.
Department of Commerce, *German Banking in Latin America*, 63rd Congress, 2nd Session, Senate Document No. 90, December 18, 1914.
Department of Commerce, Bureau of the Census, *Historical Statistics of the United States: Colonial Times to the Present* (Washington: G.P.O., 1960).
Department of State, *Papers Relating to the Foreign Relations of the United States, 1910 to 1917.*
Department of State, *Papers Relating to the Foreign Relations of the United States, The Lansing Papers*, 2 vols.
Department of the Treasury, *Annual Report of the Department of the Treasury, 1914* (Washington: G.P.O., 1915).
Department of the Treasury, Edward N. Hurley, *Cooperation and Efficiency in Developing Our Foreign Trade*, 64th Congress, 1st Session, Senate Document No. 459, 1916.
Department of the Treasury, William G. McAdoo, "Prosperity and the Future," *Documents of a Public Nature*, 64th Congress, 1st Session, 1916.
Federal Trade Commission, *Report of Trade and Tariffs in Brazil, Uruguay, Argentina, Chile, Bolivia and Peru* (Washington: G.P.O., 1916). *Proceedings of the First Pan American Financial Conference* (Washington: G.P.O., 1915)

194

United States Senate, Fall Committee Report, *Investigation of Mexican Affairs*, Senate Document No. 285, 66th Congress, 2nd Session, 1920.

United States Senate, Foreign Relations Committee, *Document Executive B*, 62nd Congress, 1st Session, June 28, 1911.

United States Senate, Foreign Relations Committee, *Document Executive C*, 62nd Congress, 1st Session, 1912.

United States Senate, Foreign Relations Committee, *Convention Between the United States and Nicaragua*, 4 parts, 63rd Congress, 2nd Session, 1914.

United States Senate, Foreign Relations Committee, *Convention Between the United States and Nicaragua: Hearings on Nicaraguan Affairs*, 62nd Congress, 2nd Session, 1913.

United States Senate, Foreign Relations Committee, *Hearings on Foreign Loans*, 68th Congress, 2nd Session, 1926.

United States Senate, Special Committee on Investigation of the Munitions Industry, *Report on the Adequancy of Existing Legislation*, 74th Congress, 2nd Session, 1936.

Works by Woodrow Wilson

Wilson, Woodrow, *An Old Master and Other Political Essays*. New York: Harper & Bros., 1893.

Wilson, Woodrow, *Constitutional Government in the United States*. New York: Columbia University Press, 1908.

Wilson, Woodrow, *History of the American People*. New York: Harper & Bros., 1902, 5 vols.

Wilson, Woodrow, *Mere Literature*. New York: Harper & Bros., 1896.

Wilson, Woodrow, *The New Freedom*. New York: Doubleday, Page & Co., 1913.

Wilson, Woodrow, *The State*. Boston: E. E. Heath & Co., 1898.

Correspondence and Collected Works

Baker, Ray Stannard, *Woodrow Wilson, Life and Letters*. Garden City: Doubleday, Page & Co., 1927-1939, 8 vols.

Baker, Ray Stannard and Dodd, William E., eds., *The Public Papers of Woodrow Wilson*. New York: Harper & Bros., 1925-1927, 6 vols.

Cronon, E. David, ed., *The Cabinet Diaries of Josephus Daniels, 1913-1921*. Lincoln: University of Nebraska Press, 1963, vol. I and II.

Fosdick, Raymond B., *Letters on the League of Nations*. Princeton: Princeton University Press, 1966.

Gwynn, Stephen, ed., *The Letters and Friendships of Sir Cecil Spring-Rice*. London: Constable, 1929, 2 vols.

Hamilton, Alexander, James Madison and John Jay, *The Federalist.* New
York: Tudor Publishing Co., 1937.
Hendrick, Burton J., *The Life and Letters of Walter Hines Page.* Garden
City: Doubleday, Page & Co., 1923, 3 vols.
Link, Arthur, *The Papers of Woodrow Wilson.* Princeton: Princeton Uni-
versity Press, 1966, vol. I.
Moore, John Bassett, *The Collected Papers of John Bassett Moore.* New
Haven: Yale University Press, 1945, 7 vols.
Seymour Charles, ed., *The Intimate Papers of Colonel House.* Boston:
Houghton Mifflin Co., 1928, 4 vols.

Autobiographies and Memoirs

Bernstorff, Count Johann von, *My Three Years in America.* New York:
Charles Scribner's Sons, 1920.
Frankfurter, Felix, *Felix Frankfurter Reminisces.* New York: Reynal &
Co., 1960.
Grey, Lord Edward, *Twenty Five Years, 1892-1916.* New York: Frederick
A. Stokes, 1925.
Houston, David F., *Eight Years with Wilson's Cabinet, 1913-1920.* Garden
City: Doubleday, Page & Co., 1926, vol. I.
Hull Cordell, *The Memoirs of Cordell Hull.* New York: Macmillan Co.,
1948, vol. I.
Lansing, Robert, *The Peace Negotiations: A Personal Narrative.* Boston:
Houghton Mifflin Co., 1921.
Lansing, Robert, *War Memoirs of Robert Lansing.* New York: Bobbs-
Merrill Co., 1935.
Lloyd-George, David, *War Memoirs of David Lloyd-George.* Boston: Little,
Brown & Co., 1937, 2 vols.
Lodge, Henry Cabot, *The Senate and the League of Nations.* New York:
Charles Scribner's Sons, 1925.
O'Shaughnessy, Edith, *Intimate Pages of Mexican History.* New York:
George H. Doran Co., 1920.
Reinsch, Paul S., *An American Diplomat in China.* New York: Doubleday,
Page & Co., 1922.
Thompson, Charles W., *Presidents I Have Known.* Indianapolis: Bobbs-
Merrill Co., 1929.
Tumulty, Joseph P., *Woodrow Wilson As I Knew Him.* Garden City:
Doubleday, Page and Co., 1921.
Wickham Steed, Henry, *Through Thirty Years, 1892-1922.* London:
Heinemann, 1925, 2 vols.

Newspapers Cited

New York Evening Post.
New York Financial Chronicle.
New York Sun.
New York Times.
New York World.

Contemporary Articles

Bingham, Hiram, "The Monroe Doctrine: An Obsolete Shibboleth," *Atlantic Monthly*, CIV. June, 1913, 721-737.

Blythe, Samuel F., "Mexico: The Record of a Conversation With President Wilson," *Saturday Evening Post*, CLXXXVI. May 23, 1914, 3-4, 71.

Hammond, John Hays, "Trade Relations with Central and South America as Affected by the War," *Annals of the American Academy*, LX. July 1915, 69-81.

House, Edward M., "The Freedom of the Seas," *Contemporary Review*. April, 1928, 416-421.

Roosevelt, Theodore, "The Trust, the People, and the Square Deal," *Outlook*, IC. November 18, 1911, 649-656.

Tarbell, Ida, "A Talk with the President of the United States," *Collier's*, LCIII. October 28, 1916, 5-6.

Wilson, Woodrow, "Hide and Seek Politics," *North American Review*, CXCI. May 1910, 585-601.

Wilson, Woodrow, "Cabinet Government in the United States," *International Review*, VI. August 1879, 46-164.

Wilson, Woodrow, "Democracy and Efficiency," *Atlantic Monthly*, LXXXVII. March, 1897, 289-300.

Wilson, Woodrow, "Cleveland as President," *Atlantic Monthly*, LXXXIX. March, 1897, 289-300.

Wilson, Woodrow, "Freedmen Need no Guardians," *Fortnightly Review*, IC. February, 1913, 209-218.

Wilson, Woodrow, "Ideals of America," *Atlantic Monthly*, XC. December 1902, 727-734.

Wilson Woodrow, "The Tariff Make-Believe," *North American Review*, CXC. October 1909, 535-556.

Secondary Books and Articles

Allen, H. C., *Great Britain and the United States*. New York: St. Martins Press, 1955.

Bailey, Thomas A., "Interest in a Nicaraguan Canal, 1903-1921," *Hispanic American Historical Review*, XVI. February, 1936, 2-28.

Baker, Ray Stannard, *Woodrow Wilson and World Settlement*. Garden City: Doubleday, Page & Co., 1922, 2 vols.

Bannister, Robert C., Jr., *Ray Stannard Baker*. New Haven: Yale University Press, 1966.

Beale, Howard Kennedy, *Theodore Roosevelt and the Rise of America to World Power*. Baltimore: The Johns Hopkins Press, 1956.

Beales, Carlton, *Porfirio Diaz: Dictator of Mexico*. Philadelphia: Lippincott, 1932.

Beard, Charles A., *The Idea of National Interest*. New York: The Macmillan Co., 1934.

Beer, Max, *The League on Trial: A Journey to Geneva*. Boston: Houghton Mifflin Co., 1933.

Beers, Burton F., *Vain Endeavor: Robert Lansing's Attempts to End the American-Japanese Rivalry*. Durham: Duke University Press, 1963.

Bemis, Samuel Flagg, *A Diplomatic History of the United States*. New York: Harcourt, Brace and Co., 1943.

Blakeslee, George H., *Recent Developments in China*. New York: F. C. Steckert Co., 1913.

Blum, John Morton, *Woodrow Wilson and the Politics of Morality*. Boston: Little, Brown & Co., 1956.

Bond, H. Frazier, *Mr. Miller of 'The Times'*. New York: Scribner's, 1931.

Bowers, Claude, *Beveridge and the Progressive Era*. Cambridge: Riverside Press, 1932.

Buehrig, Edward H., *Woodrow Wilson and the Balance of Power*. Bloomington: Indiana University Press, 1955.

Buehrig, Edward H., ed., *Wilson's Foreign Policy in Perspective*. Bloomington: Indiana University Press, 1957.

Buelk, R. L., "The United States and Central American Stability," in Foreign Policy Association, *Foreign Policy Reports*, VII. July 8, 1931, 161-168.

Burlington, Edgar, *Neutrality: Its History, Economics and Law*. New York: Columbia University Press, 1936.

Calderon, Francisco Gracia, *Latin America: Its Rise and Progress*. London: Unwin, 1913.

Calegeras, José Pandia, *A History of Brazil*. Chapel Hill: University of North Carolina Press, 1939.

Callcott, Wilfred H., *The Carribbean Policy of the United States, 1890-1920*. Baltimore: The Johns Hopkins University Press, 1942.

Calvert, Peter A. R., "The Murray Contract: An Episode in International

Finance and Diplomacy," *Pacific Historical Review*, XXXV, 2. May, 1966, 203-224.

Clapp, Edwin J., *Economic Aspects of the War*. New Haven: Yale University Press, 1915.

Clark, Dan E., "Manifest Destiny and the Pacific," *Pacific Historical Review*, I, 1. December, 1932, 1-17.

Clark, John Bates, *Philosophy of Wealth*. Boston: Ginn & Co., 1887.

Cline, Howard F., *The United States and Mexico*. Cambridge: Harvard University Press, 1953.

Cochran, Thomas C. and Miller, William, *The Age of Enterprise*. New York: Macmillan, 1942.

Coletta, Paolo E., "Bryan, McKinley and the Treaty of Paris," *Pacific Historical Review*, XXVI. May, 1957, 131-146.

Cox, Isaac Joslin, *Nicaragua and the United States*. Boston: World Peace Foundation, 1928.

Croly, Herbert, *Willard Straight*. New York: Macmillan Co., 1925.

Croly, Herbert, *The Promise of American Life*. New York: Macmillan Co., 1921.

Crosby, Gerda, *Disarmament and Peace in British Politics, 1914-1919*. Cambridge: Havard University Press, 1957.

Curry, Roy Watson, *Woodrow Wilson and Far Eastern Policy, 1913-1921*. New York: Bookman Associates, 1957.

Daniels, Josephus, *The Wilson Era*. Chapel Hill: University of North Carolina Press, 1944-46, 2 vols.

Dennett, Tyler, *Americans in Eastern Asia*. New York: Macmillan Co., 1922.

Diamond, William, *The Economic Thought of Woodrow Wilson*. Baltimore: The Johns Hopkins Press, 1943.

Downing, Todd, *The Mexican Earth*. New York: Doubleday, Doran & Co., 1940.

Dulles, Foster Rhea, *Labor in America*. New York: Thomas Y. Crowell Co., 1955.

Dulles, Foster Rhea, *The Imperial Years*. New York: Thomas Y. Crowell Co., 1955.

Elbow, Matthew, *French Corporative Theory, 1789-1948*. New York: Columbia University Press, 1953.

Esthus, Raymond A., "The Changing Concept of the Open Door, 1899-1910," *Mississippi Valley Historical Review*, LXVI, 3. December 1959, 435-454.

Evans, Laurence, "United States Policy and the Syrian Mandate, 1917-1922," unpublished Ph.D. dissertation, School of Advanced International Studies of The Johns Hopkins University, 1957.

Faulkner, Harold Underwood, *The Decline of Laissez Faire, 1897-1917*. New York: Rinehart and Co., Inc., 1951.

Fisk, H. E., *Inter-Ally Debts*. New York: Bankers Trust Co., 1924.

Forcey, Charles B., *The Crossroads of Liberalism: Croly, Wehl, Lippmann and the Progressive Era, 1900-1912*. New York: Oxford University Press, 1961.

Garraty, John A., *Henry Cabot Lodge*. New York: Alfred A. Knopf, 1953.

George, Alexander L. and Juliette L, *Woodrow Wilson and Colonel House*. New York: The John Day Co., 1956.

Goldman, Eric, *John Bach McMasters*. Philadelphia: University of Pennsylvania Press, 1943.

Graham, Malbone W., Jr., *The Controversy Between the United States and Allied Governments Respecting Neutral Rights and Commerce During the Period of American Neutrality, 1914-1917*. Austin: The University of Texas Press, 1923.

Grattan, C. Hartley, ed., *Australia*. Berkeley: University of California Press, 1947.

Griswold, A. Whitney, *The Far Eastern Policy of the United States*. New York: Harcourt, Brace & Co., 1938.

Herring, Hubert, *A History of Latin America*. New York: Alfred A. Knopf, 1961.

Hirschfeld, Charles, "Brooks Adams and American Nationalism," *American Historical Review*, LXIX, 2. January, 1964, 371-392.

Hishida, Seiji, *Japan Among the Great Powers*. New York: Longmans, Green and Co., 1940.

Holt, W. Stull, "The United States and the Defense of the Western Hemisphere, 1815-1940," *Pacific Historical Review*, X, 4. November, 1941, 704-711

Hoover, Herbert, *America's First Crusade*. New York: Charles Scribner's Sons, 1942.

Hoover, Herbert, *The Memoirs of Herbert Hoover, 1874-1920: Years of Adventure*. New York: Macmillan Co., 1951.

Hoover, Herbert, *Ordeal of Woodrow Wilson*. New York: McGraw-Hill Book Co., 1958.

Ikle, Frank W., "Japanese-German Peace Negotiations During World War I," *American Historical Review*, LXXI, I. October, 1965, 62-76.

Inman, Samuel Guy, *Intervention in Mexico*. New York: George H. Doran Co., 1919.

Kenworthy, Joseph Montague and Young, George, *Freedom of the Seas*. New York: Liveright, 1929.

Kerney, James, *The Political Education of Woodrow Wilson*. New York: The Century Co., 1926.

LaFargue, Thomas Edward, *China and the World War*. Stanford: Stanford University Press, 1937.

LaFeber, Walter, "A Note on the 'Mercantilistic Imperialism' of Alfred Thayer Mahan," *Mississippi Valley Historical Review*, XLVIII, 4. March, 1962, 674-685.

Latham, Earl, ed., *The Philosophy and Policies of Woodrow Wilson*. Chicago: University of Chicago Press, 1958.

Link, Arthur S., *Wilson: the Diplomatist*. Baltimore: The Johns Hopkins Press, 1957.

Link, Arthur S., *Wilson: The New Freedom*. Princeton: University Press, 1956.

Link, Arthur S., *Wilson: the Struggle for Neutrality 1914-1915*. Princeton: Princeton University Press, 1960.

Link, Arthur S., *Woodrow Wilson and the Progressive Era: 1910-1917*. New York: Harper & Bros., 1954.

Link, Eugene Perry, *Democratic Republican Societies*. New York: Octagon Books, 1965.

Lippmann, Walter, *The Stakes of Diplomacy*. New York: Henry Holt & Co., 1915.

Livermore, Seward W., "Battleship Diplomacy in South America: 1905-1925," *Journal of Modern History*, XVI. January, 1944, 31-48.

Mahan, Alfred Thayer, *The Interest of America in International Conditions*. Boston: Little, Brown & Co., 1910.

Mahan, Alfred Thayer, *The Interest of America in Sea Power: Present and Future*. Boston: Little, Brown & Co., 1897.

Mahan, Alfred Thayer, *The Problem of Asia and its Effect upon International Policies*. Boston: Little, Brown and Co., 1900.

May, Ernest R., *The World War and American Isolation, 1914-1917*. Cambridge: Harvard University Press, 1959.

Mayer, Henry Cord, "German Economic Relations with Southeastern Europe, 1870-1914," *American Historical Review*, LVII, I. October 1951, 77-90.

Moon, Parker Thomas, *Imperialism and World Politics*. New York: The Macmillan Co., 1926.

Mowat, Robert Ballman, *A History of European Diplomacy*, 1914-1925. London: Edward Arnold & Co., 1927.

Mowry, George E., *Theodore Roosevelt and the Progressive Movement*. Madison: University of Wisconsin Press, 1947.

Munro, Dana G., *Intervention and Dollar Diplomacy in the Caribbean 1900-1921*. Princeton: Princeton University Press, 1964.

National Foreign Trade Council, *European Economic Alliances*. New
    York: National Foreign Trade Council, 1916.
Nearing, Scott, *Dollar Diplomacy*. New York: B. W. Huebsch, 1928.
Nevins, Allan, *Henry White: Thirty Years of American Diplomacy*. New
    York: Harper & Bros., 1930.
Normano, J. F., *The Struggle for South America: Economy and Ideology*.
    Boston: Houghton Mifflin Co., 1931.
Notter, Harley, *The Origins of the Foreign Policy of Woodrow Wilson*.
    Baltimore: The Johns Hopkins Press, 1937.
Nowak, Karl Friedrich, *The Collapse of Central Europe*. New York:
    Dutton, 1924.
Noyes, Alexander D., *The War Period of American Finance, 1908-1925*.
    New York: G. P. Putnam's Sons, 1922.
O'Conner, Harvey, *The Guggenheims*. New York: Covici-Friede, 1937.
Parks, Henry Bamford, *A History of Mexico*. Boston: Houghton Mifflin
    Co., 1938.
Parrington, Vernon L., *Main Currents of American Thought*. New York:
    Harcourt, Brace and World, Inc., 1927, vol. I.
Pepper, Charles M., *American Foreign Trade*. New York: The Century
    Co., 1919.
Pitkin, Hanna, "Hobbes' Concept of Representation," *The American Poli-
    tical Science Review*, LVIII, 3. June, 1964, 328-340; 4. December,
    1964, 902-918.
Powell, J. Richard, *The Mexican Petroleum Industry: 1938-1950*. Ber-
    keley: University of California Press, 1956.
Pringle, Henry F., *Theodore Roosevelt*. New York: Blue Ribbon Books,
    1913.
Reyes, Rafael, *The Two Americas*. London: T. F. Unwin, 1914.
Rippy, J. Fred, *The United States and Mexico*. New York: Alfred A.
    Knopf, 1926.
Salter, Sir Arthur, *Allied Shipping Control: An Experiment in Internation-
    al Administration*. Oxford: Clarendon Press, 1921.
Sears, Louis Martin, *A History of American Foreign Relations*. New York:
    Thomas Y. Crowell Co., 1936.
Seymour, Charles, *American Diplomacy During the World War*. Baltimore:
    The Johns Hopkins Press, 1942.
Shippee, Lester B., "Germany and the Spanish-American War," *American
    Historical Review*, XXX. July 1925, 754-777.
Simpson, Elyer N., *The Ejido: Mexico's Way Out*. Chapel Hill: University
    of North Carolina Press, 1937.
Siney, Marion C., *The Allied Blockade of Germany, 1914-1916*. Ann
    Arbor: University of Michigan Press, 1957.
Steinberg, David Joel, *Philippine Collaboration in World War II*. Ann
    Arbor: University of Michigan Press, 1967.
Steiner, Zara S., "Great Britain and the Creation of the Anglo-Japanese
    Alliance," *Journal of Modern History*, XXI, 1. March, 1959, 27-36.

Tannenbaum, Frank, *Mexico: The Struggle for Peace and Bread*. New York: Alfred A. Knopf, 1950.

Tansill, Charles Callan, *America Goes to War*. Boston: Little, Brown & Co., 1938.

Taussig, Frank W., *The Tariff History of the United States*. New York: G. P. Putnam's Sons, 1931.

Tompkins, Pauline, *American-Russian Relations in the Far East*. New York: Macmillan Co., 1949.

Turlington, Edgar, *Mexico and Foreign Creditors*. New York: Columbia University Press, 1930.

Turner, Frederick Jackson, *The Frontier in American History*. New York: Henry Holt & Co., 1920.

Vagts, Alfred, "Hopes and Fears of an American-German War, 1870-1915," *Political Science Quarterly*, LIV. December, 1939; LV. March, 1940, 53-76.

Van Alstyne, Richard W., "The Policy of the United States Regarding the Declaration of London," *Journal of Modern History*, VII. December, 1935, 435-447.

Vevier, Charles, "American Continentalism: An Idea of Expansion," *American Historical Review*, LXV, 2. January, 1960, 323-335.

Viallate, Achille, *Economic Imperialism and International Relations During the Last Fifty Years*. New York: The Macmillan Co., 1932.

Walker, Francis A., *Political Economy*. New York: Henry Holt & Co., 1883.

Ward, A. W., and Gooch, G. P., *The Cambridge History of British Foreign Policy, 1783-1917*. London: Cambridge University Press, 1923, vol. III.

Whetten, Nathan L., *Rural Mexico*. Chicago: University of Chicago Press, 1948.

White, John M., *Argentina*. New York: The Viking Press, 1942.

White, William Allen, *Woodrow Wilson*. Cambridge: Riverside Press, 1924.

Wiebe, Robert H., *The Search for Order, 1877-1920*. New York: Hill and Wang, 1967.

Williams, Benjamin H., *Economic Foreign Policy of the United States*. New York: McGraw Hill, 1929.

Williams, William Appleman, *Contours of American History*. Cleveland: World Publishing Co., 1961.

Williams, William Appleman, "The Frontier Thesis and American Foreign Policy," *Pacific Historical Review*, XXIV, 4. November, 1955.

Williams, William Appleman, *The Tragedy of American Diplomacy*. Cleveland: World Publishing Co., 1959.

World Peace Foundation, *New Pan Americanism*. Boston: World Peace Foundation, 1916.

Young, Walter, *Japan's Special Position in Manchuria*. Baltimore: The Johns Hopkins Press, 1931.

INDEX

A B C mediation, 79-81, 100-02, 108, 111, 112-15
Allied secret agreements, 163-64, 174-75
Alternate canal route, 50-51, 52, 54, 58, 59
American Bankers Association, 30
American loans, 57, 58, 59-61, 67, 68, 69, 90, 133, 136-37, 138, 147-48
American shipping, captured, 139-49
Anglo-American cooperation,
   Latin America, 87, 94-95, 114, 116, 128,
   World War I, 130-34, 139, 140-50, 155-56, 159-60, 162, 180-83
Anglo-American rivalry, 120, 132, 172-73, 174
Anglo-Saxonism, 12, 14, 15, 17, 18, 20, 22-25, 46,51, 56-57, 61, 69, 73, 75, 88, 100, 110, 174
Anti-Imperialist sentiment in United States, 77-78
Anti-trust legislation, 40
Argentina, 69, 79, 96, 115
Austro-Hungarian Empire, 132, 163, 181, 186

Bagehot, Walter, 11
Baker, George, 137
Baker, Newton D., 110
Baker, Ray Stannard, 4, 59
Balfour, Arthur James, 185
Baralong, 163-64
Bernstorff, Johann von, 88, 152, 156-57
Beveridge, Albert J., 14, 31-32
Bliss, Tasker H., 130
Blockade, 130-34, 139, 146, 147, 153-55, 159, 172, 173
Borah, William E., 59
Brazil, 69, 79, 93, 96, 115, 175
Bright, John, 11
Bryan-Chamerro Treaty, 57-61,
Bryan, William Jennings,

Nicaragua, 57-60, 69
Mexico, 75-77, 99
World War I, 131, 132-33, 138, 149-50, 156, 158-60
Bureau of Commerce, 40
Burke, Edmund, 11

Capital, center of power, 34
Carden, Sir Lionel, 72
Caribbean area, 45, 47-49, 60, 114-15
Carranza, Venustiano, 74-76. 80, 97, 99, 100, 101, 102, 108-09 110, 112.
Central America, 45-48, 51-61, 70-72
Central American Court of Justice, 52
Central American Federal Union,52
Chile, 69, 76, 79, 96, 115, 116, 175
China, 135-36, 136-38
Clark, John Bates, 11-12
Coal Strikes, West Virginia, 19
Collective Security, 141, 148-49, 154-55, 159, 162-63, 165, 173-78, 181, 186
Columbia, 74
Commerce, liberalizing force, 11
Conditional contraband, 132, 133, 139, 140, 146, 149
Congress, 12, 13, 14, 33, 34, 39
Conquest of world markets, 29, 32-33, 35-38
Constitutional Government in the United States,13, 24
Continuous Voyage, 132, 134, 135, 140, 146, 147
Contributory negligence, doctrine of, 157, 159
Cooperation of Business and Government, necessity, 34-35, 40-41
Cooperative empire, 69-70, 72, 73-74, 81, 82, 88-90, 91, 128
Corporations, reform, 31, 33, 38
Corporatism, 7, 12, 13, 14, 17, 19, 31, 32, 33, 34, 35, 37, 38, 41

Costa Rica, 52, 76
Cowdray, Lord Weetman Dickinson Pearson, 54, 68, 74
Croly, Herbert, 7
Cuba, 20, 46, 47, 57, 59, 72, 89, 93
Currency reform, 40

Dacia, 150, 158
Daniels, Josephus, 4, 76, 99
Davies, Joseph E., 119
Dawson Pact, 50, 51, *see also* Nicaragua
Declaration of London, 1909, 130-32, 135, 139-41, 146, 149-53
Declaration of War, United States, 185
Democracy, 6, 13, 15-18, 21, 22-24, 33, 34
Department of Commerce, 161, 178
Diaz Adolfo, 48-50, 52, 53, 55, 58-59, 72
Diaz, Porfirio, 49, 52, 53, 54, 67
Disinterestedness, American claims to, 3, 5, 120, 127, 190
Dodge, Cleveland H., 68
Doheny, Harry, 53, 67
Dollar Diplomacy, 45, 47, 55, 57, 59, 72-73, 87, 113, 115, 128-29, 138
Dumba, Konstantin T., 159

Ecuador, 76
El Salvador, 52, 53, 59
Estrada, Juan, 50-52
Economic concentration, 10, 31, 32, 33, 35, 37-39
Empire, American, 7, 10, 22, 41, 58, 160
European leaders, cynical, 4
Expansion, American, 9-25, 29-33, 35, 37, 38, 40, 41, 46-52, 54-56, 61, 77, 111, 114, 129, 172, 174, 176-78

Falaba, 157
Federal Reserve Act, 40-41, 118
Federal Reserve Board, 117
Federal Reserve System, 93, 117, 118
Federal Trade Commission, 41, 119, 175, 178
Federalist X, 18
Fonesca Bay, naval base, 50, 58
Foreign Relations Committee, Senate, 50, 58
Francis, David R., 181
Frankfurter, Felix, 8
Freedom, 13, 14

Frontier, role of, 6, 7, 18, 22-23, 25, 29, 35-36, 172

Gamboa, Frederico, 71
Gerard, James W., 150, 152, 178, 179, 181, 182
German-American rivalry,
    Latin America, 87, 96, 108-09, 111, 134, 175, 178
    Pacific, 175
United States abandonment of neutrality, 141, 146, 149, 160-65
Germany,
    Cooperative empire, 35, 69, 132
    Neutrality controversy, 149, 150-53, 156-57, 162-63, 180-82, 185
Gillow, Eulogio, 56
Gladstone, William, 11
Glass, Carter, 39
Great Britain,
    armed merchant ships, 163-65, 178-81
    Mexico, 54, 68, 69-72
    Pressure on U.S. trade, 172-73, 177-79, 181-83
    Q Boats, 163
    Russian Trade, 181-82
Greene, Cananea Copper Company, 67
Grey, Edward, 70, 73, 89-90, 135, 140-41, 153, 173, 184
Guatemala, 52, 76

Haiti, 47
Hamilton, Alexander, 14-15, 20, 32, 33
Hamlin, Charles S., 117
Hammond, John Hays, 116-17
Harriman, Edward H., 136-37
Herrick, Myron T., 137
Higginson, Henry L., 139
History of the American People, 29
Honduras, 52
Hoover, Herbert, 3, 4, 8
Homestead Strike, 19
House, Col. Edward Mandell
    Cooperative empire, 69, 88, 89, 90, 95, 128
    Pan Americanism, 91, 94-95, 101, 175
    Mexico, quick settlement, 108
    Anglo-American cooperation, 134-35, 150, 160, 163-64, 175
    curb British expansion, 172,

negotiation with Germany, 163, 172-73, 183-85
Huerta, Victoriano, 54, 56, 57, 67-81, 89, 101

Industrial efficiency, 33, 35
International Harvester, 100
Iturbide, Eduardo, 101

Japan, 48, 69, 136, 175, 181
Jefferson, un-American, 15
Jeffersonianism, 13, 14, 15

Kiaochow, 138
Knox-Castrillo Draft Treaty, 50, 55, 58-59
Knox, Philander C., 49, 50-51, 55, 136, 138
Krutschnitt, Julius, 67-69
Kuhn, Loeb and Company, 117, 137

Laissez-faire, 6, 7, 11, 12, 13, 17, 37
La Luz y Los Angeles Mining Company, 49
Lamar, Joseph R., 80
Lamont, Thomas, 139
Lane, Franklin K., 113
Lansing, Robert,
    Questions league, 4, 48, 61
    Monroe Doctrine and Pan Americanism, 90-91, 97, 114-15, 122
    ABC Mediation, 100-02
    German role in Latin America, 108
    Loans to Belligerents, 132, 147-48
    British violations of neutrality, 133-34, 154-65, 174, 178-82
    German danger, 150-51, 152-53, 157, 158-60, 161-62, 165, 179, 182-83
Latin America,
    U. S. interests, 6, 30, 41, 45-47, 54-57, 59, 61, 69, 72, 93-94
    U. S. System, 54, 59, 96, 114, 118, 119
    Resentment of U. S., 59, 98, 186
    Collective security, 122-23
    German threat, 161
League of Nations, 4, 173, 176, 184
Lind, John, 70, 75, 76, 77
Liberty, 13-14, 16, 37, 78
Lodge, Henry Cabot, 77
Lusitania, 152, 158-59

McAdoo, William G., 118, 147, 177

Madero, Francisco, 54
Madison, James, 12, 15, 18
Madriz, Jose, 49
Mahan, Alfred Thayer, 87, 128
Manchuria, 136-38
Marines, 60-61, 77
Merchant Marine,
    U. S. need, 35, 36, 41, 118, 129, 130, 173-74
    Purchase of German ships, 119-21, 133, 150
    British opposition, 139
Mexico,
    Agrarian Reform Law, 1915, 97
    Annexation movement, 100, 110
    Arms embargo, 75-76, 109
    "Banditism," 68, 110
    Border raids, 109-10, 112, 113
    Coercion, 8
    Elections 67, 70, 71-72, 108
    Interests, British, 68-70, 114
    Interests, American, 46, 53, 54, 67, 68, 70-71, 74-75, 114, 116
    Intervention, American, 67-68, 71, 72, 75, 112-14
    Negotiations, 111-12, 115
    Pershing Expedition, 109-11
    Political factionalism, 67-68, 71, 72, 97
    Recognition, 67-68
    Resentment of U. S., 98
    Revolution, 67, 68, 74-75, 97, 110, 112, 114
    World War I, 93, 94, 110-11
Mixed Claims Commission, 58, *see also* Nicaragua
Mobile Address, 72-73, 91
Mondell, Frank W., 77
Monroe Doctrine, 7, 57, 81, 87, 94, 96, 100, 114, 115, 117, 121-22, 134, 161
Moore, John Bassett, 72
Moral leadership, U. S. conception, 41, 46, 53-55, 57, 58, 68-69, 73-74, 114, 120, 122
Morgan, John Pierpont, 30, 128, 133, 137, 139
Munsterberg, Hugo, 149
Murray, William H., 110

National City Bank, 68, 147, 182
Nationalism, opposition to U. S. expansion, 41, 53, 114

Negroes, 12, 39-40
Netherlands Overseas Trust, 172
New Diplomacy, 3, 4-5, 6, 45, 60, 72, see also New Order.
New Freedom, 13, 20, 37, 41, 45
New Nationalism, 7, 37
New Order, 3, 4-5, 6, 7, 46
Niagara Conference, 80
Nicaragua, 47, 48-52, 55-61, 70, 72
Norris, George, 59
Northcott, Elliott, 51, 53
Open Door, 128, 138
Obregon, Alvaro, 97, 99
Order in Council, August 20, 1914, 132-34
Order in Council, March 1, 1915, 153-55
O'Shaugnessy, Edith, 77
Overproduction, United States, 30, 35, 36,

Page, Thomas Nelson, 57
Page, Walter Hines,
    Mexico, 72-74, 111
    Wilson Doctrine, 73-74
    Cooperative empire, 88-89
    Need for Pro-British position, 94, 134, 139-41
    American world leadership, 128
    German ships, 150
    American shipping, 130
    Blockade, 152-55
    Need for Allied victory, 174
    Submarine warfare, 179
    Joining Allies, 181
Panama, 47, 88
Panama Canal, 47, 48, 50, 51, 53, 54-60, 71, 73, 79, 87, 115
Panama Canal Tolls Controversy, 70, 74, 89
Pan American Financial Conference, 117-21
Pan American Pact, 95-97, 114-16, 122, 175
Pan American Postal Convention, 119
Pan Americanism, 52, 65, 78, 81, 91, 108, 114-17, 160
Pan American Scientific Congress, 121-22
Pan American Supreme Court, 116
"Peace Without Victory," 186
Peláez, Manuel, 114
Pepper, Charles, M., 60, 65-66
Persia, 178
Petroleum Law of 1901, Mexican, 53
Peynado, Franciso, J., 119

Phelps, Dodge and Company, 67, 68
Philippines, 24
Platt Amendment, 52, 58, 59, 94, 111
Polk, Frank, 116
Progressive Movement, 19, 37
Puerto Rico, 24
Pujo Committee, 137
Pullman Strike, 19

Radicalism, 15, 16, 30-31, 34, 45-46
Redfield, William G., 118
Revolution,
    U. S. opposition to, 16-17, 48-49, 50-51, 54-56, 61, 97
    Controlled by U. S., 47, 102, 108
    "Legitimate," 78, 97
    Pan American Treaty, 95, 122
    Repression of revolution, 186
    Threat to U. S., 56, 88
    Wilson Doctrine, 73
Roberts, Samuel, 147
Roosevelt Corollary to Monroe Doctrine, 47, 51, 52, 57, 72, 75, 81
Roosevelt, Theodore, 6, 14, 19, 37, 38, 45-48, 51, 52, 67, 77, 87
Root, Elihu, 51
Root-Takahira Note of 1914, 138
Russo-Japanese Treaty of 1912, 136

Santo Domingo, 119
Self-determination, 6, 8, 16, 24-25, 181
Self interest, American pursuit of, 29-30
Seligman, J. and W. 58, see also Nicaragua
Seward, William H. 48
Smith, Edward N., 111
Socialism, dangers of, 34
Southern Pacific Railway Company of Mexico, 67
Spanish American War, 21, 23-25, 29, 35, 36, 47, 54
Speyer, James, 67, 88
Spring-Rice, Cecil, 153
Straight, Willard, 128-29, 147
Stone, William J., 159
Strict accountability, doctrine of, 151
Submarine warfare, 151-53, 157, 161, 163-64, 173, 178, 181
Suez Canal, 87
Sun Yat-sen, 137

Tampico Incident, 76-78

Taft, William Howard, 8, 45, 48, 50-51, 55, 57, 60, 67
Tariffs, 32, 35, 38, 40, 128, 178
Tariff reduction, 32, 38-39
Thompson, Charles Willis, 8
Tirpitz, Alfred von, 89, 181
Tumulty, Joseph, 61
Turner, Frederick Jackson, 6, 7, 17-18, 22
Tyrell, Sir William, 73, 89, 90

Underdevelopment, 7, 32, 48
United States,
    abandonment of economic independence, 148
    commercial supremacy, 128
    expansion of armed forces, 173-74
    economic commitments in Latin America, 46-47, 53-54, 97
    economic stagnation, 30-33, 35-36
    intervention, 53-55, 70, 74-75, 78, 88
    neutrality, 127, 130-33, 135, 139-41, 146-50, 153, 159, 176, 182
    solution to problems found abroad, 6, 7, 8, 9
    War Risk Insurance Bureau, 139
Uruguay, 76

Vanderlip, Frank, 137, 139
Vera Cruz Incident, 76-77, 79
Villa, Francisco (Pancho), 73, 75, 97, 101, 102, 109
Visit and Search, 163-64

Walker, Francis A., 11
Warburg, Paul, 117, 118
Washington Conference of 1907, 52-53
Webb-Pomerene Act, 41, 178
West Indies, 46
White, Henry, 4
William II, 90
Williams, Edward, T., 135
Wilson Doctrine, 74-75, 79, 97, 127
Wilson, Henry Lane, 68, 75
Wilson, Woodrow,
    Allied victory necessary, 162
    Allies in Mexico, 100-01
    Anti-Imperialism, 3
    Black suffrage, 12
    cabinet government, 12, 13, 14
    Calvinism, 10-11, 17, 21, 81

class interest, 31
colonialism, 56
corruption of local government, 10, 12
democracy, 6, 13, 14, 15, 16, 17, 18
disruption of balance, 10, 12, 13, 30-31, 37, 38, 46
early years, 10-11
efficiency, 10, 32-33, 36-38
enlightened conservatism, 11, 39, 46
expansion, 9-25, 29-33, 35, 37, 38, 40, 41, 46-52, 54-56, 61, 77, 129, 172, 174, 176-78
factionalism, 7, 10, 12, 13, 14, 16, 20, 21, 29, 33-38
George Washington's Farewell Address, 22
Alexander Hamilton, 14-15, 32
ignorance of Mexican affairs, 67, 81
Thomas Jefferson, 13, 14, 15, 20
lack of consistency, 8, 45
laissez-faire, 6, 7, 11, 13, 17, 37, 38
leadership, 7, 10, 12, 13, 14, 17, 20, 21, 21, 23, 24, 33, 34, 36, 46
liberty, 13, 14, 16, 37, 78
limits on competition, 11, 37-38
neo-corporatism, 7, 33, 37-38, 41
New Diplomacy, 3, 4, 5, 7, 45, 49, 60, 72
opposition to Congress, 10, 12, 13, 14, 34
protectionism, 32-33
social legislation, 7, 39, 40
Peace Note, 185
Princeton, 11-13
reform, 45-46, 54
representing people of Europe, 5
representing people of Mexico, 70
representing people of the world, 127
revolution, 47-52. 54-56, 60, 76, 80, 98-100
Scotch-Irish, 21-22
social legislation, 7
split with Bryan, 160
Southerner,.10-12
States Rights, 7, 20, 32
underdevelopment, 7, 32, 48
vagueness of rhetoric, 5
Wilson Doctrine, 24-25, 75, 79, 97, 127
Wood, Leonard, 67
World War I, outbreak,
    economic effects at start, 92-94

World War I (continued)
    danger of German victory, 94
    destroys balance of power, 130
    jeopardizes Open Door, 138
    need for Mexican settlement, 108, 111, 113

Zapata, Emiliano, 97, 101
Zelaya, Jose Santos, 48-50, 52, 57, 70
Zimmerman Telegram, effects on U.S.-Mexican relations, 113, 186